CHOOSE POSSIBILITY

CHOOSE POSSIBILITY

How to Master Risk and Thrive

SUKHINDER SINGH CASSIDY

Macmillan

First published 2021 by Houghton Mifflin Harcourt

First published in the UK 2021 by Macmillan
an imprint of Pan Macmillan
The Smithson, 6 Briset Street, London EC1M 5NR
EU representative: Macmillan Publishers Ireland Ltd, 1st Floor,
The Liffey Trust Centre, 117–126 Sheriff Street Upper,
Dublin 1, D01 YC43
Associated companies throughout the world
www.panmacmillan.com

HB ISBN 978-1-5290-6642-5
TPB ISBN 978-1-5290-6643-2

1 3 5 7 9 8 6 4 2

A CIP catalogue record for this book is available from the British Library.

Book design by Emily Snyder
Infographics by Christie Young

Typeset in Minion Pro by Jouve (UK), Milton Keynes
Printed and bound by CPI Group (UK) Ltd, Croydon, CR0 4YY

Visit **www.panmacmillan.com** to read more about all our books
and to buy them. You will also find features, author interviews and
news of any author events, and you can sign up for e-newsletters
so that you're always first to hear about our new releases.

To my parents, who showed me
the power of love and possibility every day

When nothing is sure, everything is possible.

— MARGARET DRABBLE

CONTENTS

FOREWORD

Early on in my career, when a start-up I'd cofounded was failing, a mentor passed on some wisdom he'd received when *his* business was failing. "There is a fine line," someone told him, "between success and failure. When you're succeeding, never think you're as good as everyone is telling you that you are. And when you're failing, never think you're as bad as everyone is telling you that you are."

These words have helped me enormously, grounding me during the good times and comforting me during the bad. So imagine my delight to find that my friend Sukhinder Singh has done my mentor one better. *Choose Possibility* shares a powerful risk-taking framework Sukhinder developed over the course of a successful Silicon Valley career. Underlying this framework is a keen awareness of the fine line separating success and failure. But Sukhinder not only observes this line and explains why it exists. She also helps us understand better *how* to put this wisdom into practice so as to move in the direction of our dreams.

The truth is, we seldom appreciate the close connections between success and failure. Failure is painful and threatening to our egos, so much so that we find it impossible to glean in it the seedlings of our future success. We can't understand the blessings of the class we've failed or the start-up that doesn't catch on or the job from which we've been fired. Rather, we panic and become paralyzed. *Choose Possibility* helps you recover from your stumbles or missteps so that you can risk it all again and keep growing. Sukhinder shows you how to "pick yourself up and dust yourself off and get back in the saddle."

With real compassion, Sukhinder explores how to manage the "ego risk" of failure. How can you inoculate yourself from this most dangerous of fears? For example, when I had just finished writing *Radical Candor,* someone told me, "You shouldn't publish this book. It makes you look stupid and insecure." Ouch! I had to wrestle my old fear of making a fool of myself to the ground if I was going to move forward. And eventually, I did. Even if people did think the stories in my book made me look ridiculous, I stood by what I'd written. Sukhinder offers a way to think about the ego risks of failure, and how to inoculate yourself so that you can take positive action more easily. How I wish I'd had her book then!

Of course, the risk of failure and rejection plays out differently for all of us. Right out of college, I had a very specific career goal: I wanted to work in Moscow on the issue of military conversion—a fancy way of saying that I wanted to help turn swords into plowshares. There weren't a lot of jobs in this area, to say the least. I took a job with a Russian think tank to write a paper on this topic, but the pay was measly — six dollars a month. There was exactly *one* American company working on this issue, and my letters to them went unanswered.

I got this company's address and marched into their front door to ask for a job. For me this wasn't a very big risk. I marched back out that door with a job offer in hand. My risk there was only ego risk — there was very little risk of bodily harm to me walking in the door. That is privilege, and it's unjust.

Contrast my experience with that of Shaun Jayachandran, an Indian American man. When he walked into the World Bank offices to inquire about an internship opportunity, the guards drew their guns on him. Decades later, the memory still brings tears to his eyes. But he used that experience to deepen his commitment to making the world more just. Today, he is founder and president of Crossover Basketball and Scholars Academy, an international basketball program in India that provides educational opportunities for all students regardless of socioeconomic status. Shaun chose possibility. And his choice has had a positive impact on many people.

I hope that reading *Choose Possibility* will help you, too, to take failure in stride. Learn Sukhinder's tools and techniques. Absorb her wisdom. May you move more boldly in the direction of your dreams, learning from both your successes *and* your failures, and making the world just a little bit better.

Kim Scott

INTRODUCTION

Have you ever suffered through a really tough job search, absorbing multiple blows to your self-confidence? That was me during the fall of 1992. I was twenty-two years old and had graduated the previous May with an undergraduate degree from the Ivey Business School at the University of Western Ontario in Canada. All of my friends had landed positions at prestigious investment banking and consulting firms, but I hadn't. I had gone abroad my senior year as part of an exchange program, missing most of the on-campus recruiting season. Upon returning home I scrambled for interviews, and of the few I landed, none led to anything. By graduation, I'd been forced to take the same temporary job I'd had the previous summer, selling conference space for a hotel in our small university town of London, Ontario. Meanwhile, my friends were starting their impressive careers.

I decided I needed another shot at recruiting, so I stuck around London to participate in the fall on-campus recruiting season, stalking the job boards right beside students the year below me who hadn't yet graduated. I landed several "prestigious" interviews — Goldman, McKinsey, Monitor — but still didn't receive any offers. I had been a ridiculous overachiever in high school and done well in my college classes without too much trouble. Now, for the first time in my life, success eluded me. I was nine months into my job search and hiding out alone in my rented room, feeling anxious and dejected as I replayed each job application fail in my head.

Not knowing what else to do, I kept obsessively checking the job boards and applying to new opportunities. One day, I saw that a private investment firm called Claridge Investment, Ltd., was looking to hire a graduating MBA student for a position as an associate. I had no business applying for this job — I lacked an MBA, had hardly any work experience, was at least four years younger than most graduate students, and only vaguely knew what private equity was. Claridge, meanwhile, was a pretty big deal. Headquartered in Montreal, it was the investment arm of the Bronfman family, one of Canada's wealthiest and most powerful dynasties.

Still, with nothing to lose, I applied once more. I sent in my résumé, called up the hiring manager (a partner at the firm) and left a voice message. A week passed. Then another. To my great shock, the partner's office called me back, wondering if I would fly up to Montreal for an interview. "Sure, I'd love to," I managed to say. Inside I was thinking, *What just happened?*

Arriving in Montreal, I was awed by the hustle and bustle of this large, cosmopolitan city. Claridge's offices impressed me too — rich wood paneling, a multimillion-dollar art collection, amazing city views. The interview with the partner went well, and I couldn't believe it when he invited me to return for more interviews. As I was leaving, I blurted out: "Why did you call me back for this position? I don't have all the qualifications."

He smiled. "When I heard your voicemail, I just liked the sound of your voice and the way you presented yourself. I figured I'd give you a chance."

I returned for several more interviews, participating in a rigorous six-week vetting process alongside MBA students, complete with case studies and simulated exercises. Ultimately, as it turned out, I didn't get the job — they decided to give it to an MBA graduate after all. I felt deeply disappointed (not a surprise, given my natural intensity), but also strangely invigorated. My search process remained grueling, but my "near win" at a truly ambitious opportunity was a surprising highlight compared to the day-to-day misses of the regular job hunt. The small risk I'd taken failed in one sense, but it delivered a different, more meaningful reward, giving me a sorely needed boost of confidence and keeping me in the game. Months later, after several twists and turns (more on that later), I landed my "dream" job at Merrill Lynch in New York City. I was on my way.

Today, I'm a technology executive, entrepreneur, and investor in Silicon Valley, the global center of entrepreneurship and wealth creation. Over the past twenty-three years, I've started three companies, served as CEO of two others, and helped grow two of the world's largest tech giants (Google and Amazon). I've participated as an employee, leader, investor, or board member at another dozen plus companies ranging from global brands such as TripAdvisor, Ericsson, Urban Outfitters, and J.Crew to successful digital services such as Stitch Fix, Upstart, and Sun Basket to little-known startups that ran out of money and fell back into the sea. I've been lucky enough to see a company I created (Yodlee) go public and to lead another company (StubHub) to a multibillion-dollar sale. I've been heartbroken to watch a company I poured everything into (Joyus) fail, and naïve enough to join two organizations where I just didn't fit (OpenTV and Polyvore).

In short, I've been putting my hands on the wheel driving growth, sometimes successfully and sometimes not, for just about all my career. I've taken countless risks of all shapes and sizes and helped others do the same. Despite some significant and painful fails, risk-taking has delivered tremendous career returns for me along every dimension—financial, emotional, and reputational. It's also taught me one thing that I wish everyone knew: Risk is *not* what you think it is.

THE RISK-TAKING MYTHS THAT SCARE US

For many of us, risk feels inherently scary, and understandably so: By definition a risk is a dangerous situation in which one faces a "possibility of loss or injury." Of course, avoiding risk is good for us if it keeps us from serious danger or irreparable harm. Still, we know that to grow faster and achieve success we must be willing to experiment and take on new challenges. The prospect of taking a chance thus pits our hopes for progress and achievement against our need for self-preservation. Most often, the need for self-preservation wins.

Certain myths that surround risk-taking and success only heighten our anxiety. Most fundamentally and problematically, we tend to conceive of risk-taking as a discrete, monumental, and downright crazy action that a person takes and that they can't easily take back, like jumping out of an airplane, draining your 401k to start a business, or getting married to someone you met three weeks ago on Tinder. On one level, this everyday conception of risk seems legitimate — from the outside in, successful people appear to be making big, nonlinear moves all the time. Problems arise, however, when we think that this is *all* risk-taking is. We assume — wrongly — that risk-taking is a single leap that has the power to make us or ruin us. That leap better be big; otherwise we won't see much of a reward. If we're not walking a tightrope over the Grand Canyon, we might as well stay home and forgo the trip. As Helen Keller famously put it, "Life is either a daring adventure or nothing."

This Myth of the Single Choice, as I call it, puts massive pressure on us to make the *right* choice on a straight shot to glory. It also gives rise to additional, supporting myths that, I posit, are equally unhealthy. Because so much seems to be at stake, we believe we should prepare zealously, as doing so might moderate the risk or perhaps even eliminate it entirely. We strive to engineer the "perfect plan," which of course seldom materializes. To further help us cope, we tell ourselves that if we're passionate enough, hardworking enough, and perfect enough in our execution, we can surely find a way to control the outcome. If we fail, we take a massive blow to our self-esteem, convinced it was all our fault. We curl up into a ball, less likely than ever to take another risk. When we succeed, others give us all the credit, treating us as valiant conquerors. After all, there's only room for one person at the top of the mountain — and hopefully it's us.

Most often, these beliefs prevent us from taking any risk at all. Looking at the yawning chasm of uncertainty between glory or epic defeat, it's safest, we think, to sit back and not make a move this time. When the next risk-taking opportunity arises, *then* we'll jump into action. Except we don't, since we find ourselves grappling all over again with yet another myth-fueled cycle of anxiety. Stories of massive risk-taking and redemption from places like Silicon Valley don't help. Rather than diminishing our overall fear of risk, tweet-size headlines reinforce the mythical, singular nature of risk-taking. The more the world celebrates risk-taking, the less accessible it can feel to any of us.

CHOOSING POSSIBILITY

It's time to free ourselves from our "all or nothing" perception of risk-taking. In truth, risk-taking is available to everyone, and so are its rewards. My decision decades ago to apply for a job I had no business applying for was hardly an epic risk. It was one small gamble I took among many in pursuit of my goal of getting a "real" job. Although the gamble didn't pay off as I'd hoped, it produced an outsize positive impact that I hadn't anticipated. I gained a confidence boost that energized me to continue taking my chances until another risk I took finally worked out. Looking back on it, the entire job search process amounted to a long, circuitous journey of successes and failures. Although I worked hard throughout, my victorious moments didn't always correspond to efforts where I'd tried the hardest or planned the most. Sometimes I just got lucky.

Risk-taking is inherently uncertain, and any single choice we make might not work out as we intended. The power in risk-taking lies in stringing together many choices over time, some small, some big, but each producing impact and insight that inform our future choices. As Ralph Waldo Emerson once observed, "All life is an experiment. The more experiments you make the better." Secure in the knowledge that each choice offers us yet another opportunity to gain or learn from results, we can let go of the fear that a single event has the power to make or break us. Risk-taking is *not* the single, epic brush with peril that we imagine. It's a continuous *process* that we humbly but hopefully embrace, knowing that individual chances we take may be likely to fail but that our probability of overall success will increase as we iterate.

I call this process *choosing possibility.* Rather than paralyzing ourselves by contemplating single large choices, we focus on the act of consistently choosing little or big risks to take in pursuit of our goals. We don't fool ourselves into thinking that we can achieve our ultimate ambitions in one monumental stroke. We simply seek to start and stay in thoughtful motion, knowing that every choice we make helps unlock the next possibility. We succeed over the long term by tacking our way to our dreams, like sailboats in a shifting wind. While we will likely accumulate more failures than others around us who take fewer risks, we will also realize far more of the possibilities we seek.

As you'll see in this book, failure loses its conventional scariness when you think of risk-taking as the process of choosing possibility. By becoming adept at this process, we can work on building a winning season rather than worrying too much about any single game or its outcome. Even when you lose, you derive important benefits, and even if you suffer a string of losses, you ultimately win.

STAYING IN THOUGHTFUL MOTION

Many of us have no trouble understanding risk-taking as a process of iterating gradually toward success when it comes to technology. We accept that companies like Apple release products in an incomplete form, adding on new features and design elements in a series of subsequent versions. We accept that a company like Uber needed to pivot to find bigger success as a ride-sharing service than a limousine-hailing app, or that an online seller such as Amazon would evolve so many times over twenty years that today we enjoy its services as both a national grocery seller and an award-winning movie studio.

Yet our views of risk-taking on the individual level have remained stubbornly static. If we want to expand our chances for longer-term impact, we must embrace a new approach. We can learn to choose possibility, underweighting our fear of each single choice while overweighting our ability to keep choosing. Mastering this skill is not only essential to accelerating our personal success but also to finding a way to thrive in increasingly dynamic and uncertain times. Even if we choose not to embrace risk-taking, risk will still "happen" to us nonetheless.

Psychologists have observed that we all hold beliefs about the forces that control our lives — what they call "locus of control." Research suggests that we're more successful and healthier and have a greater sense of well-being when we believe that *we* have more of this control as opposed to external forces or fate. Learning to choose possibility gives us a greater sense of control over our lives, including under dynamic conditions, leaving us feeling more stable and empowered. "Freedom and autonomy are critical to our well-being. And choice is critical to freedom and autonomy," the psychologist Barry Schwartz observes. As the pace of change around us continues to increase and as old ways of working, behaving, and thinking fall away, remaining stuck in place will prove increasingly costly to our psyches as well as to our careers. We need to put ourselves in thoughtful motion, becoming ever more flexible and resilient and attuned to making choices.

I wrote this book to help you do just that. I've grown frustrated with the mystique that seems to exist around risk-taking, particularly in big bubble environments like the tech industry. Observing such expansion from the outside, any ambitious person can come away believing that only the world's biggest, highest-profile risk-takers reap the benefits of taking chances. Nothing could be further from the truth. Looking back on my career, I've extrapolated a number of key lessons in *how* exactly to take risks consistently for growth, including specific strategies you can use to begin taking risks early, make calculated bigger bets, and then keep choosing over time to maximize your impact. Whether you're looking to increase the contributions you make at work by learning to take more risk or you're evaluating a bigger move in your career and are afraid to make a leap, the tips in this book can help. You'll learn how to *get going, get smarter,* and *get rewarded* over the course of your career. Just understand that having choices in life is a *privilege,* and if we're fortunate enough to have them, we should exercise them.

Sometimes we reach for growth proactively through our choices. At other times, we react to the systems and forces around us (including challenging situations of bias and inequality). Either way, we can still choose from a number of responses. If we're lucky to find that possibility is already abundant, our job is not to waste it by failing to choose, knowing that many people lack such abundance. If accessing possibility seems difficult today, our job is to forge ahead by making even the smallest of choices that will open up new pathways.

For too long, we've romanticized risk as a mythical mountain, one that takes every ounce of courage on our parts to climb and that affords us a direct route to the summit. Instead of helping us to get started, this vision leaves most of us wanting to stay at base camp. What my own journey has taught me is something much different. Risk-taking is not only for the thrill-seekers of this world. It's for all of us. If you've been struggling to move ahead, now is the time to take stock of how you think about risk.

Stop imagining making one large and dangerous choice and instead simply put yourself into motion. We don't have to be mighty or perfect in our choices. We simply need to keep choosing our way through possibilities. Apply for that unlikely job opportunity. Get in the game and start striving. When I started out, I had enormous career ambitions but very little understanding of how to achieve them. As it turns out, I didn't need the grandest of plans, nor did I need to take a single, perfectly orchestrated risk. I simply started making small choices and larger ones, and over time kept choosing my way imperfectly through possibilities. You can do it too.

Sukhinder Singh Cassidy
Fall 2020

PART I

Get Going

Nothing will ever be attempted if all possible
objections must be first overcome.
— SAMUEL JOHNSON

| DITCH THE HERO'S JOURNEY

Have you reached an inflection point in your life or career only to feel terrible pressure to make a choice? My older sister Nicky can identify. In 2010, she was running her own optometry practice in a suburban mall. Caring and giving by nature, she loved to serve patients and took immense pride in her office and small staff, whom she treated like family. For a decade, her business prospered, but more recently it had struggled due to macro conditions. Foot traffic to the mall was declining, local competition had intensified, and more customers were opting to purchase glasses online year after year.

With no break in her fixed costs, Nicky's practice was generating less profit each year, and she strained to save money for the future. Meanwhile, her lease required that she keep her office open until the mall closed at nine p.m. each night. Her husband was an executive with an international company who spent much of his time traveling, and between sports and school their two sons had busy schedules. Most nights, my sister came home around ten p.m., fixed dinner for her two hungry boys, chased them to finish their homework, and fell into bed around one or two a.m. The next day, she got up and did it all again.

Concerned about her well-being, I pressed Nicky to consider her options, which included shutting down or selling her practice, going to work for someone else, combining her practice with another doctor's, or keeping her practice but finding a new location. As exhausted and stressed as she was, Nicky couldn't bring herself to make a move. All she knew was running her own practice in its current form and in that mall location. She had built a large base of patients, sunk capital in inventory and equipment, and assembled a team of people who looked to her for their livelihood. "I took a super big risk in buying and building out this practice," she said. "Sure, I could make a change, but going to work for someone else might be an even bigger mistake. I'd be giving up everything I've built." It was too scary to think about doing something different.

Nicky felt burdened by the sense that everything rode on the choice before her — that it was make or break. Without realizing it, she had given herself over to the Myth of the Single Choice (Figure 1). So many of us fall into this trap. We struggle to chart a new path because of the seeming weightiness of a single decision before us. Risk-taking, we think, boils down to one big move, and we fear that choosing poorly will prove ruinous. Our anxiety heightens when we're already grappling with a challenging situation, but it's also pretty bad even when we feel stable and successful — we don't want to relinquish the great position we've managed to secure. And so, we wring our hands and suffer sleepless nights, racking our brains about what to do. We decide to stay put even as our current situation deteriorates, or we pressure ourselves to make a perfect choice to avoid ruin. Risk-taking becomes much harder than it has to be when we subscribe to the Myth of the Single Choice.

THE HERO'S JOURNEY IN OUR HEADS

Why do we so often monumentalize risk in this way? We often perceive successful people as heroes who take massive risks and vanquish enemies on an epic journey to greatness. Transposing that thinking onto our own lives, we assume we must take a massive risk to achieve outsize

MYTH OF THE SINGLE CHOICE

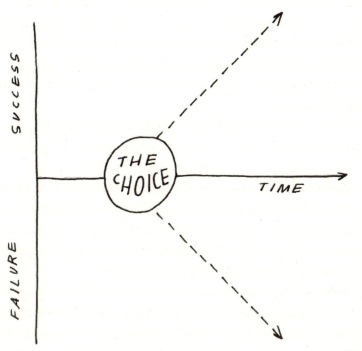

Figure 1

success. In turn, we fear the downside more than we otherwise might. The bigger the potential success, we think, the bigger our fall if our choices go awry.

Stories we encounter throughout our lives reinforce this thinking. Scholars have discerned narratives of heroic quests in ancient myths and folk tales, observing that they continue to influence the narratives we spin today in novels, television, and movies. "Throughout the inhabited world," writes Joseph Campbell in his classic book *The Hero with a Thousand Faces,* "in all times and under every circumstance, the myths of man have flourished; and they have been the living inspiration of whatever else may have appeared out of the activities of the human body and mind." Campbell interprets the hero's journey as an epic passage toward self-discovery and transformation, one that entails a brush with danger as the hero discovers their true self. "A hero ventures forth from the world of common day into a region of supernatural wonder: fabulous forces are there encountered and a decisive victory is won: the hero comes back from this mysterious adventure with the power to bestow boons on his fellow man." On a macro level, the entire quest constitutes a monumental challenge or danger the hero accepts in hopes of achieving greatness.

Look closely, however, and you'll find that the hero's journey doesn't amount to just one big risk. In fact, according to Campbell, heroes *take any number of risks big and small along the way.* They embark on their journeys, leave the ordinary world, enter a special one unknown to them, put faith in mentors, undergo a series of trials to test their skills, and much else. But in our daily retellings of the hero's journey, we often fail to recognize or process this level of detail. We continue to perceive the journey as encompassing a single, outsize risk.

Humans find the prospect of uncertainty fundamentally terrifying. "Uncertainty acts like rocket fuel for worry," one observer writes, referencing numerous scientific studies on the subject. "It causes people to see threats everywhere they look, and at the same time it makes them more likely to react emotionally in response to those threats." Psychologists posit that fear of the unknown might be our most basic fear, or as one scholar puts it, "one fear to rule them all." Some suspect that uncertainty ruffles us because it confronts us with the need to navigate more complexity in our decision-making.

Any risk carries uncertainty, but if you believe everything rides on a single big choice, the prospect of uncertainty magnifies your unease. Nicky felt deeply uncertain about her future — she had no way of knowing if any risk she might take would work out, and as she saw it, her future depended on her decision.

A final psychological factor that intensifies the effects of the Myth of the Single Choice concerns *our perception of loss.* As the behavioral economist Daniel Kahneman and the cognitive psychologist Amos

Tversky famously argued, our fear of losing what we already have feels more compelling to us than the boost we might feel from notching a potential but uncertain gain. If you already regard risk-taking as a single, high-stakes bet, the potential downside seems massive. Add in your aversion to loss, and the downside might seem so overwhelming as to render the risk impossible to take in your mind.

MANY CHOICES MAKE A CAREER

As crippling as the Myth of the Single Choice might be, you can actually dispel it quite easily. The next time you watch a movie with a clear hero's journey plotline, take a moment to chart the risks a hero takes along the way. You'll find there are many — large and small, successful and not. Likewise, if you scrutinize the careers of successful people, you discover that success usually unfolds progressively as a result of many risks of different sizes. You also find that a person's overall success usually arises out of multiple failures as well as wins along the way. Successful people tend to *iterate* their way to cumulative success through failures and achievement in equal measure.

To reach a dream is to string together a long series of choices, large and small, well advised or not. I can count at least twenty-three choices I made over a career spanning almost three decades. Figure 2 boils these down to the ten most important choices that have led me to my present circumstances. As you'll see, some of these choices worked out, some didn't, but my overall career flourished. Over time, I managed to achieve many more of my dreams than I would have with more limited risk-taking.

If you find yourself terrified of a seemingly big risk, conduct a similar analysis of your own life or career to date. You'll likely find that your success to date didn't come from a single big risk, but from many of them, with a much larger number of smaller risks nestled in.

As you register the complexity of your career path or those of people

MY KEY CAREER CHOICES

KEY CAREER CHOICES	SIZE OF OVERALL RISKS	YEAR
ANALYST MERRILL LYNCH, BRITISH SKY BROADCASTING	★	1993-1997
UNEMPLOYED SILICON VALLEY	★★	1997
MANAGER OPENTV	★	1997
MANAGER JUNGLEE/AMAZON	★	1998-1999
FOUNDER & SVP YODLEE	★★★	1999-2003
DIRECTOR, VP, PRESIDENT GOOGLE	★	2003-2009
LEAVE GOOGLE	★★★	2009
CEO POLYVORE	★★★	2010
FOUNDER & CEO JOYUS	★★★	2011-2017
FOUNDER & CHAIR the BOARDLIST	★★	2015-PRESENT
ANGEL INVESTOR	★★	2011-PRESENT
PRESIDENT STUBHUB	★	2018-2020

Figure 2

whom you know or admire, notice that any different number of permutations might have unlocked your or their present level of success. We tend to idealize clear, fixed "tracks" to success. If you want to become a successful corporate attorney, you must get into a top law school, then obtain a summer position at a major New York City law firm, then land a permanent job at one of these firms, then work your way up to partner.

If you want to be CEO of a big company, you obtain some initial business experience, then earn your MBA, land a job at a big company, and just keep climbing. Although such traditional "recipes" might comfort us, they also frighten us, because everything seems to ride on one or a few "big" choices you make: where you go to law school, or the job you land upon graduating, or whether or not you accept the riskier new role your current company is offering you.

A generation or two ago, these so-called key choices might have been critically important. But the good news is that, today, tracks to success don't matter nearly as much as they used to. Millennials and Gen Zers are crafting individualized, nontraditional career paths by working "side hustles" or jumping between industries. In one study of female business leaders, an overwhelming majority—86 percent—regarded nontraditional moves as important to their success. If you're stressed about taking a particular step on the way to your goal, don't worry so much about it. I might have become a CEO and tech leader via my twenty-three decisions, or by an entirely different sequence.

Some CEOs rise up by following the well-worn track of "work experience, fancy MBA, killer job offer, work your way up." *But this is less and less common.* Anjali Sud, called by one observer a "master of the nonlinear career," experienced a number of successes and failures en route to becoming CEO of Vimeo, despite an academic pedigree that includes degrees from Harvard Business School and Wharton. As she recounts, "I did everything from investment banking to being a toy buyer to marketing diapers online to coming to Vimeo to do marketing and finding myself in my dream job now as the CEO." Along the way, she leveraged opportunities to create new ones. When Amazon hired her as an intern in business development, for instance, she parlayed that into an opportunity in merchandising, which in turn led to a marketing position. She counsels that people have "faith that you can affect your career path at any point," understanding that "opportunities come from places you could never imagine. I wish I had known that. I think I would have been more chill."

Research bears out the wisdom of a more free-flowing approach to crafting a career. As the authors of a decade-long study of CEOs note, leaders who reach the top job more quickly than others "don't accelerate to the top by acquiring the perfect pedigree. They do it by making bold career moves over the course of their career that catapult them to the top." These moves include taking a smaller job in order to gain new skills or experience, taking on a job for which they felt unprepared, or signing up to tackle a big, uninviting business problem. Other research, including a large LinkedIn study of hundreds of thousands of people who worked in management consulting, found that people with diverse job experiences advance more quickly than those who toil away in a single specialty or business function. As an article in the *New York Times* put it, "The quickest path is a winding one" when it comes to those seeking to become CEOs.

For me, the journey of risk-taking to career success unfolded across different chapters (Figure 3), each defined by its own broad ambitions. In every chapter, I made a series of choices to help me move toward the ambition in question, generating in turn a series of outcomes. As time passed, each new chapter also built upon the previous ones in ways that appear logical and preplanned to others now, but that were not nearly so clear as events unfolded.

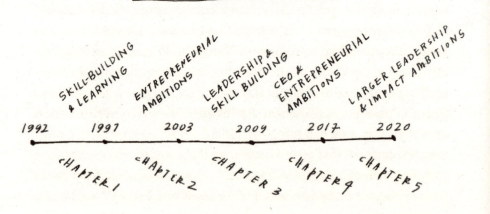

Figure 3

GROW OR GO

As long as a career risk you take results in some sort of positive impact (more on that later), it moves you forward, enhancing your skills and opening up several more potential opportunities than you could access previously. Even when a given choice results in failure, it still likely illuminates new paths to get you where you want to go. In fact, the riskiest career choice of all might be the one that seems "safest": not moving at all. The German poet Goethe put it well when he said, "The dangers of life are infinite, and among them is safety."

If your present situation is already deteriorating, staying put only allows it to worsen. Life might also create situations in which we have little choice but to take risks, even if we didn't seek them out. On the other hand, if you're coming off a success yet envisioning an even greater goal, staying put carries ever-increasing opportunity costs. As you linger in place, you fail to develop new skills and capabilities as quickly as your peers, making it increasingly harder to compete going forward. As I've found many times over, taking a chance, even if it fails to pan out, usually allows you to learn more quickly than remaining in a more comfortable situation that no longer challenges you.

When interviewing job candidates, I often ask them to name their biggest career regret. Curiously, most candidates point not to their failures, but to the business they didn't start, the job opportunity they didn't grasp, the service they hesitated to launch, the employee they failed to let go, and so on. There's an important lesson to be learned from this.

Even on the organizational level, research shows that over the long term companies that remain relatively static are far more prone to failure than companies that make multiple choices, successful or not. In researching their book *Strategy Beyond the Hockey Stick,* the McKinsey partners Chris Bradley, Martin Hirt, and Sven Smit studied companies over a fifteen-year period to determine which achieved longer-term, nonlinear success. As they found, the biggest predictor of a company's long-term success was its consistent ability to grow and evolve through moves like mergers, initiatives to improve productivity, and the like. As the authors remark, "Not moving is probably the riskiest strategy of all." The overall lesson for companies, and indeed for all of us: You need to Grow, or you just might Go.

WHEN THE MYTH STOPS, EVERYTHING CAN START

Throughout 2010 and 2011, Nicky's monthly revenue growth declined. Her landlord, despite increasing store closures in the mall, still refused to lower her rent and pressured her to renew her lease for another three years. In December 2012, after numerous phone conversations, Nicky and I agreed to spend a weekend together poring through all her financials, identifying new business options in great detail, and modeling them on a spreadsheet. By the end of the weekend, Nicky understood how much her current choice was "costing her" and how other possible choices stacked up financially and emotionally, at least in theory. We agreed on the many steps she could take in parallel to explore these choices further.

Over the next few years, Nicky took some of those steps in fits and starts. She began investigating other practice locations but concluded that this option wouldn't work well for her or her patients. Seeking out a new location would carry plenty of risk, and it would burden her with costly setup expenses. Meanwhile, she would continue to feel the stresses of being an entrepreneur. Nicky sometimes heard of practices in the area that had room for another doctor, but they weren't well suited to her business. In 2015, Nicky finally went to her landlord and refused to sign a new long-term lease. She renegotiated a short-term lease with month-to-month options, thus allowing flexibility to make a future move. Her landlord agreed, and for the first time in recent years, Nicky began to form an exit strategy from the status quo.

In early 2017, we had a conversation that finally shook everything loose for her. More worried than ever about the mall's declining prospects, Nicky made a bold decision: Rather than waiting any longer to decide on her next move, she put her practice on pause so she would have time to step back and put her full energy into determining the best new options for her and her patients. Pausing her income and letting her patients know was a daunting thought. But she understood that a new possibility would only begin to unfold when she fully let go of the choice she'd lived with for so long. Her relief at exiting her current situation was palpable.

Slowly, she began to become excited about what might come next. She also let others in her network know that she was finally moving on. Serendipity stepped in to help: A friend told her of a new medical clinic opening up much closer to her home, part of a larger venture-backed medical company opening locations throughout the region. Each location offered combined medical and optometry services, and the company was seeking optometrists to build out these practices.

Nicky went in and interviewed, informing the company of the many strong patient relationships she had built over her seventeen-year run. Impressed, Nicky and the clinic agreed on a mutually beneficial and highly lucrative contract for her to work with them. The deal, which Nicky accepted, was financially compelling, and it allowed her to work closer to home, maintain a more reasonable weekly schedule, and continue to serve her existing patients (with more comprehensive services, additionally). Only by taking a risk and shutting down her mall practice had Nicky finally opened a pathway for new possibilities to materialize. Happily, one did, an opportunity she'd never imagined, after years of stress and difficulty.

Nicky's success didn't happen overnight. Rather, she pieced together smaller and then bigger choices over several years to unlock an entirely new career possibility, one that leveraged her experience as an entrepreneur and optometrist in a whole new way. By finally letting go of her fear of the Single Choice, Nicky gained the courage, flexibility, and momentum she needed to start her next journey.

If you've been struggling to move ahead, now is the time to take stock of how you think about risk. The Myth of the Single Choice prevents us from moving both in challenging situations and at times when choices abound. It falsely persuades us that we're better off doing nothing, when in fact that is likely our riskiest move. It keeps us married to the hero's journey of our imagination, distancing us from life as it really is. Luckily for us, the number of choices and combinations of choices that can move us toward our goals is virtually infinite as long as we're willing to put ourselves in motion. When the myth stops, everything really can start.

POSSIBILITY POINTERS

- Many of us believe that a single large choice determines our ultimate success or failure (the Myth of the Single Choice).
- In truth, careers unfold over a long series of risks and choices, large and small. Multiple combinations of moves unlock success.
- Our biggest risk is inaction. Grow or go!

2 | PUMP YOUR RISK-TAKING MUSCLES

If you to want to learn the basics of risk-taking, there's nothing better than learning how to sell. My own education began in the summer of 1989, when, after completing my first year of university, I returned to my hometown of St. Catharines, Ontario, Canada, to get a summer job. I'd always worked in my parents' medical office, and my father wanted nothing more than for me to continue that, but I had other ideas. That summer, I wanted to stand on my own two feet and land an office job outside of the family. Scanning the local newspaper's job postings, I applied for secretarial jobs at small businesses. The local Filter Queen franchise hired me to answer the phone, and I was on my way.

If you haven't heard of a Filter Queen, I don't blame you — I hadn't either. During the 1980s, it was the Rolls Royce of vacuum cleaners, with its "patented cyclonic action system" and nifty attachments capable of cleaning any corner of your home. Although many a homemaker knew of these devices, many others didn't, and neither did they understand why they should pay many hundreds of dollars for the privilege of owning one. To help them understand, salespeople demonstrated the product at home, convincing people that their lives would be very much the worse without a Filter Queen.

Day one on the job turned out to be quite eye-opening. I entered a nondescript building, no company logo anywhere in sight, and made my way to the shabby chairs and desk in the front office where I'd be sitting. John, the owner of the franchise who drove a pretty sweet green Jaguar, had his office right behind my desk. With little fanfare or training, he asked me to start answering the phones. It didn't take long for me to understand where the real action happened: off to the right, in another small, equally bare room with a few tables and desks, a whole lot of yellow pages directories, and four or five salespeople trying their hardest to make some magic happen.

There were Gary and Sarah, the husband-and-wife team who often brought their new baby into work. Sarah would spend hours calling to land appointments on the phone and then send Gary out to do the demo and to close in person. There was Donny, a young, cocky salesman with blue eyes, a big grin, and a whole lot of charm. He could close sales like no other. And there were a number of new sales recruits in the office each week, each trying their hand at making a living dialing for dollars. A few made it, but many didn't.

The selling itself was as nitty-gritty as it gets. Starting at nine a.m., each rep would open the phonebook and cold-call total strangers, trying to convince them to take forty-five minutes out of their day to witness the magic of the Filter Queen in their homes. They'd dial a number and get hung up on before they even got out a few sentences. They'd dial a number and find out that the line had gotten disconnected. They'd dial a number, give their full pitch, and then get hung up on. They'd dial a number, give their pitch, encounter resistance, give another pitch, and another, and then get hung up on.

I witnessed my share of dubious tactics, and also had to handle a fair number of unhappy customers myself who felt they had paid too much for their Filter Queens. But by the end of the summer, I had gained respect and appreciation for this quirky tribe of which I'd been a small part. Every day, these folks put their egos at risk to make a living, handling rejection again and again in order to achieve an ultimate success. While many people fear facing even one failure, these individuals were willing to take lots of little chances every day and had learned to let little fails roll off their backs. Rather than a slog, life in the Filter Queen office was pretty damn fun, and funny.

The lesson on the value of learning to sell stuck, and I went on during college to make a small career of it myself. I started in retail sales at the local mall while in school, and the following summer began selling conference room space to businesses for a hotel in London, Ontario (where I attended university). I cold-called, pitched, closed, taking little risks every day to make something happen. Like my old friends from Filter Queen, I developed some risk-taking muscles, especially when it came to overcoming the fear of selling and rejection, becoming quite comfortable taking chances again and again, failing much of the time, but still succeeding enough times to become a pretty good salesperson.

If you want to buck the Myth of the Single Choice, a great way to start is by making a habit of taking smaller risks in your daily life. Before you take bigger, bold chances, get some practice when the stakes are lower. You don't have to take a sales job, but you do have to consciously look for reasons to take risks in order to become more comfortable with it. Eleanor Roosevelt advised us, "Do one thing every day that scares you." I think that putting yourself out there on the line just a little bit at a time — *but doing it lots of times* — is a great way to build risk-taking muscles.

REFRAMING RISK

As we've seen, the definition of *risk* invokes the looming specter of loss. I believe most people think about risk similarly, as a dalliance with danger. Interestingly, *risk-taking* is defined in a much more balanced way: as "the act or fact of doing something that involves danger or risk in order to achieve a goal." While acknowledging the uncertainty of any move, this simple definition directs equal attention on the positive objectives of most risk-taking. It suggests that every day we have the opportunity to take chances, big and small, to further our goals.

No matter where we are in life, taking micro-risks first can empower us to take more and bigger risks and to achieve more. We don't need to begin the journey to possibility by imagining imminent danger or large loss. Worse yet, we shouldn't wait until the unfortunate day when we face a potentially life-altering decision to take our first risk. We can begin now and start small in pursuing the simplest of positive goals.

Looking back on it, I feel like I was exposed to a very "normalized" and positive view of risk-taking as a child, well before my first pre-career foray into sales. I have my parents to thank for that. At a glance, you would be hard-pressed to call Drs. Singh and Ahluwalia risk-takers. They certainly took one big risk before I was born, moving to Canada from Africa later in their lives. In Africa, they had enjoyed a successful joint medical practice and a great lifestyle. After their move, they had to recertify their medical training and start over financially in a new country. Once settled in Canada, however, they lived a fairly conventional life as proprietors of a modest medical practice. I grew up solidly middle class in the small town of St. Catharines, Ontario, where my parents' main mission was to provide a great education for each of their children.

Behind the scenes, though, my father was an entrepreneur and dreamer of possibilities who gave me an early education in risk-taking and its benefits. From the moment he first taught me to do his taxes (yes, you read that right), starting at the age of eight or so, I understood running a small business not as an inherently risky and mysterious endeavor but as a repeatable process that involved continuous doses of risk-taking. Some of these risks were small, as when he tried build a brand for his medical office by calling it the HealthCare ServiceCenter long before consumers would understand what it even meant to have branded health care services. Others were larger, as when he took out a mortgage to buy a new building that could house multiple doctors in the hopes of establishing the area's first walk-in clinic. (He did this a good ten years before this innovation would take hold and become the basis for many new and large medical corporations.)

At a macro level, several of these risks didn't work out the way he imagined—my dad never achieved his dreams of outsize business success. But my enduring memory of my father is that of a man who felt fulfilled and was happy to take chances small and large in the pursuit of business possibility. He never talked about risk-taking with me —he didn't have to. It was simply what he did every day as an entrepreneur and small business owner. He was equal parts pragmatic and ambitious in his approach to taking chances, and this shaped my worldview, too.

RISK-TAKING FOR UPSIDE

Even when our lives are perfectly fine, opportunities exist to find and take small risks to accelerate our growth and build our risk-taking muscles. Reflecting on my childhood experiences and my career since, I've identified four simple reasons why most of us take risks (Figure 4).

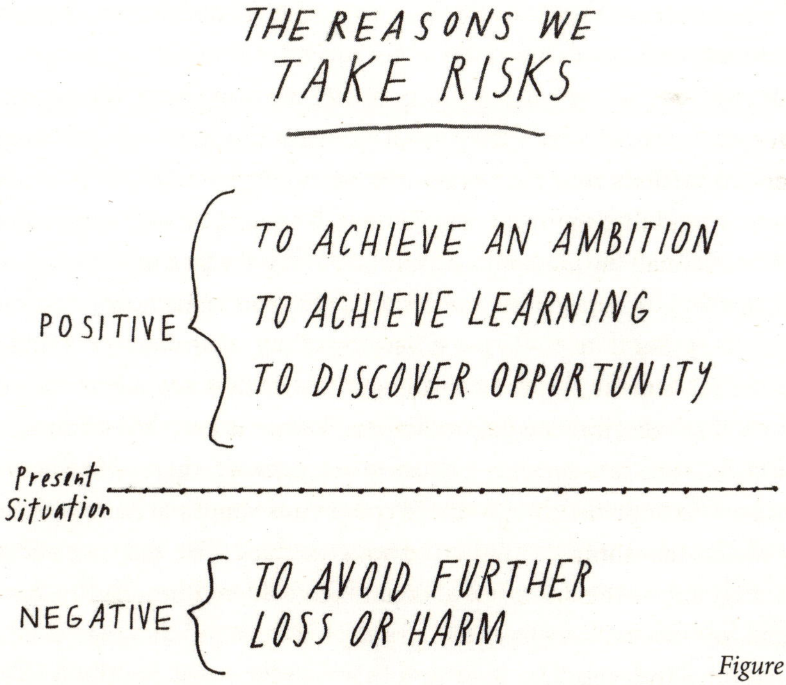

THE REASONS WE
TAKE RISKS

POSITIVE
- TO ACHIEVE AN AMBITION
- TO ACHIEVE LEARNING
- TO DISCOVER OPPORTUNITY

Present Situation

NEGATIVE
- TO AVOID FURTHER LOSS OR HARM

Figure 4

When we find ourselves in a stable or positive place, risk-taking serves as an accelerant that we can use to discover new opportunities, unlock new learning, or achieve an ambitious goal. I call this *risk-taking for upside,* and it can help us achieve greater career benefits when we already have a grand plan and even when we don't.

Let's say you're in an okay or good job. You have a vague idea of your upcoming career choices but aren't sure what they really entail. Taking small chances to discover new opportunities is a simple way to begin. Reach out and try to talk to someone who might be able to help you. In sales, I prospected to maximize my chances of success, holding exploratory conversations with groups or companies. We can do something similar in our careers, from asking to sit in on meetings in areas we want to learn to asking someone on LinkedIn for a short conversation to discover what's interesting or possible.

A second reason to take risks when life is relatively good is to learn and grow. We've been trained to think that all risk-taking is about the pursuit of a specific, large ambition. But taking small chances to accelerate our learning is worthwhile as a goal in its own right, and it might potentially open up pathways to larger success. I watched my father experiment continuously in his personal life, spending small amounts of time and money to satisfy his natural curiosity. Fascinated by investing, financial markets, and innovation, he pored over stock tickers in the newspaper, calling up his broker, Tom, to "buy some AOL" long before I knew what the tech industry was. Often we'd get roped into his tinkering, whether he was pulling apart the dryer to show us how it worked and then seeing if he could put it back together, or helping me to build a working model of the human eye for my second-grade science fair in our rural garage (you can guess who was doing most of the building).

Either way, the message I internalized growing up was the same: The main benefit of trying something new was simply to increase your knowledge. How well you did something mattered less than your ability to simply get out there, take a shot, and learn something. As the theologian John Henry Newman remarked, "A man would do nothing if he waited until he could do it so well that no one could find fault." I've taken this lesson to heart as an adult, taking on roles in order to learn new skills or industries, often as lateral moves without the promise of more pay or a better title. Not only have these experiences strengthened my leadership capabilities, but in many ways they have led to new career opportunities that I never contemplated.

Last, you can make a habit of small risk-taking to achieve large, specific goals you might already have in mind. Describing his early career, my friend Adam Zbar, cofounder and CEO of the subscription meal delivery service Sun Basket, told me about a critical life decision he made in his twenties. After he completed a two-year analyst program at the top consulting firm McKinsey & Company, the firm offered to pay for Adam's MBA and then to hire him back in a well-paying role after he graduated. He had already gained admission to the University of Chicago Business School, so it was easiest to just say yes to McKinsey's offer. However, despite having learned a lot from his McKinsey experience, Adam realized that "while many things in life are hard, few are interesting," and he wanted to pursue a different path connected to his love of storytelling and filmmaking. He turned down McKinsey's generous offers so he could follow his dreams and pursue his goal of going to film school.

Although this decision was a big one, Adam proceeded toward his goal by taking a number of smaller risks. Lacking an academic background in filmmaking, he realized he'd never get into a school if he applied right away, so he decided to take some classes as a nonmatriculated student and build a portfolio over a period of one to two years. Returning to Utah, where he'd spent part of his childhood, he enrolled in a creative writing class at the University of Utah to give himself a solid background in storytelling. Then Adam moved twice: first to Minneapolis to study dramatic writing at the Playwrights' Center, and then to New York City to take graduate-level classes as a nonmatriculated student at New York University. All along, he supported himself by working part-time as a management consultant. When he felt like he'd finally gained enough experience, he applied to UCLA's School of Theater, Film, and Television, one of America's best film schools, where he went on to earn an MFA in film production. This string of smaller risks would help build Adam's confidence, setting him up well to take much larger risks later on.

Of course, not all risk-taking happens for positive reasons. As my sister Nicky discovered, we sometimes need to take chances to escape difficult or deteriorating situations, recognizing that sticking with the status quo would cause us more pain or loss. In these cases, too, taking small risks first rather than jumping straight to a giant risk can feel less daunting. Other times, a situation might seem so negative already that risk-taking feels like it has only upside, driving us to get started without fearing further loss. Ironically, difficult situations tend to jump-start risk-taking of any kind far more than stable ones do, leading to the popular adage that we should never "waste a good crisis."

EARLY AND OFTEN: THE MULTIPLIER EFFECT

Once you begin taking many smaller risks on an ongoing basis, you'll find it gets progressively easier as you build your risk-taking muscles. We don't need to be risk-takers by nature in order to become competent at the process of experimenting in our daily lives. Some of our tries will succeed while others won't. When we take chances for the purposes of learning or discovery, we might even learn to feel our failures less, helping us to fear them less as well. When I was a child, small failures like getting shot down in class after daring to speak up left me stewing for a while. But later, as I began taking more small chances, my worries about personal insult in the face of failure ebbed. When I began cold-calling, my tolerance for rejection increased even more. By teaching us to put failure into perspective, early, habitual risk-taking prepares us to pursue more and bigger risk-taking over time.

Early and habitual risk-taking also makes risk-taking easier over time by helping us become successively smarter about the topic at hand. When pursuing any goal, particularly ambitious ones, our second, third, and fourth tries stand a better chance of succeeding, since they're in-formed and shaped by the results of preceding efforts. We come to think of our first small tries as positive or negative signals that we process as we make our subsequent moves toward something complex or auda-cious. When we're pursuing simple goals, small risk-taking can yield quick answers to our questions, allowing us to move on efficiently to other areas of focus. But by staying put, we learn nothing.

THE VIRTUES OF FULL-ON FAILURE

Although we can and should take small, positive risks to establish a risk-taking habit, a single, large failure can also jump-start the building of these muscles. A friend of mine whom I'll call Gina, cofounder and CEO of a highly successful software company, faced exactly that situa-tion when she dropped out of high school in the tenth grade. She didn't do so to start a software company and become a billionaire. This was a full-on failure, complete with Fs and Incompletes on her academic rec-ord, not to mention some serious parental pushback. For months after she stopped going to school, Gina whiled away her time playing video games in her room, reading books, and wondering what to do with her life. As she remembers, she had felt suffocated by the intense pressure her parents put on her to perform academically. She reached a point where she just couldn't take it any longer. "I felt like I had hit rock bot-tom in some sense," she remembers. "It wasn't like I was going to be able to bounce back and apply to college with a good grade point average."

Gina's terrified parents convinced her to enroll in a boarding school in Europe. After spending two years there and becoming re-engaged in academics, she returned home to finish up high school. She applied to colleges and was rejected by virtually every big-name school except one. She did well there, earning a computer science degree and even joining the women's basketball team as a walk-on player. After graduating, she joined some of her college friends at a tech startup, working as a software engineer. She spent two and a half years there, learning the basics of tech entrepreneurship. In 2008, she quit to start a company with a college friend, and eventually achieved success.

Gina's struggles in high school and her time at a boarding school didn't set the stage for her later success by exposing her to computer science, mathematics, and coding—she had already gravitated toward these subjects. It did so by demystifying failure, which in turn increased her tolerance for subsequent risk-taking. For her, every failure now seems like the window into a future success. "I guess I'm always thinking about how do I take a situation and make this the best thing that ever happened," she says. "It might take thirty years to reframe it, but there's a reframing of it where it is a turning point, and it becomes a milestone." Her experiences as an entrepreneur have only confirmed the value of this attitude toward failure. "We've had lots and lots of brushes with failure that we've worked through, and we've learned from, and that we've gotten stronger as a result of." Gina's high school failures didn't cause her to shrink back from risk-taking. In fact, *just the opposite:* It emboldened her to take even more risks large and small.

Over time, demystifying failure also helped Gina by allowing her to feel comfortable on teams packed with more accomplished performers. Speaking of her basketball career, she notes that at every level of competition she has "always been the bottom average player" in all the teams she's played for. When she reached a certain level of competence, she'd take a risk and jump to the next level, finding herself mediocre again relative to her teammates. At her college, one of the NCAA's premier college basketball programs, she was one of the weaker players and spent her time riding the bench. But at least she was on the team, improving her skills and knowledge by practicing with elite athletes. Afterward, when she played recreational basketball in her spare time, she realized that although she wasn't pro basketball material, she had become an exceptionally strong and seasoned player relative to the general public. Because she had made her peace with failing, she could surround herself with better players and improve her own skills. No matter what goals you're aiming for, making risk-taking a habit and developing a healthy attitude toward failure can help you in turn take even more risks and speed up your growth trajectory.

If you've ever wondered how high-profile entrepreneurs can risk billions on a single big idea, or how successful professionals can muster the courage to throw away successful careers to try something entirely new, or how climbers can free-solo the face of the world's most dangerous rock faces, you now know the answer. Most likely their biggest risk wasn't their first, but number fifty or even five hundred. The risk-taker who hits a grand slam in his first and only time at bat is not the rule but the extreme exception. The folks you see taking big risks today have been taking risks all along — small ones, even microscopic ones. They've built risk-taking as a muscle long before anyone noticed.

If you're curious about new career opportunities, reach out to five new contacts in hopes of making a connection. If you're working in a corporate job, decide to speak up in a meeting at the risk of sounding foolish, asking the question everyone else is secretly pondering. If you have some savings and a deep passion for following certain companies or industries, invest a little of your cash in a stock trading account, trying your hand at using your knowledge to generate incremental financial rewards.

My friend Reshma Saujani, the best-selling author of *Brave, Not Perfect,* turns to sports and other physical endeavors as a way of flexing and building her risk-taking muscles. Once every month or two, she'll try out a new sport just for the sake of experiencing it. She's tried surfing, she says, even though it didn't seem like the thing for her: "I can't swim, I don't like cold water, and I don't like doing things that I'm not good at." She's gone to dance classes, the only forty-something boogying down among a crowd of limber twenty-somethings. The point is simply to *keep taking risks,* confronting yourself with the shock of the new or the unfamiliar. As Reshma points out, risk-taking doesn't just become easier the more you do it — it can be fun, too. "There's something about feeling alive and getting a rush" by taking a risk, she says.

More important than any single chance we take is the commitment we make to start taking small risks every day. If you're in a relatively safe, secure, and positive environment, you're in the best position to be-gin taking little chances to grow. But any time is a good time. As we gain practice in building knowledge iteratively and dealing with small failures, we become more adept at choosing possibility. When the time comes for us to make a truly significant choice, as it invariably will, we'll be ready.

POSSIBILITY POINTERS

- Taking small risks early and often helps you to build risk-taking muscles, with compounding benefits.
- Rather than focusing solely on the potential for loss, we can re-frame risk as decisions we make that afford us considerable upside potential.
- There are four key reasons we can take risks: to discover opportu-nities, to learn something new, to achieve a new goal, or to avoid further harm.

If you think you must prepare endlessly or have absolute clarity about your goals before you can take risks effectively, then I have a story to tell you. Throughout my school years, I knew exactly what it took to succeed, but as I approached my graduation from university, I found myself shockingly unclear about what to do next. Even the ambition I identified — becoming a prestigious investment banker or management consultant, replete with power suits, CEOs as clients, and a big paycheck — was a copycat goal. My closest friends were seeking jobs in these areas, as were a number of other classmates, so because I didn't know what to do, I figured I should seek that kind of job too.

I wish I could tell you I'd even heard of these roles before, let alone contemplated them deeply before my job search began. I wish I could tell you I'd put in motion all the steps to achieve this goal by starting much earlier in university, such as joining the Economics Club or Debate Club, bolstering my résumé with leadership positions like class president, or getting a summer internship with a global corporation. In truth, between being a secretary for the local Filter Queen and doing local retail and hotel sales, I had amassed few of the impressive college accomplishments I'd need to compete with the best of the best of my peers. Their educational and career moves seemed perfectly orchestrated and executed. Not mine.

My anxiety during that fall of 1993 was running high, and I felt terribly depressed, having failed to secure a position the previous June when I graduated with my peers. My experience interviewing at Claridge had given me a temporary confidence boost, but by the end of November I still hadn't landed my dream job in global investment banking or consulting and felt once again like I was on the brink of failure. My fortunes turned in December, but just a little: I finally received an offer from TD Bank, a Canadian investment bank in Toronto. I accepted, far more grudgingly than I should have. Although I was glad to have lined up a job, my less enlightened younger self still felt that I had fallen short of what others had accomplished and what I had presumed I could achieve as well. I made plans to move to Toronto in a few weeks, but I wasn't happy about it.

At around this time, I heard from my friend Bertram, who was living in New York City and working at Merrill Lynch, one of the largest and most aggressive of the Wall Street investment banks. While Merrill didn't formally recruit at Canadian universities, Bertram had conducted an independent job search and managed to get himself in the door. Hearing the dejection in my voice, he encouraged me to try once more for a global banking job. "Send me your résumé and I'll pass it on. You have nothing to lose." After my Claridge experience, I knew he was right, so I didn't hesitate. I also knew that the chances of receiving any kind of response were slim at best.

A week or two passed, and in the middle of December I received a letter conveying the classic noncommittal response. Merrill suggested that were I "ever in New York," I would be welcome to come in for an informational interview to "learn more about the firm."

Sitting around the dining table at my parents' home in rural St. Catharines, I sighed and uttered, "Well, that's that."

"What's what?" my father asked.

"Another rejection, this time from Merrill." I handed over the letter for him to scan.

"That's not a rejection," he said. "They invited you in."

"Dad, it's just a courtesy. They're being polite. If they wanted me, they would have offered me a real interview and asked me to fly down to New York."

My father handed me the letter back. "Maybe, but I say you buy a train ticket to New York and take them up on their offer." Like Bertram, he reminded me I had nothing to lose, and he paid little mind to the fact that I'd already accepted a job. *In short, he was encouraging me to take a risk.*

Two weeks later, I found myself in Merrill's sparkling new world headquarters in Lower Manhattan, located directly across the street from the Twin Towers. About fifteen minutes into a thirty-minute informational interview, the recruiter asked if I would stay longer to meet with a colleague of hers. I agreed, and by the end of the day, I walked away with an invitation to participate in Super Saturday, the grueling final round of Merrill's competitive, multi-round vetting process. Top students from elite U.S. schools would converge on Merrill's headquarters for an afternoon of high-pressure interviews and exercises. Somehow, I'd bypassed the usual process and secured a coveted chance to compete with the best of the best for a prestigious Wall Street job.

Super Saturday would take place about a month later. As I set about mentally preparing, I also completed my move to Toronto and started at TD Bank. Given how unenthused I was about that job, I resolved to pursue multiple opportunities in parallel, and I didn't stop with Merrill. If I couldn't fulfill my dream of landing a job at a leading global investment bank (and after failing so many times, I feared I wouldn't), I wanted to pursue some other, equally ambitious goal. I still didn't know precisely what kind of career I wanted, but still not content with having only one new option I was excited about, I began putting my energy into researching brand-new opportunities. The three possibilities that rose to the top of my reignited ambitions were as diverse as one could imagine: joining the Canadian Foreign Service, attending law school, or enrolling in medical school. Secretly I applied to McMaster University's medical program and managed to secure an interview on the basis of my overall academic achievements despite having never taking the MCAT or any college science courses. I simultaneously sat for the Foreign Service exam and managed to pass, securing an in-person interview in Ottawa in February. And I walked into the LSAT exam as well, only to walk out five minutes later when I realized that I would never, ever wish to work as an attorney. In retrospect, I should have begun methodically exploring these options months earlier, at the very beginning of my job search and pipeline, but better late than never. I found myself relieved to have new choices to consider, and the exercise also validated my continued excitement for Merrill.

In the middle of January, I took the train down to New York again and participated in Super Saturday. Although intimidated by the caliber of the other applicants, I competed aggressively and felt good about the day. Apparently, Merrill's recruiters felt similarly about me. A couple of weeks later, on a frigid winter's evening that happened to be my twenty-third birthday, my original Merrill interviewer called me personally to offer me a full-time position as an analyst at the company. I'd start in June — that is, if I was interested. I could barely contain myself. After a year of struggle, I had finally landed my dream job. "I'd love to work at Merrill," I managed to say. I was ready for this exciting new chapter in my career, my conviction in my choice strengthened by the multiple avenues I'd pursued in parallel.

I promptly canceled my in-person interviews with the Foreign Service in Ottawa. While it would make for a better story to tell you that I rejected med school as well, the truth is that I never ended up getting in. I'm reasonably sure my fumbling for answers regarding my passion for medicine left them reaching for much better candidates after our interview.

If the path to success is an ongoing process of risk-taking, don't presume it favors only those with the biggest goals or the most clarity. One of the most useful ways to begin risk-taking even before we're sure what we want is to pursue multiple options at once to find out. Salespeople often kick off a sales process by creating the widest "funnel" of prospective customers they can, taking multiple chances at the same time to explore the possibilities. You can do something similar in your life, taking a series of small risks in multiple directions simultaneously. By deliberately pursuing a path of discovery to experiment with a full spectrum of opportunities and risks, you can actually identify and clarify your goals, potentially winding up with even more options to consider than you realized, as well as more information to use when the time comes to finally make a big choice. If you've already determined your goal, you can use this period to pursue the one-in-ten bets alongside the one-in-a-hundred or even the one-in-a-thousand, keeping your options open for as long as possible in case any of these paths might ultimately materialize.

I've used this technique of discovery-based risk-taking — or *pipelining in parallel,* as I call it — throughout my career to discover and clarify my goals while also putting myself in motion early to pursue them. I've benefitted enormously from the approach, maximizing the opportunities available to me, minimizing large risks by making multiple bets at once, and setting myself up emotionally to pursue my goals. Let go of the idea that risk-taking starts only once you "know" exactly what you want to do. Use risk-taking to help you discover and validate your goals and to open up new and unforeseen pathways toward achieving them.

PIPELINING IN PARALLEL

On the face of it, the tactic of pursuing multiple risks of various kinds at once should seem familiar. Financial professionals often try to offer investors optimal returns by creating diverse portfolios that include both higher- and lower-risk classes of assets. By taking multiple risks, they maximize investment opportunities while lowering the overall risk of the portfolio on any single bet. Likewise, as parents research colleges and take their children on campus tours, counselors encourage them to apply to many schools in parallel, from the safest of safety schools to the most elite colleges and universities, so that they may maximize their odds of success while diversifying their risks. At work, many of us are familiar with creative problem-solving techniques that call for exploring a wide range of ideas at once, a critically important step before ranking possible solutions and making an effective decision.

As pervasive as this logic is, the sad truth is that we often ignore it when planning for our own professional lives, constraining our choices too early. Research suggests that having too many choices can feel overwhelming and hamper our motivation to act. Seeking to avoid discomfort, we home in on a choice very early and then energetically execute a singular plan to achieve it. Performance coaches, psychologists, and others advocating focus can reinforce this instinct to keep our perspective very narrow from the start. If we don't discipline ourselves to focus, they suggest, we'll become scattered and get nowhere, not least because we possess limited willpower to use when executing our goals.

It's certainly important to focus deeply on a goal and pursue it doggedly after we've chosen a given path of action. But when we take the time *before* choosing to explore *all* potential paths of opportunity, we usually achieve much better results. In addition to allowing us to identify or validate our overall objective and to uncover multiple pathways to success, pipelining in parallel can help us to mitigate risk. By diversifying our efforts, we lower the risk we would have run had we pursued only a single path of action. We might need to tap our inner salesperson to do it, optimistically pursuing the highest and lowest probability opportunities with equal vigor, while remaining skeptical enough to know that we stand only a slim chance that all of these opportunities will work out. We have nothing to lose at the beginning of any new chapter by prospecting broadly, and much to gain.

Relatedly, parallel pipelining of opportunities helps us by opening the way for serendipity to assist our efforts and create new, unforeseen opportunities to achieve our goals. I only received my dream offer because I was constantly putting bait in the water during my job search, and because I responded to nudges from Bertram and my dad despite my own paralyzing skepticism.

Finally, discovery and pipelining deliver important emotional benefits. If we pursue safer choices in parallel with riskier ones, we can stay ambitious and hopeful while also remaining pragmatic. When it comes time to make a decision, the information we gain via pipelining can give us more confidence and conviction as we finalize our goal and plan.

Taking small risks before committing to a given path also puts us into motion earlier, giving us a sense of momentum heading into decision-making and then execution. Last, taking risks to maximize opportunities can feel liberating given the intense pressure we often feel once we've made a big, important choice and told people about it. When we take the time to learn, try something new, and pursue long-shot opportunities as part of a discovery process, we give ourselves some permission to fail, since we haven't yet committed to our final choice.

FROM ZERO TO ONE

I see entrepreneurs use pipelining in parallel all the time to drive amazing results, both for their personal careers and for their companies (much of the time, these are one and the same). Ashvin Kumar, founder of the mobile shopping marketplace Tophatter, recounts that he originally got started in 2008 when he and a friend quit their jobs to found a technology company. That in itself was a massive risk, but they also faced an equally big decision: which technology to pursue as the basis for their business. Rather than develop a single app or feature and market that, they decided to build a whole slew of them to see what came up and only then pick one to commercialize. "We didn't really know what we were going to build," he says. "We just knew that we were committed to building something. We really enjoy building the ship as much as we do sailing it to a specific destination. We sort of leveraged that enjoyment and said, 'Look, let's not worry too much about what exactly we're building.'"

Discovering that they liked e-commerce, the two spent about eighteen months building, testing, and launching fifteen to twenty products in that space. These were small risks — the two didn't require much capital to quickly launch a product (good thing, because they didn't have much). Many of these experiments didn't amount to anything, but that didn't matter. Through the process of pursuing possibility, the two were honing their skill and their own interest: "We were trying to find what we enjoyed doing, what mountains we had the energy to climb. We were learning about ourselves in the process, and what markets were interesting. With each experiment, we got better." The two knew they weren't going to experiment forever — at some point they would have to make a decision to get behind one of their products. But rather than pin down a specific end date, they kept working, checking in periodically with each other to gauge how they were feeling and whether they were ready to end their discovery period.

In 2009, one of their inventions gained traction. Blippy was a social network that allowed people to share information about their purchases on sites like Amazon or iTunes with their friends and also see what their friends were buying. Investors poured millions of dollars into the project, allowing Ashvin and his partner to hire a team, build out the product, and give it a real launch. Unfortunately, Blippy didn't catch fire, so within a year Ashvin and his partner went back to discovery mode. They pipelined in parallel to uncover opportunities, this time mobilizing all that they had learned from Blippy and previous experiments. After about nine months, they launched Tophatter. From the very beginning, the product "had a magic that none of the other stuff [they] had built had." The time had come: The two were willing to commit as never before. Because they had undertaken such a prolonged and rich discovery period, they could move ahead confidently.

You might hear a story like this and fear that you'll never exit discovery mode once you enter it. Year after year you'll spin out possibilities, searching for the "perfect" choice and never leaving your current one. You can avoid this trap by defining a clear deadline up front for ending your discovery period. Often, necessity will set a time limit for you. I gave myself a year to keep trying for the job of my dreams but couldn't have gone much longer for both financial reasons and for my résumé.

Remember, too, that you run a greater risk of never choosing if you pursue opportunities *sequentially* than if you get moving in parallel. When you process choices serially over an extended period, it's easier to say no to every single one in anticipation of the ever elusive "perfect choice." When you start actively pipelining and putting safer and riskier bets in motion alongside one another to see what happens, choices and knowledge come at you more rapidly and in waves. As a result, you build the conviction that you've "seen enough" to choose and feel a sense of momentum toward making a change.

When my friend Jonathan was in his mid-twenties, he graduated with a law degree and went to work at a leading law firm as an associate. Months into it, he realized that he hated the daily grind and couldn't imagine spending years rising up the ranks at a law firm. Unsure what to do, he worked relationships he'd built in college to conduct informational interviews across a variety of jobs and sectors. Reasoning that his legal background would allow him to negotiate effectively, he explored opportunities in business development at technology companies, and he also looked into working as a sports agent (he'd always been a diehard sports fan). Jonathan looked into a third option: opportunities in corporate development forging strategy around mergers and acquisitions. Meanwhile, a fourth option unexpectedly opened up when one of his current clients called him to ask if he'd consider joining the firm's in-house legal department.

After spending a few months researching these paths and the specific opportunities available to him, Jonathan decided to take the leap into business development. Not only did this option interest him more than the others; he learned that he could transition into this career quickly and land a good job without having to undergo years of additional training. By contrast, it would take him years to build a career as a sports agent. Working in-house at a company wouldn't require much additional training, but it also didn't fire up his passion that much. By pipelining in parallel, he had been able to compare disparate opportunities with one another. He felt sufficiently informed to make a great choice, so he didn't hesitate to take the leap.

PIPELINING LIKE A MASTER

Over the years, I've become better at pipelining, learning to stay open to possibility longer and resisting the inclination to choose "big" before I have multiple choices on the table. I've also developed some tactics that have helped me get the most out of discovery mode, and that can help you, too.

First, *create your own timeline for discovery instead of reacting to everyone else's schedule.* As we field opportunities, particularly those that come inbound and faster than we thought, we often feel compelled to respond quickly and urgently to the people or companies who offer them. Instead, step back and ask yourself why a given opportunity has captured your attention. Was it because of genuine interest on your part and a sense that it serves your larger goals, or because someone else was pressuring you? Do your best to be responsive to others, but also make it clear (diplomatically, of course) what your timeline is for exploring choices before making a final decision. This will also help uncover their true timeline and how much flexibility they really have before making the decision at their end.

Second, if an opportunity feels urgent to you because it will free you from an unpleasant or deteriorating present reality, first *try to articulate the loss you would sustain if you didn't make a choice now and the status quo continued.* What does this "downside scenario" look like? As a second and separate step, think about the "upside opportunity" — the positive outcome you would like to pursue if you were in a "neutral" situation. If you can arrive at rough definitions of the downside scenario and the upside opportunity, you'll identify more readily whether you're choosing something now to satisfy one or both ambitions.

Distinguishing among your goals in this way, you can avoid conflating the choices you're making with multiple objectives in mind. You'll be able to identify many more possible moves you might make in sequence or in parallel to push yourself forward, including some that you might not have considered to line up behind each goal. Using this process will help you identify at least one option that allows you to fix what's broken in your current situation while also analyzing what options you might consider to move yourself from "neutral" to your dream. You might realize that abandoning your present circumstances entirely in favor of something new isn't your only or best path forward.

Yet another tactic to adopt when entering the discovery phase is to *find a brainstorming buddy for your career.* Choose someone who can understand your ambitions, who is adept at generating possibilities, and who can help you to stay optimistic. This person might not be your best friend, biggest confidant, or life partner. Early in my career, I relied on my father and certain friends as brainstorming buddies, but as I advanced I found an executive coach as well as peers who were going through similar situations and brainstormed with them (what I'll describe a bit later on as "professional priests"). We all have wisdom to glean from different people at different stages of our journey. Seek out a tribe of people who enhance rather than diminish your ability to generate ideas in any particular phase. Make sure they're open to listening to your list of opportunities in an unbiased and nonjudgmental way, and to contributing to that list as well.

A final tip for taking pipelining to the next level is to *embrace the art of passive pipelining.* Staying in discovery mode even when you're not looking to make a big decision or choice can prove immensely valuable. It can help you to keep current on the opportunities around you and to stockpile knowledge you might need later on. Some of the best career opportunities I've received have resulted not from purposeful efforts on my part to pursue a new goal, but from simply accepting invitations to connect with interesting people and companies regardless of whether they could contribute to my current goals.

When leading companies, I've always held exploratory conversations with smart prospective hires sent my way even if no roles were open at the time. I've hired several of these people along the way, whether at that same company or the next one. (If you find yourself on the other side of this equation, make sure you say yes to a trusted introduction you've been offered.) Likewise, several of my more successful investments in startups originated because I was keeping an eye on companies in my areas of expertise that were doing interesting things, or because people I trusted referred people or companies to me they thought might fit with my interests or strengths.

The practice of taking small risks to maximize choices *before* you commit to a big choice in your life has only upside. When I was twenty-two, I possessed none of this wisdom and stumbled my way through this approach in a time of need. I certainly didn't examine my obsessive pursuit of a prestigious global banking job as my one "true north." I also swung like a pendulum in pursuing options that I felt were equally ambitious and worthy while remaining unclear about what I really wanted from a career. While I wouldn't wish this anxiety-fueled process on anyone, the tactic of pursuing diverse possibilities at once delivered results for me nonetheless. You have the opportunity to unleash this process earlier and more deliberately than I ever did.

Pipelining in parallel can help each of us to maximize both our opportunities and our knowledge at the start of a new journey, empowering us to make a better choice when we're finally ready to commit.

POSSIBILITY POINTERS

- You don't need perfect goals or clarity to start taking risks.
- Pipelining in parallel allows us to uncover new ambitions, clarify our options, pursue high- and low-probability bets, and build momentum.
- To master the process of discovery via risk-taking, own your timeline, find a brainstorming buddy, and embrace the art of passive pipelining.

4 | WHY PROXIMITY BEATS PLANNING

After landing my dream job at Merrill in 1993, I was determined to prove my worth, so I put in long night and weekend hours, doing my best to anticipate and exceed my boss's expectations. I knew my time at the company was limited — Merrill's analyst program lasted only two years, after which participants typically left the company and either found new jobs in the industry or went back to school for their MBAs — so I had a short time to do it. Serving as an analyst in the Financial Services group, I worked hard, and it paid off. Based on an exceptional first-year review, Merrill offered me a coveted assignment for my second year: an opportunity to move to London and cover European banks.

I immediately accepted, excited about my next big career chapter. I also excelled in London, and when my year there was up, I opted to take another small risk and find a great role within a UK-based company. Most of my peers in investment banking were taking the traditional route of using their job experience to secure admission at an elite graduate business school. Instead, I wanted to learn how to operate and grow part of a big business, not just serve on a team advising it.

Researching potential employers, I set my sights on British Sky Broadcasting (or Sky, as it was known), one of Britain's leading entertainment firms. Founded by the media mogul Rupert Murdoch, Sky was a highly innovative company that had disrupted the cable industry by providing movies, sports, and other programming via satellite dish. Although Sky had struggled initially, at one point losing millions each week, it had grown rapidly thanks to aggressive pricing and marketing, eventually becoming the crown jewel in Murdoch's global empire. After focusing on banks and other financial institutions at Merrill, the prospect of working at a successful media company seemed incredibly glamorous. I was also intrigued by Sky's high-profile leadership duo of the CEO, Sam Chisholm, and the deputy managing director, David Chance. An Australian by birth, Chisholm was famous in Britain for his aggressive and blustery personality, while Chance was known as a much more cool-headed and diplomatic business operator.

With the help of a referral from Merrill, I landed a job as a financial analyst with Sky's chief financial officer. I would not stay in this position very long. After about six months, I found myself on a team presenting a marketing plan directly to Sam, the CEO. We ventured out to Sam's country house on a Sunday evening, and as the meeting proceeded, I mustered the nerve to speak up, taking a small risk to try to contribute my opinions to the conversation. The next morning, Sam called me into his office. "Sukhinder," he said gruffly, but with a twinkle in his eye. "Do you know why you're here?" When I confessed that I did not, Sam praised my comments from the night before and then promoted me on the spot, asking me to come work directly for David, Sky's chief operating officer. "He needs someone just like you," Sam proclaimed, and just like that, I was moved up to the executive floor and assigned to work as David's right hand on special projects.

The perks on the top floor were amazing: fully catered lunches, access to a butler, daily exposure to the company's management team, and more. It wasn't long, though, before I became disappointed and a bit antsy with my prestigious new gig. Although I had expected to work closely with David on big, important initiatives, he was used to being a lone wolf and didn't use me very much at all. He had managed pretty well on his own before my arrival and I suspect had been equally surprised when Sam promoted me and assigned me to him. As the months wore on, my days at work seemed increasingly empty and a little lonely, quite a contrast with my busy first few months at Sky.

I was also feeling empty outside of work. Upon first arriving in London, I shared a flat on Kensington High Street with three other women expats from the U.S. and Canada, who had become my closest friends. When we all finished our analyst positions at different banks, all of them had returned home to get their MBAs. Since then, I had made new friends in London, but was starting to wonder where I wanted to live longer term myself. With so much time to myself, I began to think about my own potential move back to North America and also about leaving the corporate world.

Even though I was in my mid-twenties, I had already begun dreaming of starting my own business. My father always extolled the virtues of "working for yourself," and undergraduate business school exposed me to case study after case study of successful entrepreneurs. Now, as the mystique of corporate life started to wear off, I thought about whether I too could build my own company. Before I started at Sky, my roommate Laura and I tossed out new business ideas to one another, just for the fun of it. When she went home to the States to get her MBA, I continued these musings with my sister Nicky, who had married a Brit and was living in England herself at the time.

At one point, I went so far as to design a new product: fashionable cuff links women could use to add glamor and excitement to business attire. Given the staid and conservative suits we had all worn on Wall Street and the lack of fun options to spruce them up, I thought these cuff links could succeed, and that I'd feel passionate about building a business around them. My sister was an enthusiastic supporter and encouraged me to try. I bought some fabric and created a rough prototype of a cuff link with patterned feminine fabrics embedded in it. I went on to mock up different company names and logos on my computer and even found someone to manufacture more cuff link molds into which I inserted more patterns. After a few months, though, I stalled out, not knowing what to do next or how to get the cuff links distributed or marketed. I would keep those molds in a Zip-loc plastic bag for another ten years, taking them with me from home to home, a reminder of my first mini entrepreneurial attempt.

Watching David and Sam at Sky whet my entrepreneurial ambitions further; the two had built the company as if it were their own business, moving quickly and aggressively to grow the business virtually from scratch many years back and maintaining a shorthand between the two of them that continues even now. I envied their success story and dreamed of creating one of my own. I just didn't know how exactly to make it happen.

Unsure of how to start a new service from scratch myself, and without a great idea, I began to think that being around entrepreneurs might be my next best alternative to figure it out. When another roommate of ours, Jen, returned to her home state of California to attend Stanford's Graduate School of Business (in 1995), I had taken the opportunity to visit her almost right away, and had fallen in love with the Bay Area. The vibe of people innovating and starting companies everywhere seemed pretty magical, especially when coupled with the sunny skies and great lifestyle.

On a fall morning in October 1996, I walked into David's luxurious glass office and resigned from Sky; he was taken aback as I explained that I felt underutilized, and he offered to include me more. But weeks of thinking about it had left me determined to make a change and to take a risk. I told him I was headed back to North America, and specifically to California to figure out my next role.

Although summarily quitting a job to pursue a vague dream might seem like a crazy thing to do, I didn't see it that way. After three successful years at great companies like Merrill and Sky, plus a tough job search that I had survived out of college, I felt pretty confident that I could find a good job in California too. I had $10,000 saved up and parents who would help me if I needed it. So, I just made a move, heading in a rough direction toward my ambitions and trusting that I'd find my way once I got there.

In fairly short order, I did. Four months after quitting at Sky, I arrived in the beautiful San Francisco suburb of Mill Valley, located directly to the north of the Golden Gate Bridge. I came by way of Whistler, British Columbia (where I had spent a month going from zero to hero as a skier) and Los Angeles (where I briefly considered jobs in entertainment). My other expat roommate from the UK, Laura (with whom I'd dreamed up business ideas), was also a California native, and her parents generously agreed to put me up for free in their Mill Valley home until I found a job. It took a few months, but in the summer of 1997, I convinced an interactive TV startup called OpenTV to try me out as a business development manager. Thus began my journey toward entrepreneurship. Two years later, I would get the opportunity to start my own first company, and I've since gone on to start two more and invest in numerous others.

While overall planning has its benefits, popular culture would have us believe that we can't succeed in taking risks unless we have a perfect and precise plan already in place. But I've found that *proximity to opportunity* can benefit us even more than planning in many cases. When we only have a vague idea of our goal or how to achieve it, quickly getting ourselves closer to our dreams may be far more valuable than constructing a precise yet abstract plan from afar. Everyone's circumstances are different, so your version of "close" need not be the same as mine. I quit my job and moved across an ocean in order to surround myself with entrepreneurs. You likely can get proximate to your goals by taking less drastic steps. Still, the lesson is the same: When we don't yet know how to score ourselves, getting onto the field and closer to those who do (and have already) can teach us a lot of what we need to know, including insights we didn't even realize we needed to learn.

THE MYTH OF PERFECT PLANNING

To understand why we shouldn't wait for a sharply defined goal to take action, let's unpack the broader Myth of Perfect Planning. A plan is simply a theory of how our future might unfold assuming a certain defined starting point. Because we frame plans as an antecedent to action, planning itself can seem like a way of getting closer to our dreams. We think that the more precise the plan, the more likely we are to succeed in achieving it. Conversely, when our ambitions are rough and half formed, we presume that we lack permission to act. We haven't done the "hard" work of constructing our plan and thus aren't fully prepared to meet an opportunity.

We also tend to presume that the more specific our plan is, the more likely we will be to achieve it. When we subscribe unconsciously to this thesis, we pour increasing amounts of effort into plotting our goals, then our actions and the expected results, then the next action, and so forth, trying to perfectly predict our future before making any move. Even when we're fuzzy on our goals, we are tempted to plan away, as creating the perfect plan can somehow make us feel highly productive, and even more positive.

Even when we do take action, placing too much emphasis on planning can hamper us as we move toward our goals, locking us in and preventing us from grasping unexpected opportunities. Shea Kelly, a veteran human resources leader at companies such as Citibank, Hewlett Packard, GE, Thomson Sun, Wize Commerce, and Sumo Logic, has seen many talented people plot out their career moves years, even decades early. They decide they want to become a senior leader in some capacity and map out all of the steps they must take to get there. "I think what they can miss along the way is that they might have opportunities to learn and change their perspective. And if you're too prescribed going in, you're going to shut that down," she says.

Kelly offers the example of a well-regarded engineer who was determined to become the head of his company's engineering division. Recognizing that he understood customers and the business well, leaders wanted him to step away from engineering midway through his career to become a product manager. The engineer resisted, fearing that it would undermine his long-term goals and unsure if he'd succeed in a new function. Kelly counseled him to take the risk, arguing that deviating from his plan would allow him to gain a range of new knowledge that he could eventually put to use in a more senior engineering role. After a number of conversations, the engineer took the risk. Good thing: After six months, it became apparent that he was "killing it" in his new job. If this engineer had clung too tightly to his long-term planning, he wouldn't have made what is turning out to be a stellar career move.

As rational as planning seems, personal feeling more than logic tends to drive the elaborate process of mapping out the future. "What motivates our investment in goals and planning for the future, much of the time, isn't any sober recognition of the virtues of preparation and looking ahead," observes Oliver Burkeman, author of the book *The Antidote: Happiness for People Who Can't Stand Positive Thinking.* "Rather, it's something much more emotional: how deeply uncomfortable we are made by feelings of uncertainty. Faced with the anxiety of not knowing what the future holds, we invest ever more fiercely in our preferred vision of that future — not necessarily because it will help us achieve it, but simply because it helps rid us of feelings of uncertainty in the present."

THE POWER OF PROXIMITY

The intellectual act of planning in and of itself doesn't actually shrink the distance between ourselves and our loosely formed ambitions as much as we think. What often does shrink it are certain actions that we take in service to planning. When attempting to plot out the future, we'll often perform desk research to learn how others have achieved something similar to what we want. We'll even go so far as to perform informational interviews, taking a small risk to find out more about things we aspire to. As important as this work is, the next important step is to insert ourselves in an environment filled with people who routinely do what we're struggling to imagine.

Drawing close to these people benefits us in at least three important ways. First, it helps us to further *visualize* what it is we think we want by allowing us to see it in action. If you dream of being an entrepreneur generally, you can read about entrepreneurship in a book, but you can also find a side hustle, figure out a way to follow an entrepreneur, or take a job within a startup. Each of these experiences will allow you to understand better what your goal really looks and feels like, helping to clarify in your own mind if the goal is really for you.

Second, if you have a relatively clear goal but lack a plan for executing it, you can learn more about the specific executional steps you need to take by helping someone else execute their plan and learning by watching, copying, and doing. Historically, we'd call these learning roles *apprenticeships*. In fields such as academia, the arts, and the manual trades, young aspirants have traditionally learned their crafts by serving as the right hand to established practitioners and helping them on their own projects. In recent years, U.S. policymakers have looked to expand apprenticeships and internships as a means of helping more young people build skills and careers, in many cases looking to Europe for inspiration.

Research in psychology and neuroscience also points to the value of learning by helping someone else. A school of thought called "social learning theory" holds that people learn by copying others' behaviors, and neuroscientists have discovered that social learning occurs via a specific neural pathway in the brain. One research study brings more nuance to the social learning theory, arguing that people learn by watching others because those others "inadvertently filter information, so that copiers learn behaviors that have proved successful." Thus, getting close to those people who have mastered what you aspire to do or become might make for more efficient learning, allowing you to more quickly distill your ambitions down to clear, actionable goals and then form realistic plans.

Third, when we insert ourselves into environments where people with ambitions similar to ours have succeeded, we increase the odds that we'll access more opportunities to advance our ambitions simply by virtue of our proximity to them. In his book *Superbosses,* the Tuck Business School professor Sydney Finkelstein describes a group of highly successful practitioners across industries who serve as master teachers to the younger people who work for them. These practitioners not only aggressively advance understudies and support them as they go on to build careers; they create what Finkelstein calls "networks of success" made up of former protégés who open doors and otherwise help one another.

Finkelstein develops the example of the restauranteur Alice Waters, creator of the famed Berkeley, California, restaurant Chez Panisse, whose network in the culinary world is particularly large. As one of her protégés said, "You go anywhere and somehow, someone knows somebody that worked there or they've heard of Alice or one of the cookbooks. It even opens doors when you want to go cook in other countries." If you want to reach a career goal, putting yourself in close contact to those who see or have a lot of opportunity can be just the break you need.

THE ART OF MOVING *BEFORE* PLANNING

In January 2020, Alyssa Nakken became Major League Baseball's first full-time female baseball coach, and the first to ever appear on the field during a game (I had met Alyssa several months before, through our partnerships with the San Francisco Giants at StubHub). How did she achieve such a distinction? Did she frame a clear goal at the outset, craft a brilliant plan, and diligently hack away at it?

Not exactly.

As a child growing up in the small town of Woodland, California, about fifteen miles from downtown Sacramento, Alyssa had dreamed of going to college and playing Division I softball. She achieved her goal, attending California State University in Sacramento on a softball scholarship. Upon graduating in 2012, she didn't quite know what to do other than play it safe and get a well-paying, nine-to-five professional job in the local area. She landed a position as a financial planner in Sacramento and enjoyed it well enough, particularly the chance to meet with clients and forge relationships with them.

It wasn't too long, however, before Alyssa found herself pining for more. Many of her older clients told stories about their career adventures — the cities they'd lived in, their unexpected career moves across companies and industries. Listening to them, she realized that she wanted to have career adventures of her own rather than settle passively into a comfortable job for the next thirty years. She wanted to feel *passionately* about her career and to experience risk-taking in pursuit of her passion. "I was inspired by these clients and all of the different risks they took," she says, "whether it was to start their own business or blow all of their savings to invent something. Rather than play it safe, I started to reimagine what my life could look like."

Although Nakken loved the business of sports and working on teams, she had no clue about which specific goal to pursue. So, she took a leap and moved directionally. Taking a risk and quitting her job, she moved to San Francisco and enrolled in the University of San Francisco's graduate sports management program with an eye toward learning about the sports industry and its opportunities. Her parents supported her decision, encouraging her to take an iterative approach to learning through risk-taking. Recalling their conversations, she says, "It was always like, 'Okay, you've got to try this, learn about it, if it's something you don't like, adjust, readjust, and go a different way.'"

As a student, Alyssa tested out parts of the sports industry by landing internships with the Oakland Raiders (the team has subsequently moved to Las Vegas), Stanford, and the University of San Francisco. Initially, she thought she might like to become athletic director at a university, but after these experiences and an in-class visioning exercise, she decided that this goal didn't quite fire her passion. She would have to continue to experiment to see if she could find out what did — a stressful proposition at times. "You're getting into your mid-twenties and people are asking, 'Well, what are you doing? What's next?' And I'm like, 'Oh, I don't know.' Meanwhile, my friend who I grew up with is now almost done with medical school."

In 2014, Alyssa secured a position as a baseball operations intern with the San Francisco Giants organization. It wasn't glamorous: She worked long hours and immersed herself in the administrative minutia of running a baseball team. But having experienced other organizations, she found that she loved the Giants and could see working there for some time. She also resolved to make the most of the internship as a learning experience so that she could continue to iterate new possible moves.

To get a better handle on the opportunities available in an organization like the Giants, she borrowed a tactic she had learned in graduate school. As part of the visioning exercise she'd performed, she'd had to imagine an ideal job and conduct informational interviews with people who currently occupied that job or others like it. Taking the initiative, she began knocking on the office doors of seasoned Giants executives and asking them about their careers. "You quickly realize that no path is the same. So many people think you have to take this step to get up to this step and then eventually get to that end goal, but that's not the reality. The reality is that a curve ball gets thrown your way, and you can either use that to your advantage and learn and grow and adjust, or you can crumble and fail and give up."

When her internship ended, Alyssa finished her degree and took time off to travel. The following year, the Giants called and asked if she'd help with a short-term project. That went well, and later that year they offered her a full-time job helping them run a series of health and wellness initiatives. A longtime health and fitness buff, Alyssa accepted. "People talk about passion projects. I was like, 'Man, this is a passion project, but I'm actually getting paid for it.'"

Alyssa stayed in that role for four years. All along, she still lacked a particular long-term career goal. Toward the end of that period, during the summer of 2019, she was feeling itchy for something new, so she again began to hold informational interviews within the organization. In November, the team hired a new manager, Gabe Kapler, and she knocked on his door (literally and metaphorically) and asked to discuss his coaching philosophy and vision for the organization. They had a series of conversations over the course of a month, and Kapler began bouncing ideas off her. She didn't know it, but he was actually interviewing her for a position on his coaching staff. In January 2020, he offered her a job as an assistant coach working with the team's outfielders and base runners, making her the first female assistant coach in the MLB.

About six months into this job, Alyssa loved what she was doing, yet she still couldn't identify a specific end goal she had for her career. She was in "more of an exploratory mentality," bent on continuing to learn about opportunities open to her and not wishing to box herself in unduly by defining a particular goal. Her selection set had narrowed somewhat — over the long term, she was envisioning potential opportunities within baseball and coaching in particular. But she was as content as ever to keep her options largely open, to stay alert to how she felt about what she was doing at any given time, and to iterate her way ever closer to what she loved.

A small percentage of us do have clear plans that come to us during childhood or at some point in our careers. If you fall into that category, the next section of this book will show you how to choose and pursue risks to maximize your opportunities. But if you don't, Alyssa Nakken's story evokes all that we might accomplish by identifying the general direction we want to pursue, launching ourselves in that decision, and then iterating our way forward as best we can, learning from each choice. If Alyssa had waited until she knew precisely what she wanted out of a career, she might have languished for years or even decades in her uninspiring financial planning job. Instead, she took a leap, accepting a certain amount of risk and then moving little by little in the general direction of her dreams.

One of the best analogies I've heard on moving directionally comes from a fellow CEO and tech entrepreneur I know here in the Bay Area. As this veteran risk-taker observes, making our way to any destination is like being on a set of monkey bars in a local playground. When we're on the course, we don't need to see all the rungs in detail. We can begin to progress simply by reaching for the rung right in front of us while letting go of the rung behind us. It's time to simply stretch an arm out and the rest will follow.

WHITEBOARD YOUR WAY TO YOUR FUTURE

Just to be clear: The idea of moving directionally first doesn't mean we should throw out the process of planning entirely. We can still use it — we just have to develop the right *kind* of plan for the phase of the journey we are in as we reach toward our next major ambition. There is no better tool to begin planning with than the whiteboard. We can use an actual whiteboard, an iPhone screen, a chalkboard — whatever we have handy, so long as we have the ability to save, erase, and edit what we write. Use your whiteboard to sketch out the roughest of plans, including your general ambitions and a few bullet-pointed paths you might take to get there. Your ambitions will likely be both extrinsic (wealth, say, or occupying a position of power) and intrinsic (achieving fulfillment or personal joy). As we've noted, learning can be its own goal as well as a tactic you deploy to achieve a larger goal. In a single sitting of a couple of hours, do your best to identify your top and subordinate dreams.

A whiteboard markup is the "zero" draft of a plan, a few words that give voice to a general ambition for your future and a few different hypotheses or ideas for how to achieve it. If you've performed background research or informational interviews and have made detailed notes, stow that away in a separate folder and use it to inform the several line hypotheses written on your whiteboard to the best of your ability. All you need to make a first move is a starting point; resist the urge to keep adding endless details until your whiteboard is so filled with words that it is impossible to read. A more detailed plan can come later, evolving to a full-fledged framework as you add the learnings from getting proximate to opportunities first.

A whiteboard plan is a living, evolving thing — the *opposite* of the Perfect Plan. Its mere presence reminds us that the most *relevant* plan is one that we can alter, modify, update, or erase altogether as we gain more insight. A whiteboard plan isn't precious in the least. It's simply a tool, one that becomes more useful if we keep it current. Whiteboarding usually identifies the essence of a framework for future action more quickly and efficiently than lengthy and more complex planning methods, helping to get us roughly prepared and moving first to get closer to our ambitions before refining our thinking down the line. And when we're just starting out on our risk-taking journeys, that's exactly what we want to be doing, moving directionally and gaining more precision as we go. Rather than developing precision as an untested theory through prefect planning, we'll do so much better if we derive it directly from lived reality.

POSSIBILITY POINTERS

- Moving closer to our goals helps us far more than creating a perfect plan from afar.
- Proximity helps us visualize our ambitions more clearly, become apprentices, and gain access to interesting opportunities.
- A great plan is simple, efficient, and capable of evolving as we go. Whiteboard your way to the future.

5 | FOMO > FOF = ACTION

And the day came when the risk to remain tight in a bud
was more painful than the risk it took to blossom.

— ATTRIBUTED TO ANAÏS NIN

While letting go of the Myth of the Single Choice and starting to take smaller risks to build our "muscles" might make sense intellectually, we might still confront one major challenge: fear.

The reason we often don't take risks, even small ones, isn't because we don't see the potential upside of a choice. It's because we fear the downside far more. While reframing risk-taking as a continuous series of positive, incremental moves might be the best advice logically, we still may not take action if we cannot conquer and control our anxieties.

A set of simple equations can help us understand whether or not we are likely to act when evaluating a risk (Figure 5). They go something like this:

$$FOMO = FEAR\ OF\ MISSING\ OUT$$

$$FOF = FEAR\ OF\ FAILURE$$

$$FOF > FOMO = INACTION$$

$$FOMO > FOF = ACTION$$

Figure 5

As these important equations suggest, if our fear of missing out on opportunities (FOMO) exceeds our fear of failure (FOF) in trying something new, we'll act. Otherwise, we simply won't. Risk-taking isn't about cultivating fearlessness or denying that our fears exist. It's about accepting our vulnerability and negotiating the relationship between these two anxieties we might feel at any given moment. When we feel discomfort, it's as much because a "positive" anxiety — the fear of missing out — haunts us as much as a "negative" one — the fear of failure. We'll remain unsettled until we make a definitive decision, often experiencing these dueling feelings for extended periods.

When I decided to leave London for California, I moved directionally toward a large opportunity, one made even more attractive given the discontent I felt at Sky.

I calculated that my risk of failing to find a good job when I arrived in California was objectively quite low. I also realized that I'd be unlikely to fail financially if it took me longer than anticipated to find work, since I had some savings, a free place to stay, and my parents to fall back on as a last resort. Overall, the urgency I felt to get to the West Coast far outweighed my fear of walking away from a good job in the UK, so I acted. Think of an important choice you made at some point in your life. What fears did you feel? How or why did your fear of missing out outweigh your fear of failure?

Conventional wisdom holds that we should spend all of our time thinking in a positive manner when attempting to pursue goals. "I am the greatest," Muhammad Ali apparently remarked. "I said that even before I knew I was." Winston Churchill is said to have pointed out, "The positive thinker sees the invisible, feels the intangible, and achieves the impossible," suggesting that strong positive beliefs are essential to pursuing anything truly ambitious. But the truth is, positive thinking alone won't get us where we need to go if we can't stomach the thought of failure along the way.

In her book *Rethinking Positive Thinking*, Gabrielle Oettingen, professor of psychology at New York University and the University of Hamburg, reports on research showing that positive thinking alone often "impeded people in the long term from moving ahead. People were quite literally dreaming themselves to a standstill." When you aim for a goal based on past experience, you can perform better if you temper positive thinking with an awareness of key obstacles in your path. When it comes to risk-taking, visualizing positive outcomes can incline us to take action by growing our FOMO, but it does nothing to conquer the anxiety we feel about suffering a potential loss. Looking failure squarely in the face and thoroughly imagining its consequences can actually help ease our fears, boosting the chances that we'll act.

My executive coach, David Lesser, a veteran practitioner whose clients include CEOs of Fortune 50 companies and startups alike, suggests that understanding and honoring our fears is instrumental to acts of risk-taking and leadership. Each of us have what he calls an "inner risk manager," a voice inside our heads that is "always scanning for dangers, and threats, that part of you that whenever you aspire to something, always tells you what could go wrong and why you should hesitate." As Lesser argues, entrepreneurs in particular spend so much time fighting with or dismissing our inner risk managers because we've been trained to believe that we must only visualize the positive. As a result, "most people have an immature relationship with risk . . . Being a risk manager inside a highly positive person has got to be a hard gig!"

Instead of antagonizing the voice inside telling us to "be careful," we stand to gain by communicating more openly with our own inner risk managers about the downsides. That way, we can take on ambitious goals while also taking reasonable steps to keep ourselves safe in case events don't transpire as we'd hoped. Whether you're just starting out or have already progressed in your career, make a point of listening more carefully when doubts arise about a course of action. Go even further and begin a dialogue with your inner risk manager, asking them to run down the risk they see so that you can "talk them through." Once we bring risks to the surface, we can use the following tactics to manage our fears of failure and finally get the fear equation working in favor of action.

1. IMAGINE THE "CHOICE(S)-AFTER-THE-CHOICE"

Curiously, when we confront the full range of potential "failure" scenarios for any risk we face, something powerful happens. Rather than turning away from our fears, we move through them and begin identifying the *choice-after-the-choice*. That is, we visualize what we would do to recover from loss or minimize its impact after a failure occurs. We might find that we have one good follow-up choice, or several. The more we come to realize that failure won't destroy us and that we can spot multiple options for getting back up on our feet, the less scary failure seems.

In a famous 1997 letter to shareholders, Jeff Bezos, founder of Amazon, articulated a similar strategy for lessening fear. Describing Amazon's approach to decision-making, risk-taking, and failure, he observed that two kinds of decisions exist: those that you *can't* reverse (what Bezos called Type 1 decisions) and those you *can* (Type 2).

Type 1 decisions are "one-way doors," and so you must make those decisions "methodically, carefully, slowly, with great deliberation and consultation. If you walk through and don't like what you see on the other side, you can't get back to where you were before." In contrast, because Type 2 decisions are reversible, you can make them more quickly, worrying less about the consequences.

As Bezos recognizes, most decisions are Type 2. But even when the moves we make aren't entirely reversible, we might still have plenty of room to maneuver if we fail. That's why it's so important to contemplate the *choice(s)-after-the-choice*. With little effort, we can imagine steps we might take that would leave us no worse off than where we started — either retrenching or moving forward in another direction.

Let's say you have a successful career with an important role at a large company, and you're contemplating whether to move to a similar job in a different industry or at a startup. Although you hope to learn more or to accelerate your wealth by gaining equity, the switch carries some risk. While you are imagining the upside, imagine in parallel a disaster scenario in which you fail to thrive in your new job. If that happens within a few months, you'll likely have at least two choices if not more. You might be able to return to the organization where you previously succeeded, or given your experience, you might find a similar role to your previous one with another, larger company in the industry. If these *choices-after-the-choice* exist, it's quite likely that what you originally perceived as a bigger risk probably wouldn't damage your overall career trajectory or finances very much, while the upside remains high.

When we take the time to analyze Type 1 (one-way door) decisions, we will likely find that we actually have two or three new actions we could take in case of failure, even if we still bear a cost. Clarifying the paths and the costs will empower us more in our choice than if we dismissed bigger opportunities out of hand as "too risky."

2. NAME *ALL* OF OUR RISKS AND FEARS

It's so important to be specific about the *kinds* of risks we're taking and the associated fears they generate within us. If we can name them and also consider them in the context of our current circumstances, we're more likely to tackle them individually, look at them more realistically, and size them up appropriately.

There are generally three kinds of risks we face in any career choice: *financial, reputational/ego,* and *personal.* If one of our career choices goes sideways, it's because we might lose money, we might experience a hit to the image that we have of ourselves or others have of us, or we might lose something we value deeply on a personal level (work that gives us joy, or time spent with our family). Personal risks are sometimes thornier than the other two; in a world of endless career ambition, we can feel embarrassed to name them or grant them validity. But personal risks affect our happiness immensely and are thus important to assess.

In general, the most emotionally powerful risk we confront continuously throughout our lifetime is *ego risk.* From childhood, we strive to build our self-esteem by mastering skills, tackling challenges, and impressing ourselves and others. When we fail at a challenge, we take it personally, questioning our innate potential, personality, and even our soul. We might lose money or perceived status when we fail in business, but what is that compared to our identity and sense of self-worth?

Although ego risk is intangible, it constantly holds us back in small and big ways, preventing us from trying new things. Yet fears related to ego risk are perhaps the easiest to overcome, since ego risk resides almost entirely within our own psyche. If we can find a way to feel good about ourselves even when we fail (stay tuned!), we can minimize our fear of taking ego risk, unleashing ourselves to act and to flourish. "Give me the young man who has brains enough to make a fool of himself!" Robert Louis Stevenson once said. It might not be brains so much as an ability to shift the meaning we attach to our actions and their results.

We should note that the nature of our fears changes over time, although they don't necessarily diminish in strength. As an example, early in our careers, the biggest risk we face when making choices might be financial: We're trying to establish ourselves and earn enough to live independently and to save. As our careers progress and we ascend professionally, ego and reputational risk might take hold; we might begin to fear that we might lose the stature we've gained. By the time we reach mid-career, having established ourselves and built families, we might find ourselves confronting all three risks and their attendant fears. With our partners and children to consider, the financial and personal costs of our choices would rise significantly.

As I navigated my own career, untangling and naming these fears helped me to tackle them. It's all too easy to lump our fears together when making choices, which makes them seem bigger and more powerful. Separate them out, and you can take steps to mitigate some of them. In my case, ego and reputational risk moved to the forefront of my thinking as I approached mid-career, becoming no less scary than financial risk had been earlier on. And, as fate would have it, I fell in love, got married, and had children just as my professional life started to peak, so the personal risk of my career choices grew (I risked time with family and my sense of a healthy work-life balance).

Instead of leaving the risks unspoken, I found myself negotiating at work and at home to find tolerable solutions before making any final choices. For example, I spent a year negotiating with my husband about how we could have a third child while I pursued my goal of becoming a tech company CEO. Such efforts allowed me to feel more comfortable when it came time to making decisions. By the time I said yes to an opportunity, I knew I'd optimized the tradeoff as much as possible, even though no decision would address all these risks at the same time. Nevertheless, my fear of failure shrank while my fear of missing out remained high, so I was ultimately able to take action.

3. SIZE OUR RISKS

It's as important to put risks in true perspective as it is to name them clearly. This starts with honestly assessing our present situation and the room we have to fail, including the availability of choices after the choice that would allow us to recover. When evaluating the reasons why we're taking a risk, we can also identify our current situation and mental state, which helps determine how weighty the risks we're taking really *feel to us now.* Depending on our present situation, a given choice might affect our lives more or less than it would someone else's. The magnitude of risk isn't absolute, but is relative to our present circumstances.

When we find ourselves in a neutral to positive position — that is, our careers are on track and acceptable to us or even quite fulfilling — we take risks to realize a positive benefit. In these situations, we can often fail and still recover. If many choices-after-the-choice exist, the risks we're taking are probably quite small. If the choices-after-the-choice will leave us somewhat worse off than where we originally started, the risks we're taking are probably medium-size.

But if we're in a bad place when taking a risk (our well-being is deteriorating and we could suffer further losses), we're usually trying to avoid further losses and are trying to make our way back to a neutral or positive position. In this case, too, we might regard a risk as small if it promises mostly upside and we can't imagine things getting much worse. When a choice we make could plunge us deeper into negative territory, it represents a larger risk. Similarly, when we make a significant choice that is a one-way door, offering few if any viable choices-after-the-choice and possibly leaving us meaningfully worse off than we currently are, that's also a bigger risk, whether we start from a positive, neutral, or negative state.

Let me give you an example. My friend Ade Olonoh, founder of the workplace productivity platform Formstack, took "a pretty big risk" in January 2006 when he left a stable, well-paying job to become an entrepreneur. The timing wasn't ideal — Ade wife's had quit her job, the two were expecting their first child, and they only had six to nine months of expenses saved up. But Ade was miserable in his job, and his wife encouraged him to "follow his passion." Ade had run a startup with some friends for a couple of years after college, and although the venture ultimately failed, he had enjoyed it immensely and yearned to start another business.

We can classify this as a large risk. Yes, Ade would be worse off over the short- to mid-term if his entrepreneurial venture didn't work out. With the family dependent on his income, their financial circumstances would have been precarious. But Ade had some choices-after-the-choice that could help him recover, including performing some technology consulting work as a freelancer or returning to a job similar to the one he'd had. To mitigate his risk, Ade decided to consult part-time while building his new business (Formstack). It all worked out: Ade built Formstack, continuing to freelance for a couple of years until he was able to raise some investment money and run the company on a full-time basis.

Naming and sizing our risks allows us to understand objectively how well we might tolerate a failure, taking into account our present reality, the availability of options should our risk-taking choice fail, and the magnitude of any losses we might experience. I run through this analysis mentally (sometimes even turning it into a simple spreadsheet) whenever I am trying to evaluate my choices.

4. PLAN FOR THE DOWNSIDE
MORE THAN THE UPSIDE

I've negotiated hundreds of contracts during my career, both for very simple deals and extremely complex ones. I've found that the most expert of negotiators look at contracts with a very distinct purpose in mind. That is, they put all of their effort and energy first, before a deal is inked, into mitigating the risk of future failure. To me, that makes a lot of sense. We should all do the same when we're planning to make any choice that carries major risk. In these cases, we ease our fears by paying more attention to planning for the *downside* instead of the upside.

Over the years, I've also seen hundreds of highly ambitious plans that lay out in minute detail the initial steps people will take, the predicted results, the subsequent steps they'll take, and so on. Yet these plans say little if anything about what happens if actions fail to yield the promised results. They all but presume that actions always work out and that we're best served by mapping out every successive and successful move we'll make.

A better approach to planning is asymmetric to the downside: We pay more attention to what might go wrong rather than all that we will do if things go right 100 percent of the time. How much effort should we invest in thinking about contingencies? When taking small to medium risks and starting from a positive place, simply identifying the choices-after-the-choice mentally is likely enough to allow you to take action. When we're contemplating larger risks or starting from a difficult position, you'll want to act fast, but taking some time to perform detailed planning before risk-taking makes tremendous sense. You'll want to evaluate all of your available alternatives, playing out which variables might go further "negative" with each choice and comparing the downsides of alternatives with one another.

When my sister Nicky and I confronted her challenging business conditions, we constructed multiple scenarios on a spreadsheet, identifying the range of financial outcomes, best case to worst case, for several choices she might make. Detailed financial modeling for each choice might seem like overkill, but it made it abundantly clear that several choices Nicky was contemplating, including restarting her practice in a new location, were fraught with downside repercussions as bad as or even worse than staying put.

Downside planning kept Nicky from taking a new entrepreneurial risk she couldn't afford. Just as important, having each alternative on paper with pros and cons and the range of possible financial outcomes eased her fears, better preparing her to see which actions would yield far more upside than further potential loss. With her fears diminished and confronted, Nicky could then get moving, feeling both excited and fully prepared.

Most people dislike spending time and mental energy looking at the downside. It's a lot more fun thinking about all the ways something will exceed our expectations. But if you ask some of the world's biggest, most successful risk-takers and negotiators, you'd find that they value skillful downside planning far more than upside planning, precisely because it fuels their conviction to act.

Let me give you an even more unusual example of risk-taking where the downside was severe. On October 24, 2014, my friend and former colleague Alan Eustace jumped from the stratosphere to set the world record for the highest-altitude free fall jump. Meeting Alan, a happy, bespectacled computer scientist who served as Google's SVP of Engineering from 2002 to 2015, you'd have a hard time imagining this builder of code as a daredevil of any kind. But after taking a sabbatical from Google in 2011, originally to create a manmade flying suit, Alan teamed up with a group of scientists to pursue a jump from the stratosphere. Unlike the previous record holder for the world's highest skydive, Felix Baumgartner, Alan had no previous experience with such risky stunts. "I kind of liked the idea of an old, ancient engineer setting a world record for skydiving," Alan later remarked.

For the next three years, Alan and a technical team designed the parachute and life support and balloon systems needed to achieve his goal. As Alan noted, he approached skydiving from an engineering standpoint, creating a highly detailed, carefully conceived test plan (Baumgartner, by contrast, had relied instead on an almost superhuman skydiving ability). "We probably ran two hundred and fifty tests" during the three-year period, he said, "the vast majority of them unmanned but some of them manned. Every one of them, we worked really hard to be able to get the maximum amount of information we could and be able to buy down the risk the entire time so that when we got to something that somebody else might've thought was risky, we could look at it and say, 'Yeah, but we did all these other things to be able to mitigate that risk or understand that risk.'"

The testing was so rigorous that Alan found it "agonizing" at times. On five separate occasions, for instance, the team tested Alan's flight suit to make sure that it could withstand the cold of the stratosphere, exposing him to temperatures as low as –120 degrees Fahrenheit. He notes, "You have to have a list of all the things that could possibly go wrong, and then you have to look at what are the mitigation that you're taking for each of those things." Only once Alan and his team had thoroughly tested the various pieces of equipment individually and in combination and prepared for all conceivable contingencies did he complete his jump from 135,000 feet, a full twenty-five miles above the earth's surface.

During the jump itself, Alan wasn't paralyzed by fear. Astonishingly, his heart rate remained fairly low throughout, a little over sixty beats per minute. That's because he and his team had done their homework. As he puts it, "Daredevils are people that try to do crazy things where there's a lot of variables that are unknown and the chances of being injured or killed are really high. I was mostly being saved by incredible technology that my team designed. It's not one hundred percent safe, but it's as close as humans can come."

In short, Alan had mapped out all the risks and fully confronted them. As a result, he went into his jump psychologically knowing that he had fully prepared himself for success, not failure.

HOW TODAY'S OMG CURES TOMORROW'S FOF

While imagining the choice-after-the-choice, planning more for the downside, or naming our specific risks can minimize our fears dramatically, there is nothing like actually surviving failure for enabling future risk-taking. Small risk-taking can build our tolerance for handling all types of outcomes, instilling an experimentation mindset, but managing through a larger failure can prove far more positive and empowering than we realize, reducing our FOF going forward. Painful as it is, experiencing failure teaches us powerful lessons about how capable we truly are at bouncing back and figuring out what to do next.

Ade Olonoh, the entrepreneur, can attest to our ability to learn through failure. Ade initially positioned his company, Formstack, as a data management system that allowed people to easily create forms online for use on their blogs and websites. Formstack did well at first, but one part of its service was growing much faster than others. Bloggers using Formstack were using forms to pose questions to their audiences, asking them to contribute topics for upcoming blogs. Thinking that this was a neat application of Formstack, Ade created a new platform with his team as both an experiment and a fun end-of-the-year team-building exercise. On Formspring, as Ade called the new platform, other users could ask you questions, and your responses were published on a profile of you on the site or on other social media platforms.

Ade anticipated that they'd perhaps get a couple of thousand people to sign up. Boy, was he wrong! In just forty-five days, a million users joined Formspring. The demand was so great that the costs of hosting so many people risked bankrupting Ade's small company.

I met Ade in early 2010 when I joined his board at Formspring. By then, the company was a hot new startup, raising over $16 million from top-tier Silicon Valley investors to grow it. Finding it difficult to run both companies, Ade hired a CEO to run Formstack, then moved with his wife and two kids from Indianapolis to the Bay Area and dedicated himself full-time to running Formspring. "It definitely felt pretty risky," he remembers, "packing up the entire family to go out there. We didn't really know that many people out there or anything like that, so it was kind of crazy."

At first, this risk seemed like a good move. Formspring grew rapidly, reaching almost 28 million users by early 2012. The company was flying high. Later that year, however, it hit turbulence as teen bullying memes cropped up on the site, damaging the company and its reputation in ways Ade never imagined. In addition, Facebook changed its algorithm to de-emphasize content from third-party sites such as Formspring.

Almost overnight, the company's growth stalled; the traffic generated by Facebook — which accounted for about one-third of Formspring's total traffic — disappeared. To address the bullying, Ade changed certain user features (like anonymity), but doing so also diminished its growth.

In December 2012, Ade laid off his entire workforce. The following May, some four years after his big bet on Formspring, Ade sold the firm for pennies on the dollar. He was devastated, feeling like he'd let everybody down. Fortunately, his wife was supportive. "She was really just concerned with how I was handling it and wanted me to be happy. She wouldn't accept my conclusion that Formspring's failure meant that I was a failure."

In 2013, Ade went back to work at his original company, Formstack, working remotely from the Bay Area before eventually moving back to Indianapolis. That two-way door was luckily still open to him, allowing him to reconnect with his original roots at the company. Today Formstack is profitable, serving more than 500,000 users in 112 countries, and Ade is continuing his journey as a serial investor and entrepreneur.

Ade looks back on Formspring and his move to Silicon Valley as the biggest failure of his career. But at the same time, he also sees it as one of his biggest successes. At one point, he notes, Formspring was the fast-est-growing social media platform in history. "It's pretty rare and I don't know that I'll ever be able to replicate it personally," he says. In addition, Ade's attitudes toward risk changed fundamentally through surviving this failure and other lesser ones in his career. He now feels "much more comfortable with risk" than he formerly had, and recognizes that that comes with experience: "The time horizon is truly long, whereas early in my career it probably felt like every decision I made that ended in failure was going to wreck the rest of my career."

WORK THE FEAR FORMULA TO YOUR ADVANTAGE

No matter how experienced you are at risk-taking, you need to under-stand and accept that *fear never goes away entirely.* But you can learn to choose possibility by addressing both sides of the fear equation. Rec-ognize the galvanizing fears like FOMO, and actively manage the more negative emotions like of FOF. Embrace your ambitions while also look-ing at failure first and identifying ways of mitigating it. If you do, you'll likely come away feeling more positively about your chances than you would have otherwise.

Many people regard optimism and faith as mindsets we must inject into risk-taking, but in fact they often emerge as *by-products* of choos-ing possibility once we've identified recovery strategies for ourselves. You can become a realistic optimist, remaining realistic over the short term and optimistic over the long term, as you recognize that you can keep choosing your way through failures, too. There's nothing like hard-won experience to teach us this and related lessons. If we sustain a ma-jor failure and can learn to embrace it, we'll emerge with a diminished fear of failure going forward. Before then, managing our fear equation when contemplating a choice will dramatically increase the odds that we'll move.

POSSIBILITY POINTERS

- We take action when our FOMO outweighs our FOF.
- Embracing our inner risk manager helps us face our fears instead of avoiding them.
- Imagining the choice-after-the-choice, naming and sizing your risks, and planning more for the downside are powerful ways of managing the fear equation and getting into motion.

PART II

Get Smarter

Take calculated risks. That is quite different from being rash.

— GENERAL GEORGE PATTON

6 | PUT *WHO* BEFORE *WHAT*
WHEN TAKING A RISK

Let's return to the summer of 1997, when I first began working in Silicon Valley. I was twenty-seven years old and had taken a decent-size risk by quitting my job in the UK and moving without one to California. It seemed like that risk was going to pay off. I landed a job as a business development manager at an interactive TV startup called OpenTV. I had been recruited by Shea Kelly, the charismatic human resources executive I mentioned earlier who would become one of my dearest friends and peers. Eager to learn about an exciting new part of the television industry (which I still found very glamorous), I arrived full of enthusiasm and was ready to kick butt on day one.

That enthusiasm didn't last. On day two, my new boss, one of the company's male senior leaders, pulled me aside to tell me half seriously that I was "scaring the secretaries." I wasn't sure what that meant. How could I have possibly made them so nervous in just forty-eight hours? I'd come from two companies — Merrill Lynch and British Sky Broadcasting — both with aggressive, male-dominated cultures, and in both cases my bosses had praised and promoted me. Now that I had arrived in the Valley, the first feedback I received was that I might somehow be too outspoken or hard-driving for my environment.

My experience deteriorated from there. Rather than receiving more responsibility than my job title would indicate, I got less. OpenTV had hired me to help grow its platform by forging partnerships with other companies. Instead of assigning me that work, my boss gave it to a male colleague with a volatile style, asking me to perform more mundane tasks instead. I apparently was "too scary" for their culture, but this male colleague wasn't. It felt unfair to me.

Frustrated, I struggled with what to do. One night, as my boss and I headed to the parking lot, I opened up and shared my concerns. He tried to placate me, saying smilingly that I was the "rookie on the team who needed to be coached." I pushed back, arguing that over the first several years of my career I'd been rewarded and promoted at two incredibly successful global companies and given increasing amounts of responsibility with little oversight.

After that conversation, my despair only increased. I began to wonder if I was really cut out for Silicon Valley, for a business development role, or both. When an external vendor came into OpenTV to offer sexual discrimination training, I took a risk and mustered the courage to request a private conversation with the trainer. I described my experience and asked if I was facing gender bias. She hedged, reluctant to give me a straight answer. Ultimately, the label we gave it didn't change the underlying issue. My boss and I very much differed in our expectations about my job, and I had little confidence I could thrive at the company while working for him. He wasn't going anywhere, so I felt like I had to.

While pondering my choices and my risks, I received a call from a tech headhunter who was recruiting people to serve as product managers for a startup called Junglee. I was wary of responding; the company's tagline, "The Internet Is the Database," could not have sounded more foreign to me, or for that matter, more boring. Junglee's vision of technology was geekier than anything I'd ever heard. By building little "spiders" (bots) that could venture out across the Internet and copy or "scrape" bits of information from any web page, Junglee could create new online services that aggregated all of this information in a single place. As its first application of the technology, Junglee patched together bits of jobs listings from thousands of company websites across the Internet, collecting them in a single job board service on

Yahoo.com's site, which allowed job-seekers to search for opportunities much more easily.

I knew nothing about the product manager role the headhunter described, and I'd never ever envisioned anything like it for myself. Product managers are folks who help design and determine which features an online service or product should have in order to help it appeal to customers. They also work closely with engineers writing the actual code, helping them understand these requirements. While many tech companies don't require product managers to be coders themselves, others do, since technical know-how can make working with the engineers much easier. This recruiter convinced me I didn't need to know how to code — I just needed to be smart enough to figure out how to talk to engineers in their language (good thing, since I didn't know a lick of coding).

Despite my initial reservations, I agreed to interview at Junglee. I came away impressed. In a tiny, bare conference room in Sunnyvale, California, almost an hour south of San Francisco, I met with Venky Harinarayan, one of Junglee's founders. He held a PhD from Stanford's esteemed computer science program, known for churning out successful entrepreneurs. Previously, he had graduated from one of India's top technology schools. Beyond his intellect, I admired his candor and his understated style.

I was equally excited several days later when I met his cofounders, Ashish, Anand, and Rakesh, and even more so when I learned they had managed to recruit Ram Shiriram, a successful former sales executive from the early Internet darling Netscape, as the company's president. Collectively, these leaders were extremely smart and also plainspoken; compared with my current boss, they felt far more credible, straightforward, and hungry to hustle. I received an offer and quickly signed on as product manager for Junglee's jobs service, quitting my job at OpenTV with a huge sigh of relief.

My day two experience at Junglee was the opposite of what I had experienced at OpenTV — almost comically so. As I walked into our Sunnyvale offices, eager to learn the fundamentals of product management, Venky and Rakesh asked if I'd feel comfortable making a last-minute job switch. Junglee was about to launch a new e-commerce service on Yahoo's site that helped consumers compare prices on items across dozens of shopping sites. The founders were scrambling to get the service up and running as quickly as possible and wanted me to serve in a business development manager role. It would be my job to hop on the phone and persuade shopping sites to partner with us formally, and pay us if we sent them a new customer through our service. Forget coaching, training, or management oversight: Venky felt confident that I could figure out this new role and help the company grow. Not only didn't the founders ask me to "tone myself down"—they wanted me to lean into my sales ability and step up as soon as possible. Thus it was that I went back into a business development job in tech without ever meaning to.

Over the next several months, I hustled, cold-called, and helped Junglee sign up almost a hundred online merchants as partners on the new service. Our efforts gained the attention of Amazon, whom I also cold-called, and who at the time was mostly selling books, music, and videotapes online but had much larger ambitions. Jeff Bezos, then a charismatic young founder and CEO, imagined a day when Amazon would help you find products from any seller on the web, whether or not Amazon stocked these products itself. Junglee seemed to have the technology necessary to help achieve this vision.

During the summer of 1998, six months after I joined the company, Amazon acquired Junglee for $280 million as its very first step toward building Amazon Marketplace. The online merchant partnerships I had built were a key part of the acquisition, and Amazon offered me a job post-sale to persuade more online sellers to list and sell their products on Amazon. Along with almost every other full-time employee at Junglee, I moved from San Francisco to Seattle to work for our new parent. The Amazon stock I received as part of our sale made me a million dollars, a staggering amount for anyone, let alone a twentysomething like me.

My decision to move from OpenTV to Junglee taught me an important early lesson in taking smart risks, one that has been reaffirmed multiple times in my career: When making critical career choices, we can't

overestimate the value and importance of the "people" factor. I originally signed on at Sky and OpenTV because I loved the idea of becoming part of the television and entertainment industry. As a passionate
consumer of entertainment, I saw these jobs as fun and exciting. I felt
far less passionate about Junglee at first (although in short order I did
develop a passion for the services I was building). That didn't matter:
I succeeded because I surrounded myself with people I respected and
from whom I could learn, while also thriving in the culture they created.

As you ponder which risks to take in your career, always recognize
that "who" we align ourselves with influences our ultimate success far
more than the "what" we have picked to focus on. Don't be so sure that
falling in love with a given field, job type, or industry will take you most
quickly to the mountaintop. Pay much more attention to the individuals
who will accompany you on the journey.

THE TROUBLE WITH "WHAT"

Whether at school or at work, we all aspire to work on subject matter we
find interesting or intriguing. We presume we'll feel more motivated to
work hard when we're engaging with topics we love or find exciting —
our "passions" (more on this later). We often put ourselves through endless soul-searching and machinations to align what we work on with our
deepest desires. Although this approach is logical, we spend most of our
time on the job working in teams with peers, direct reports, leaders, and
sometimes external partners. These others will influence *what* we actually get to work on, and *how* we work as well. Factoring heavily into our
ability to succeed is whether the process of working is joyful, fulfilling,
or inspiring, or overly inefficient, uncollaborative, or depleting.

If all of us worked alone, perhaps the *what* of a job would make all
the difference between success or failure, but we don't. Instead, the *who*
in our risk-reward equation significantly influences our day-to-day in-
teractions and mechanics. Great people around us can actively increase
our engagement and excitement for any goal, making us more curious

about the subject matter we're dealing with. Even if at first we don't find a given line of work all that interesting, it can become more interesting to us if we find ourselves surrounded by engaged, motivated, and inspiring people.

HOW GREAT PEOPLE CHANGE OUR CHANCES

We talked in chapter 4 about getting around the goal when you don't know how to score — by simply getting proximate to the right people and opportunities. When we surround ourselves with people who have the expertise we lack, they can help us raise our game more quickly than if we were to try to figure out everything on our own via trial and error. This accelerated learning happens in at least four distinct ways: via *osmosis, active challenges, coaching,* and *social learning.*

When we are learning through osmosis, we simply get to observe and emulate people with desirable skills and capabilities. Bosses can also challenge us to attempt something we've never done before, stretching our capabilities and risking our egos, albeit with the immense value of a safety net. When we work with leaders who ask us to take on new challenges, we get the best of both worlds: the chance to attempt something ambitious while also asking questions or requesting support when we find ourselves at a loss. We often believe that bosses who push us into new territory are setting us up to fail in the short term. More often than not, they're actually setting us up to succeed over the longer term, accelerating the development of our problem-solving skills and agility.

When we learn through coaching, we benefit from working with leaders who pay attention to our development and goals, who give us consistent feedback, and who sometimes slow down daily activities to bring us along or to help us build a skill in the moment. When we learn socially, we benefit from leaders who themselves attract skilled and diverse teams, giving us the opportunity to learn faster through lots of discussion, debate, and other interaction with our peers.

However the learning happens, the most important benefit we gain when we follow great people is the chance to develop more quickly than we might otherwise. While we're working extra hard to keep pace, they're teaching us how to work smarter. We don't even realize how much we've absorbed until we look back on it much later. The opportunity to work with great people or leaders is often the very best reason to join any innovation or startup opportunity: These ventures attract individuals who might dream larger and think completely differently from the way we do. Even if the venture fails, we're sure to build our capabilities more quickly and expand our own capacity for such thinking.

The great people with whom we work also become our single best source for more opportunities, so long as we do great work. When I was running Joyus, an employee once wrote in a survey on employee satisfaction, "The reward for great work at Joyus is more work." Although I'm reasonably sure this feedback was *not* offered as praise, I couldn't help but agree. As a leader, I tend to give more work (and in my mind more opportunity) to folks on my team who have earned my respect, extending trust and responsibility at a faster rate.

In these cases, I've spotted talented people whom I want to develop further, and this is my way of doing it. We tend to believe that positive feedback always takes the form of verbal praise, but I've found that the folks who keep out-executing others and quietly garnering increasing amounts of responsibility are actually receiving the highest form of true acknowledgment.

YOUR SINGLE BEST NETWORK

Great people themselves also tend to become opportunity magnets, receiving new offers from other companies at an accelerated rate. They can't take all of these opportunities, so they usually pass on these leads to folks in their own networks who've performed well for them. This is why I regard bosses, colleagues, and associates as composing our single best career network.

Business books often advise that we network aggressively at business events or in social situations, trying to meet or get close to people who have achieved dreams close to ours. I understand the merit of such cold-calling — we take a small risk to make a great first impression, receiving as our reward a new opportunity that might never otherwise have transpired. But for all the pressure we put on ourselves to make cocktail connections, our greatest chance of finding an exciting new career opportunity comes from our own deepest professional connections. When we've apprenticed alongside someone, having learned quickly and shown our willingness to work harder for them, they're more likely to put their own reputations on the line to vouch for our abilities. As the management professor David Burkus puts it, "Your old friends are better than your new friends" when it comes to generating opportunities.

The founders of Junglee went on to open doors for me, sending opportunities my way that I never could have anticipated. Using their newfound wealth from the Amazon acquisition, they then began investing in other startups. When they met an enthusiastic computer science professor from the University of California at San Diego who was starting his next venture utilizing technology similar to Junglee's, they were quick to fund him. When the founder asked his new investors for help finding the first businessperson to join him as a cofounder, I got the opportunity to start a company of my own — Yodlee.

Five years later, as I began contemplating my future life after Yodlee, the executive team from Junglee was again happy to help. Junglee's former president Ram Shriram (the Netscape executive I mentioned earlier) was Google's very first angel investor and a member of its board. When he learned I was looking for my next job, he was quick to suggest that I reconnect with Google's founders (whom I had met at startup-related events) and the company's top business executive. Soon after, I went to lunch with Omid Kordestani, Google's chief business officer. I told him of my interest in founding a startup instead of joining a company like Google, which, with its then nearly a thousand employees, seemed massive to me.

Eight months after that meeting, I was still at Yodlee pondering my next move. Omid called again and described a new opportunity within Google to build a "greenfield" business — a product to compete with Yahoo Maps, AOL's Mapquest services, and the traditional, multibillion-dollar yellow pages industry (remember those thick yellow business directories, dropped on your doorstep?). Performing some research, I realized how massive a business like this could become and agreed to an interview. Within two weeks, I had received an offer to become Google's first general manager of Maps and Local Search, and I accepted the job, surprising even myself. I have Ram to thank for investing in Yodlee, but also in large part for this amazing new chapter of my career.

While my own network has expanded immensely since those early days, now including colleagues at Yodlee, Google, Joyus, StubHub, and more, I still count Junglee's founders as among my best mentors in Silicon Valley. Whenever I've faced substantial professional crises, it's Venky whom I've called for advice. At the same time, when I've had an opportunity to do a favor for one of them, I've been happy to say yes. I hope they'd now include me in their best networks too, simply because I had the chance to work closely alongside them as leaders and entrepreneurs early in their own career journeys.

As my career has grown, I've come to think of my own network as composed of three rings. The outermost ring comprises folks I don't know at all personally but whom I always appreciate for having the gumption to cold-call me on LinkedIn, ask me a question on Twitter, or otherwise try to engage me as they strive in their own careers. I try to respond to most of the messages I receive, even if I can't say yes to everyone. In my second order network are acquaintances of mine, former business colleagues or people who are associated with individuals I trust. I also try to help these members of my network when asked, if I can do so relatively quickly and efficiently. I've passed along résumés to members of my professional network and taken meetings with folks in this network when asked. Choosing possibility has taught me the power of serendipity, and I'm happy if I can serve as a catalyst in some small way for people in my broader professional networks.

I reserve my most vocal support for people in my innermost ring, whom I know well and deeply — my first order or what I call my "best" network. I place people into this network not because of their rank or prominence, but because we've worked together closely in a deep and meaningful way. I'll put my own credibility on the line to help them succeed because I really can vouch for the work they've done, I have insight into their strengths and areas to develop, and I can attest to their potential to rise even further. Your best network will stand up for you, too, when you've lived through successes and failures together and forged an authentic connection.

THE "TELLS" OF GREAT LEADERS

Leaders who might supercharge your career are special people, and they come in some pretty unexpected packages. In *Superbosses*, Sydney Finkelstein describes an elite class of bosses who have an unusual ability to develop talent. These "superbosses" are incredibly diverse, displaying different personalities, hailing from a variety of countries and backgrounds, and operating in disparate industries. "Aside from their basic humanity," Finkelstein writes, "and their uncanny ability to innovate while also developing all-star performers, we might wonder if superbosses have much of anything in common at all."

When I think back to my first, highly positive work experience at Merrill Lynch, I would not have characterized my new boss, an eccentric young managing director named Henry Michaels, as a superboss-style leader who could somehow supercharge my career journey. But he did accelerate my career journey in ways for which I am still grateful.

I first met Henry "Hank the Crank" Michaels when I was assigned as an analyst in the Financial Institutions Group, affectionately known as FIG. A pipe-smoking, intense New Yorker with a love of lucites (the beautiful small desk trophies awarded every time the bank advised on a successful IPO or merger), Henry rose quickly up the ranks from associate to managing director (the seniormost role in investment banking). He was responsible for dealing with savings and loan companies — or thrifts, as these banks were known — and trying to help them go public or acquire other entities.

At first, I was disappointed to be in the FIG group. I wasn't interested in studying the workings of banks and brokerage companies, let alone obscure financial institutions like thrifts. But because I felt so grateful to have landed my dream job on Wall Street, I accepted the assignment and was determined to work hard and prove myself.

Henry turned out to be meticulous and highly detail-oriented, and he fully expected me to be the same. My primary job was to prepare his "pitch books," the thick tomes he took to meetings with potential clients. These books presented Henry's thoughts on the industry, the company, its competitors, and last, his and Merrill Lynch's credentials as potential advisors to the client on their financing or mergers and acquisitions strategy. My fellow analysts and I spent most days and nights preparing these books, working with word processing and graphic design groups sitting deep in the bowels of Wall Street skyscrapers. We were Power-Point jockeys, striving to deliver the perfect pitch book for any given meeting.

I knew Henry would make sure every font color, size, and script was correct on every page, and that he would spot-check my calculations of a company's financial metrics to ensure they were not only perfect but showing the right number of decimals in each column. I worked hard to meet his expectations of precision, and this is how I learned the key numbers and ratios for the savings and loan industry and its individual companies, pitch book by pitch book.

Before long, I came to anticipate what Henry liked and wanted in his pitches. He in turn didn't have to spend as much time instructing me on the basics, which he appreciated. He was also happy to school me personally on the business, skipping the traditional hierarchy of the office that put at least two levels of people between us. He told me the story of this thrift or that while smoking his pipe, describing which company he was pitching and why and taking me along to key client meetings so I could listen in and learn. Like any good analyst, I was expected to carry all the heavy pitch books, but I appreciated the exposure he gave me both to him and to the large company CEOs with whom he met.

Soon after I started, Henry won the business of a large Long Island savings and loan that wanted to go public and needed an advisor. On this occasion, he asked Merrill Lynch to staff me directly on the project — a rarity for young analysts, who often spent a year or so on pitch books before ever participating in a "live deal." An associate (an MBA graduate who worked at the firm on a permanent basis and was a few years older than me) was also assigned to the team, and she didn't seem too happy when Henry continued to give me work assignments directly and would bring me along to meetings, bypassing her at times and at other times treating us as equals. The more exposure he gave me, the more I hustled and the faster I learned. By the end of my first year, I not only had helped take a company public but became one of the top-ranked analysts across all groups at the bank. This in turn led to the opportunity to move to London that I've described earlier.

Henry was not easy to work for, but he kept giving me more chances to experiment and learn, to take more responsibility, and to feel like my work had impact. I couldn't have asked for a better experience and model for leadership starting out in my career.

So if leaders like Henry are so diverse and quirky, how do you spot them? As Finkelstein notes, superbosses tend to display some common personality traits, including authenticity, confidence, integrity, and imagination. In my experience, and drawing as well on other parts of Finkelstein's research, there are three additional signs that I would highlight as marking leaders worth following.

The first has to do with the company these leaders keep. Good leaders attract smart people and can sell a vision that attracts them to sign on. *Great* leaders are true talent magnets, surrounding themselves with people who are equally smart, confident, and diverse in their capabilities. Further, great leaders can *retain* these people and leverage their expertise. When you see a strong team of people who debate, disagree, but reconvene repeatedly in good spirits, you can be pretty sure that their leader knows how to develop, harness, and mobilize their skills.

The second telltale signal that someone is worth following has to do with their strengths, skills, and capabilities relative to our own. Leaders certainly don't have to be perfect, but when we encounter people who think differently from how we do and who have styles and capabilities we admire but also lack, we can be pretty sure they'll be able to teach us new things. From my father, to Venky at Junglee, to my boss Omid at Google, the leaders I've followed have all had qualities different from my own, including deep patience and diplomacy, an understated style, and an ability to make others feel heard (for better and for worse, I tend to be aggressive, share opinions early, and bring high energy to any situation). By complementing my own tendencies, these leaders have allowed me to exercise my own greatest strengths in a safe and trusted environment while also teaching me new ways to handle situations more productively.

To spot whether a boss is worth following, I would also assess whether their values appear to overlap strongly with our own. If a leader shares underlying values with us, we're more likely to understand and respect them. In turn, we'll be more likely to stick around long enough to make meaningful contributions, deal with their quirks, and still learn the utmost. It's hard to discern whether a person shares our values when we first meet them, but we can research their track record (including how they have handled difficult situations), gleaning their reputation from current and former colleagues or direct reports. We can also ask about their values directly, comparing their answers with what our research has turned up to get a sense of their own self-awareness, as well.

The former TaskRabbit CEO Stacy Brown-Philpot spent an important phase of her career serving in leadership roles at Google. In describing her decision to join the company, she describes how she underwent a daylong series of interviews with leaders at Google and emerged blown away not just by the intelligence of the people she'd met, but their "values match" with her. She cared about doing more through her work than just making money, and she found that folks at Google were similarly focused on a higher mission. As she recalls,

> Every single person was very accomplished already, but spoke with this sense of humility and also they wanted something bigger than themselves. They wanted something better than themselves ... They really cared about [Google's] mission, it was bigger than them. They were going to work with a lot of other people to make this mission a reality. And I was drawn to that. I was drawn to people who care about something bigger than themselves, and want to work with others to make something like that a reality.

One of the high points of the day came at the end, when she met with Sheryl Sandberg, the leader who would serve as her boss. Here, too, Brown-Philpot spotted a strong values match, this time related not just to a mission focus but to her approach to management. Brown-Philpot notes that Sandberg didn't spend much time asking her about her capabilities or past experience. Rather, she focused on *why* Brown-Philpot wished to work at Google. "She really showed that she was more interested in what my motivations were than my competencies. I think that's a hallmark of a really good leader, to not just understand how smart somebody is, but what drives them and what motivates them."

Looking back on my own career, I believe that values alignment motivated me to do some of my best work, while in a few instances, mismatches led me to struggle. Two of my most important values—authenticity and hustle/lack of entitlement—turned up in leaders and cultures I encountered at Merrill Lynch, British Sky Broadcasting, Junglee, Google, Yodlee, and more. At OpenTV, I struggled to work with a leader whose values I (later) judged as different from my own. Later in my career, I made another painful mistake around values alignment that proved more costly (more on that to come).

If you're going to follow someone when taking a major risk, make sure they're worth it. As Finkelstein writes, "Superbosses are the great coaches, the igniters of talent, and the teachers of leadership in most industries. In effect, superbosses have mastered something most bosses miss — a path to extraordinary success founded on making *other* people successful." Whether we find a true Superboss or just a super boss, our number one job in taking smart risks is to make sure we value whom we are working with as much as what we are working on.

WHO + WHAT = *AMAZING*

As we weigh whether to take a risk on the *who* or the *what* of a choice we're contemplating, we should bear in mind that we often don't have to make a tradeoff. We can find work that is interesting in and of itself *and* do it with people who supercharge our own learning and impact. When people inquire about my own career journey, I often tell them that "doing great work for great people" has unlocked both professional fulfillment as well as rapid progress for me. But in prioritizing our search for people who can teach us, complement us, challenge us, and motivate us to learn disproportionately, we will likely find ourselves more engaged in and stimulated by whatever it is we decide to focus on.

POSSIBILITY POINTERS

- To take smarter risks, overvalue the "people factor" in your choices.
- Great people help us learn via osmosis, active challenges, coaching, and social learning.
- To spot your own potential superbosses, look at the talent they attract, their strengths and skills relative to yours, and the extent to which your values overlap.

7 | IT'S NOT ALL ABOUT YOU

Over the decade that followed my risky move to California, my career flourished. From a junior business development manager at a technology startup I rose to become one of the highest-ranking executives at Google. Along the way, I helped build another startup that successfully sold to Amazon, launched my first tech company, and helped Google launch and scale several businesses, including its international operations and Google Maps.

I've been given a lot of credit for turning my career into a rocket ship of opportunity and growth. It's true that I immersed myself in the process of choosing possibility, working relentlessly, racking up both successes and failures, and building capabilities and leadership skills. But on a basic level, I got *extremely lucky.*

In 1997, when I arrived in the Bay Area, the Internet was just starting to explode.

Amazon went public that year as an online bookseller, having launched just three years earlier. Google, today's search giant, wasn't even founded until September 1998. (Yahoo.com, based on the idea that a single portal could aggregate all the day's news, sports entertainment, and stock tickers for you in a single place, was the giant of the time.) Venture capitalists were pouring money into any new services consumers might want to get online, while entrepreneurs were dreaming about what you might soon do on smaller, mobile devices. At the time, the most popular mobile device used for transmitting data was the BlackBerry, a handheld with a full keyboard on it used by the busiest executives to send and receive mobile emails. In 1997, the startup Unwired Planet worked with the three biggest cell phone companies of the time — Nokia, Ericsson, and Motorola — to identify a standard called WAP that would allow companies to transmit data across networks better so that the industry could grow.

I wish I could say I was a genius who foresaw the rate and magnitude of the Internet's growth and who knew which segments of the technology industry would expand most rapidly, but I'd rather not BS you. While as a consumer I knew larger tech names like AOL or Yahoo, I had no insider knowledge. I was mostly focused on snaring an entrepreneurial opportunity for myself. That didn't matter: The whole industry was accelerating, and it took me along with it, opening up enormous opportunity. Glancing back, I liken my journey to that of Nemo catching the East Australian Current all the way to the shores of a vast new continent. The truth is, I simply rode one of *the largest business tailwinds imaginable,* the growth of the Internet itself.

Individuals most adept at taking chances are more alert than most to what *isn't* about them — the external environment. Recognizing that external forces can disproportionately influence their odds of success, they try to anticipate those forces when choosing which risks to take and which to avoid. They seek to identify and ride tailwind trends that might accelerate their probabilities of success and avoid headwinds to the extent they can. We should all strive to do the same. To become smart risk-takers, *we must lift our heads up and out to evaluate how changing circumstances around us should inform our choices.* We must try to identify the currents of external possibility that might provide us with fuel to help us get where we want to go.

THE MYTH OF CONTROL

If you find it strange to think about big, external trends when making choices, you're not alone. Many of us tend to neglect our surrounding environment as factors in our success, focusing instead on ourselves and our ability to craft the perfect, airtight plan. Society teaches us to value freedom, self-determination, autonomy, and perseverance, so we presume that risk-taking is all about us and factors that lie entirely within our control. If we work hard enough, we think, plot out our actions carefully enough, and execute our plans diligently and persistently enough, we'll surely succeed. Similarly, we internalize any failures we experience as our own. If we can't turn our dreams into reality through our own intelligence and grit, we must be fundamentally flawed in some way.

As researchers and philosophers have observed, we humans have an emotional and even biological need to feel in control over our destinies. When we lack the ability to make choices, we lose confidence in our abilities, feel helpless, and are more prone to depression and other illnesses. As scholars have argued, "The need for control is biologically motivated, meaning that the biological bases for this need have been adaptively selected for evolutionary survival." Certainly the notion that we can forecast and control our own outcomes helps us to stay motivated to pursue goals amid challenges. If we can't choose and manifest our own destiny, if we're simply beholden to circumstances around us, why even bother to pursue any ambitious goal at all?

The opportunity before each of us is to shape our destiny through our choices, actions, and responses, acknowledging that we don't control our environment. We might presume that external conditions are static or "neutral," but this seldom holds true. If we persist in subscribing to this Myth of Control, we risk frustrating our own efforts. We impede our learning for the next time, failing to identify and understand the forces around us that skew the results of our choices. By continuing to funnel all of our energy into our internal plans, we can also miss the chance to find and respond to developing opportunities presented by our environment.

In this way, subscribing to the Myth of Control paradoxically gives us *less* control over our destinies. If we can wean ourselves off this myth and stay alert to tailwinds and headwinds whenever we choose possibility, we can time our choices better to take advantage of these macro trends (positive or negative), learn to anticipate new forces, and become better, more effective risk-takers.

SUBWAYS AND COCONUTS

Identifying tailwinds and headwinds doesn't mean trying to predict the future perfectly. Writing about prediction in business contexts, the management experts Spyros Makridakis, Robin M. Hogarth, and Anil Gaba suggest that we simply can't forecast the future accurately, even using advanced techniques. We can't completely extrapolate future realities from the past, since "the future is often a bit like the past, but never exactly the same." Even if we use sophisticated mathematical models to predict the future, we find that they have difficulty accounting for all the data about the past *and* predicting the future accurately. Humans don't do any better than the statistical models — in fact, we're worse, a problem compounded by our ignorance of our own deficiencies. Possessing reams of specialized knowledge doesn't help, as experts generally don't out-predict the average well-informed person.

What we can do, given the imperfect similarities that exist between the past and the future, is evaluate the trends that already exist before we make our choices, identifying conditions visible today and extrapolating from them to make rough guesses about what will happen next. In their analysis, Makridakis, Hogarth, and Gaba distinguish between events that are utterly unpredictable, and those that, although unpredictable, have qualities we can anticipate. We can statistically model variations in the promptness or tardiness of our subway train when we're headed to work, factoring these variations into our planning (for instance, by resolving to arrive five minutes early each morning). But no matter how sophisticated we might be in our forecasting, we can't predict and plan for freak occurrences, like a coconut dropping on our heads when we're on vacation. As these authors observe, freak occurrences are "less rare than you'd think," and they can be positive (winning the lottery, for instance) as well as negative (that darn coconut).

To become smarter risk-takers, we should try to anticipate the bigger, "subway"-type trends that can affect our choices and factor these into our decision-making. These trends are macro developments such as the growth in size of a consumer behavior (like gaming on our mobile phones) or of an industry we are thinking of joining. They might be more specific trends, like the size and rate at which a company or division's profits are growing and shrinking and why. *To ride current tailwinds or to avoid current headwinds,* we want to observe what is actually happening today and can reasonably assume will likely continue in the same direction. We won't perfectly anticipate the size of these trends or the rate at which they'll change, but that's okay. Roughly identifying what may help or hinder the bets we're thinking of making, we'll still increase the odds that we'll choose in ways that acknowledge these conditions. We'll unlock more opportunity for ourselves, quickening our success.

WHY TAILWINDS RULE

Analysts have written volumes about the impact of macro-environments and conditions on companies' long-term success. As research has shown, companies that identify and exploit external trends tend to grow much faster than competitors who focus only on themselves and seek to make small improvements to their operations. Similarly, when companies try to outrun large and significant headwinds by making only small operational improvements, they are more likely to fail over the long term.

How companies participate in macro trends has important implications for us in our own career risk-taking. When we find ourselves at companies that are riding tailwinds, we'll also likely see a disproportionate jump in the career opportunities available to us. Individual job roles will grow in scope and size as the company struggles to hire fast enough to keep pace with its growth. Competent people will receive new challenges and management roles more quickly, including opportunities to move up and to move laterally to new areas within an organization. Even those inside slower-growing organizations might experience outsize career growth as new divisions or groups crop up to try to take advantage of new business trends.

In my experience, professionals focus more on the absolute size of businesses rather than on important business trends when making career decisions. Why leave a job at a large-scale business unit already regarded as important to join a brand-new team that is small but growing fast? Such moves might feel like a demotion, but they frequently become some of our best opportunities to advance disproportionately by finding and riding new tailwinds.

Consider for a moment how one of the world's most famous CEOs, Microsoft's Satya Nadella, rose to the top of his organization by taking advantage of a powerful and very specific tailwind. In 2011, Microsoft's then CEO, Steve Ballmer, asked Nadella, a trusted leader and veteran at the company, to take over one of Microsoft's cash cow businesses, the Server and Tools business. This unit oversaw products, such as Windows Server (supporting Microsoft's flagship product, the Windows operating system), that companies used in their large data centers. But inside that unit, a group was pursuing a brand-new bet: Microsoft's Azure cloud platform. Although in its infancy at Microsoft, this service would eventually disrupt Microsoft's major revenue streams, since it would undermine companies' need to purchase more and more software and servers for their data centers.

As a result, this caused a lot of consternation internally, since it essentially would compete with the billions in software and server sales that was the bread and butter of the division. As Nadella notes in his book, *Hit Refresh,* "The organization was deeply divided over the importance of the cloud business. There was constant tension between diverging forces. On the one hand, the division's leaders would say, 'Yes, there is this cloud thing,' and 'Yes, we should incubate it,' but, on the other hand, they would quickly shift to warning, 'Remember, we've got to focus on our server business.'"

Instead of shying away from this new business area, Nadella recognized hosting services in the cloud as a massive macro trend and concluded that Microsoft had to be a part of it in order to win. Already Amazon Web Services (the market's biggest cloud hosting player) was one of Amazon's fastest-growing segments and profit centers. Spotting opportunity, Nadella began spending a disproportionate amount of his time on Microsoft's cloud offering, trying to help the company pivot into this important tailwind despite all the internal skepticism. "I had a very good idea about where we needed to go," he recalls.

Did all of this represent a major risk to Nadella and his corporate track record? Of course. But he also sensed that there were disproportionately great rewards to be achieved, as well, by tuning in to the massive trend of cloud computing.

Microsoft began losing its sleepy reputation as the cloud division boomed, and in 2014 Satya Nadella was named the company's new CEO. He would go on to lead one of the biggest turnarounds in corporate history, helping Microsoft reassert its place among the world's foremost tech giants. As he observes, "A leader must see the external opportunities and the internal capability and culture — and all of the connections among them — and respond to them before they become obvious parts of the conventional wisdom." Similarly, we as individuals must also spot the external opportunities, match them with our own capabilities, and take advantage of rising tides.

HOW HEADWINDS HURT (AND HELP)

While divisions, companies, and industries riding macro tailwinds often experience faster growth, those fighting large headwinds face constant pressure to accelerate their performance while pivoting into new areas of opportunity. Individuals within companies facing headwinds often experience similar pressures. Fortunately, we're hardly powerless in these situations. If we know what to do, we can find career growth opportunities there as well.

Our first and most obvious step is to recognize the size and magnitude of the negative external forces around us that may affect our career growth. As we saw with downside risk planning, we can only discover how to survive and possibly thrive in adverse conditions if we take the time to understand them. Identifying the bigger, more observable headwinds around might seem like it would promote a classic victim's mindset, leaving us feeling helpless and believing that everything is happening *to* us. On the contrary, honestly evaluating the external environment as well as our own past and potential responses can give us more, not less, autonomy in challenging situations.

We might find, for example, that our company's stagnant growth will mean less potential for upward mobility inside the organization or a cap on the scope of our current jobs. Alternately, we might find that our cash-strapped company will cut the majority of the resources we need to execute a new program that was our biggest goal for the coming year. With such information in hand, we can adjust our own expectations and empower ourselves to think strategically about how best to react.

One option, of course, is to simply leave, seeking a more hospitable macro-environment for career growth elsewhere. Think carefully before making this move — because challenging circumstances can often provide us with some of the best career opportunities. We might be able to identify opportunities to contribute more in our current job, accelerating our own new learning and development. Given how hard it is for companies to compete for top talent, our managers might ask us to take on new areas of job responsibility or to improve our team's efficiency. A willingness to take on new challenges and goals, including difficult ones, widens our capabilities, gives us the chance for greater impact now, and makes us far more attractive to future employers. Recruiters today rank flexibility and resilience in new hires among the most attractive traits, and headwind situations allow us to build and demonstrate these skills in ways we otherwise might not.

A glance at the career of trailblazing banking executive Jane Fraser testifies to the great possibilities that headwind situations can unlock. Serving as Citigroup's first female CEO (the first woman to ever lead a leading global financial institution), Fraser rose to power via at least two major turnaround situations in which she faced strident headwinds. In

2013, she was named head of Citigroup's mortgage business, which was still struggling to recover from the subprime loan crisis of the Great Recession. Under her watch, the company settled claims relating to bad mortgages it had fobbed off onto government lenders, at a cost of hundreds of millions of dollars. Next, Fraser led a turnaround of Citigroup's troubled Latin America business, making strategic investments and helping to transform a culture that had proven too accommodating to unethical conduct. As one media report noted, "Fraser made a name for herself overhauling Citigroup's trouble spots." Think twice about passing up headwind situations out of hand. These might be precisely the opportunities you need to rocket to the top.

In deciding whether to stay or go, we need to assess how much the headwinds will limit our career growth and weigh that against the new opportunities for contribution and advancement we'll realize if we stay. If we can build our skills and deliver more impact in a trusted environment, we might wind up maximizing our career and leadership growth more by staying than by pivoting out.

DEALING WITH COCONUTS

Most headwinds and tailwinds are just routine events in business — like a subway, they are situations or trends that we can easily identify and to which we can consistently respond. In contrast, little can prepare us for the coconut occurrences in our career — the sudden and abrupt changes in our external conditions that are impossible to predict but that can significantly alter our reality almost overnight. Although we'd never wish to encounter these unexpected forces in our lifetime, they offer some of the largest opportunities for professional and personal growth and learning we'll ever get.

In 2012, following a failed run at a U.S. congressional seat, Reshma Saujani founded Girls Who Code, a nonprofit dedicated to remedying the gender disparity in technology by teaching girls coding skills. The organization scaled rapidly, due in part to macro trends around diversity and inclusion in the U.S. By 2020, it had served 300,000 girls around the world — that year alone counting 8,500 Girls Who Code clubs, 80 summer immersion programs inside technology companies, and 80,000 college-aged alumni in its network. Then, in March of that year, a massive and unexpected headwind struck: the COVID pandemic. Since the organization's activities were all in person, they shut down almost overnight. The resulting economic crisis threatened the corporate dollars that supported the organization.

For Reshma, who was on maternity leave at the time, the crisis was a deeply personal moment of truth. "I have nearly fifty full-time staff and thousands of part-time people who depend on me to pay their healthcare and their salaries. At that moment, I had to make a decision. Were we going to pivot and buckle down and build a product that was virtual? Or would we take a pause and just ride it out?" Pivoting represented both a massive risk and a painful choice. Reshma would in effect be transforming the organization, completely redesigning its offerings to go online. It wasn't clear if they could pull that off successfully.

Judging that the pandemic wouldn't pass quickly and that virtual education would become a necessity over the short- to mid-term, Reshma and her team decided to pivot. Within eight weeks, the organization designed, built, and launched virtual afterschool clubs, a virtual summer immersion program, and a remote education learning product. As Reshma reflects, her team "was able to do what school districts across the country haven't been, which is to make a hard decision, take a risk, potentially be wrong about what you think about how long this crisis is going to last, and therefore be able to serve thousands and tens of thousands of students, millions of students." By August 2020, only five months after the pandemic struck, Girls Who Code had taught more than 5,000 girls virtually and had been noticed for building one of the innovative educational products on the national scene. "We ended up not just surviving the crisis," Reshma says, "but thriving in it."

Reshma is hardly alone in turning a "coconut"-type crisis into a hidden opportunity for learning and growth. As one study has shown, corporate executives can dramatically accelerate their path to becoming

CEOs by taking on difficult, "messy" assignments and solving around them. "When faced with a crisis," the study's authors note, "emerging leaders have an opportunity to showcase their ability to assess a situation calmly, make decisions under pressure, take calculated risks, rally others around them, and persevere in the face of adversity. In other words, it's great preparation for the CEO job."

TRENDSETTER OR TREND-RIDER?

So far, we've discussed the importance of identifying and reacting to readily visible trends when making choices. But some of the most exciting risks to take in our careers involve opportunities to move "ahead of the curve" and help to build new, disruptive services. How should we think about these opportunities? Should we start or join companies that aim to profit and grow by being the first to identify a nascent trend and change the way people behave?

Silicon Valley has long celebrated the idea of the truly "disruptive" company, and entrepreneurs have launched many a new technology anticipating that customers will love a breakthrough offering and be ready to adopt it. I wish more people could experience the process of dreaming of something and building it from scratch. Truly, it's some of the most fun, ambitious, creative, and rewarding work we'll ever do. I've bet big portions of my career on new innovations and realized a tremendous amount of personal and professional growth by challenging myself this way. But choosing to be a trendsetter is a very specific risk. It's a no-brainer as far as the opportunity we'll get to grow our skills and capacity, but when it comes to whether it actually pays financially to be first, the results are more of a mixed bag. It's worth understanding innovation's pros and cons when it comes to financial risk specifically.

In 1999, two years after arriving in Silicon Valley, and following Amazon.com's successful acquisition of the startup I had joined, I was invited to cofound an exciting new financial technology startup called Yodlee. Meeting the company's five engineering cofounders, I came away greatly impressed by the technology they'd created. As part of their service offering, thousands of technical spiders would crawl the Internet, securely accessing bank balances, brokerage accounts, bills, airline reward programs, and more. The service would then give users an aggregated view of all their personal information on a single screen. Yodlee had secured great early backing from angel investors, had twelve engineers coding day and night, and needed a businessperson to join the founding team and help figure out how to further develop the service, get it distributed, and create a business model.

Having just turned twenty-nine, I was ready to leave Amazon.com in order to achieve my dream of becoming an entrepreneur.

During the summer of 1999, we raised over $15 million from two of Silicon Valley's most famous venture capitalists on a promise of becoming "the Yahoo for all your personal information." But within a year of launching this vision, we found it challenging to get large numbers of consumers to adopt our service directly, as they would need to trust us immensely to turn over all of their personal passwords to us. We pivoted, offering our services instead to large financial institutions like Citibank and Merrill Lynch with the idea that they would market it to their consumers instead.

Yodlee eventually went on to become a business-to-business software provider, raising over $141 million and generating revenue by licensing its service to the big financial institutions. Still, consumers never widely embraced the technology through our partners in the first decade of the company, as our service was ahead of its time. Consumers were used to receiving and paying bills in the mail and had only set up a small portion of their financial accounts for online access. By giving them the opportunity to compile all of their information on one place online, we were providing them with too much functionality that they didn't yet want or value enough.

Still, Yodlee plugged along, raising more money even though revenues grew slower than we projected. Surviving the dot-com boom and bust of the early 2000s, it became a backbone service for many new financial startups, working behind the scenes to gather the data these startups needed to function. In 2007, Mint.com launched, generating great excitement for its consumer tools but also failing to attract enough users. Smartly, its founder sold the company to Intuit for $170 million after just three years in business. The service had over a million customers, but these users felt quite enthused about the product promise.

After about 2010, more and more consumers became comfortable conducting their financial affairs online. The fintech (financial services technology) industry began to accelerate, fueled by money from venture capitalists. In 2014, fifteen years after its founding, Yodlee went public, garnering a respectable $450 million valuation. But the company never became the largest service of its kind, despite being first. In 2013, a newer, well-timed software service called Plaid launched to service the industry and was acquired by VISA for over $5.3 billion in 2019. Nonetheless, as the industry pioneer and the backbone on which an industry and even bigger companies were built, I was immensely proud of what we'd accomplished.

Many of Yodlee's employees went on to receive offers from other exciting and successful Silicon Valley companies or to start their own ventures. I was no exception, leaving Yodlee in 2003, almost five years after starting the company. There was no senior role left for me at the company — the CEO spot was happily occupied by Anil Arora, the executive I'd helped recruit to Yodlee so many years earlier (over a pitch I made on the back of a napkin, incidentally). Fortunately, the reputation I'd built at Yodlee led Google to take an interest in me, and I joined Google as one of its first twelve hundred employees.

Despite all of Yodlee's success in its industry (a story told in Daniel P. Simon's *The Money Hackers*), I didn't make much money from my own company — about $300,000 in total over that sixteen-year span. My equity as the last founder was small to begin with. Given the large amount of capital Yodlee needed to raise to keep going over sixteen years, my stake became downright minuscule by the end. Overall, it was worth only about $20,000 per year pre-tax over the many years it took to realize a financial result, or about $10,000 after tax annually. At the same time, Amazon — the company whose stock I walked away from to join Yodlee

— rode the macro trend of online shopping and outstanding execution to the financial stratosphere. Between 1999 and 2020, the value of Amazon's stock rose from $97 to $3,500, for a total 2020 valuation of $1.8 trillion.

Our founding team at Yodlee could never have predicted the course and rate at which consumers would adopt financial services online. We didn't know how far ahead of the world we were in anticipating this trend. Similarly, I couldn't have predicted that Amazon would transform itself from being a seller of books to a movie studio, a delivery and logistics behemoth larger than Walmart, and a cloud computing business used by millions of businesses online. Yet none of this mattered. I reaped disproportionate career and financial rewards from Yodlee by building a company of my own, honing my leadership skills for the first time, and gaining a reputation as an innovator and leader, among other benefits. These achievements have in turn unlocked plenty of other career opportunities for me since, including the offer to join Google and build new businesses there and later to participate in the massive fintech sector as a board member and investor.

Trying to predict when exactly users will be ready for any very early and promising concept is a tricky business. Even the best teams and talent will have a hard time succeeding if their timing is off. Silicon Valley has a saying that, although a cliché, bears repeating: "Between great teams and bad markets, bad markets win." Yet if you can live with market uncertainty, innovation offers some of the largest career rewards for the risk you take to build something new. Most fundamentally, you gain an opportunity to accelerate your learning, contributions, and agility. When we go first, we face a more unpredictable path, but we learn to anticipate, assess, respond, and pivot at a superhero level, regardless of the outcome.

BRAINS IN YOUR HEAD AND FEET IN YOUR SHOES

As an exercise, evaluate your past risk-taking attempts, reviewing not only your own efforts but the macro conditions under which you operated. Conduct a similar analysis for actions taken by seemingly successful people you admire from afar. As you'll likely discover, forces are always at play around us that we might overestimate, underestimate, or fail to predict at all when calculating our risks. We are never as terrible as we might perceive in our worst outcomes, nor are we as brilliant as others think us to be when we succeed.

We can't control every outcome by sheer will, but we can always choose where we are headed next, maximizing our chances for success by continually identifying and positioning ourselves to account for the changing forces around us. We should take heart: Whether we ride tailwinds that allow us to grow faster than we imagined or find a way to take on more responsibility in the face of headwinds, we can always navigate our way to increased opportunity. In the immortal words of Dr. Seuss, "You have brains in your head,/you have feet in your shoes,/ you can steer yourself in any direction you choose."

POSSIBILITY POINTERS

- Our external environments disproportionately influence our odds of success in any choice. Beware of subscribing to the Myth of Control.
- We can anticipate headwinds and tailwinds ("subways") to find our opportunities for growth, while never fully predicting the "coconuts."
- Look for tailwinds when joining divisions, companies, and industries. In headwind situations, seek out opportunities to learn faster and contribute more.

8 | WELL, SOME OF IT IS (HOW TO BET ON OURSELVES)

A friend of mine in her forties — I'll call her Margaret — has built a career as a very successful editor in the publishing industry. She had always been a strong writer in school — in fact, a bit of a prodigy. During her freshman year in college, the professor teaching her a required writing seminar called her into his office midway through the semester to tell her she was writing at a level far above the rest of the class. He planned to give her an A+ for the course. All he asked was that she continue to participate in class and to help other students with their work.

Margaret had similar experiences in other writing-heavy courses. But she only pivoted into writing as a livelihood when she was well into her thirties. Until then, she vacillated between careers, struggling to find the right way to channel her passions, strengths, and values.

Margaret was also highly skilled as a musician, playing piano in bars and at parties on the weekends to earn extra money. Upon graduating college, she thought of pursuing a creative career in either writing or music. Her father had other ideas — he wanted his daughter to choose something "safer," "less risky."

He asked her, "What about getting a PhD in anthropology and becoming a professor?" Margaret liked anthropology and did well in it. She excelled in the structured environment of academia. As a professor, she could build a life writing research articles and playing music on the side, all while earning a stable and risk-adverse income.

Terrified at the prospect of living as a starving artist and intrigued by the chance to spend her time reading, writing, and participating in late-night intellectual conversations with students and professors, Margaret listened to her father and applied to top PhD programs. She gained admission to several and chose one that offered her a chance to earn her degree at little cost through scholarships and teaching assistantships.

But graduate school wasn't what she expected. Intellectual conversations were rare. Her fellow students competed intensely with one another, eager to ingratiate themselves with their professors and to build their careers. Plus, between teaching and her studies, the workload was overwhelming. Most worrisome, Margaret's professors didn't value the kind of stylish, creative writing that Margaret enjoyed and at which she was so uniquely talented. They coached her to produce highly researched prose that Margaret found tedious and that would only appeal to a tiny audience of academic specialists. Writing in their eyes was merely a tool for conveying ideas precisely, not an art form that could delight and inspire tens of thousands or even millions of people.

After her first year, and again each year thereafter, Margaret yearned to drop out and try something else, but her father and academic advisors told her to stick with it. She was very good at writing about anthropology, they said, and would be an amazing professor someday with a stable career if she could just get her doctoral degree. She listened but became increasingly depressed as she continued on — some essential part of herself felt smothered in academia. Still, she just couldn't bring herself to quit, afraid of lacking clear goals or structure. Besides, she told herself, she was progressing toward that magical milestone — her PhD.

After eight years, when Margaret was in her late twenties, she finally received her doctorate. At that point, she knew she couldn't abide a career in academia, so she didn't force it any longer. While her peers all applied to academic jobs, she declined. Unsure of what to do, and with her father's advice to find a stable career ringing in her ears, she applied to law school. She got in and won a nice scholarship but hated her classes so much, she dropped out after only a semester. After that, she floated for a few years, working as a researcher and then landing a corporate job.

Her "breakthrough" came after her company laid her off. For several months she was isolated, depressed, and subsisting on government unemployment insurance. One morning, she thought to herself, "I have absolutely nothing to do today." But then it occurred to her: "That means I can do anything. What do I *want* to do?" An answer popped into her head, one she had never before entertained: "I want to *write stories.*"

Rushing to her computer, Margaret signed up for a local fiction-writing class. After just a few sessions, she realized she didn't just love writing short stories — she was amazing at it. She had a unique way of seeing the world, a natural ability to empathize with others as "characters" and to project voices onto the page. Her instructor read a story she submitted — the first she'd ever written — and arranged for a newspaper to publish it.

Some months later, a literary agent saw the story and was so moved, he invited Margaret to lunch. For the first time in her life, Margaret had stopped listening to what others prescribed for her and focused instead on what *she* felt she was uniquely great at and also loved to do. Although at this point she didn't have much to lose, she set aside her fears and went for it. She published more work and wound up parlaying her writing skills into a publishing career, going on to edit dozens of books, including several bestsellers.

After the last several chapters, you might think you should focus primarily on the environment around you when deciding which risks to take. In fact, who we are and how we're wired play a critical role in our success. When we take risks, we're betting on ourselves and in our ability to decide, experiment, act, iterate, adjust, and pivot in concert with the changing environment around us. If we can identify not just our passions but our values and strengths, we can make better choices that take full advantage of who we are, increasing our odds of success. We can find the roles and environments that allow us to maximize our own intended results.

All too often, we approach parents, advisors, friends, and other trusted authorities for help deciding on career choices. Unfortunately, their advice can sometimes lead us astray if it doesn't account for our unique gifts. Like Margaret, we might opt for "safe" choices, chasing goals that superficially seem right but that align poorly with who we are. Alternately, we might find ourselves taking bold risks without considering whether they fit our passions, strengths, and values. To the extent we can connect with what makes us tick, we place ourselves in a far better position to thrive when making our choices. We're the protagonists in our own career movies — let's not forget that. While we don't control our environments, we do gain autonomy when we anticipate and respond to surrounding situations by using all of our abilities. But betting on ourselves requires that we know ourselves deeply — a much neglected prerequisite for smart risk-taking.

THE SELF-AWARENESS "SANDWICH"

Sages have long advised that we pursue lives filled with passion and a sense of purpose, and they've encouraged us in turn to delve inward to define those elements for ourselves. As Mark Twain remarked, "The two most important days in your life are the day you are born and the day you find out why." Yet in taking risks, what precisely should we endeavor to know about ourselves that can maximize our chances of success?

I think of self-awareness as a three-layered "sandwich" of self-understanding that can help guide our choices (Figure 6). At the top lie our passions, the pursuits that naturally captivate and excite us. As we've noted, passions can evolve over time, some developing and deepening and others waning. Further, what we love doing in our spare time might or might not translate well into a full-time profession. Given that we can become passionate about skills we develop or contributions we find we can uniquely make, we don't want to anchor our career trajectories too firmly to a single, fixed vision of what our passion is or *must be*. Rather, staying cued in to what we feel passionate about at any given time allows us to take into account what gives us energy or joy as we can make work choices, but not be totally boxed in by it.

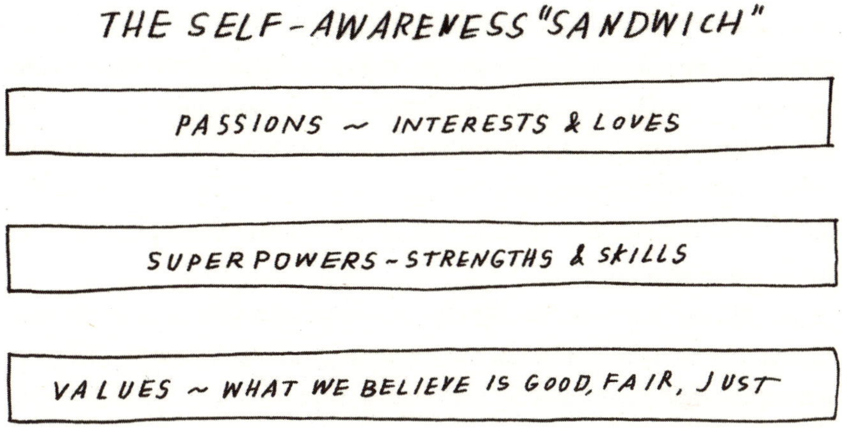

THE SELF-AWARENESS "SANDWICH"

PASSIONS ∼ INTERESTS & LOVES

SUPER POWERS - STRENGTHS & SKILLS

VALUES ∼ WHAT WE BELIEVE IS GOOD, FAIR, JUST

Figure 6

One level below passion, at the center of our self-awareness sandwich, we find the "meat" of who we are: our innate, "trademark" strengths, as well as the skills and specialized knowledge we acquire throughout our lives. While we can always build more skills (such as an ability to communicate professionally, lead a team, or deeply understand an industry) and gain more knowledge, our natural personal qualities such as our ability to empathize with others, think strategically, or behave charismatically truly distinguish us and enable us to excel at certain tasks. Of course, some of the capabilities we might acquire will capitalize on our trademark strengths and thus come easier, while others require more effort given our natural dispositions. I developed selling skills, for instance, because I'm naturally extroverted and high energy; this is a perfect example of how skills and innate qualities can be both intertwined and distinct.

In his book *Career Superpowers,* James Whittaker helps us correct a common mistake that people often make of conflating our strengths with our accomplishments. He argues that our educational credentials and experience might gain us entry into a profession, but they usually don't differentiate us. What does are the one or two qualities we possess in great abundance, "superpowers" that make us especially effective in our pursuits. Whittaker describes the art of building our careers as akin to managing a business: To accelerate your success, you need to double down on what you're great at and to stop doing what you're bad at. This presumes, of course, that you have at least a basic awareness of both your superpowers and your key weaknesses. If you doubt you have superpowers of your own, rest assured: As my friend Kim Scott, the bestselling author of the book *Radical Candor,* says: "I do not believe there is any such thing as a 'B-player' or a mediocre human being. Everyone can be excellent at *something.*"

The third, foundational dimension of self-awareness sits at the bottom of our sandwich. I'm talking about our *values,* our most cherished principles that describe what we believe to be just, right, and fair. Unlike personality traits, which describe us as individuals, values are, in the words of one group of researchers, "rather stable broad life goals that are important to people in their lives and guide their perception, judgments, and behavior."

You might be an honest person — that's a personality trait. But you might also seek out environments where people speak their minds — that's because you value transparency. Moving toward our values means finding our "tribe," like-minded people who, because they subscribe to some set of similar values, energize us and make us feel comfortable and safe in their presence. We thrive when surrounded by people who think differently and who have different strengths. But it's hard to build trust amongst diverse people over the long term if we don't find values in common amongst them also. Most of us need to feel as if the work cultures of our teams or organizations affirm at least some of the values we hold dear; otherwise, we'll struggle to operate together at our best.

As my friend Margaret took on more editing assignments, she realized she had as much freedom to choose whom she worked with as she did what she worked on. When I inquired about her values, she was quick to mention humility, empathy, integrity, and open-mindedness. When selecting the handful of book projects she works on each year, she carefully considers the values of the authors with whom she partners.

Today she feels fulfilled not just because she gets to apply her unique gifts doing work she loves, but because she identifies deeply with her colleagues and trusts them.

KNOW THYSELF

So many of us lack clarity about our passions, superpowers, and values. When I give leadership talks to MBA students or tech CEOs, I routinely ask audience members to raise their hands if they can name one or two trademark strengths they possess. Usually only a quarter of the people in the room respond. I suspect some of this reflects false modesty, but if so, it's ill advised. We're best positioned to succeed when we're more self-aware and honest about our abilities, not less. In fact, lack of self-knowledge will likely expose us to more risk; the choices we make might end in failure because they require us to behave in ways incompatible with who we are.

In a long-term inquiry into self-awareness, the organizational psychologist Tasha Eurich found that "although 95% of people think they're self-aware, only 10 to 15% actually are." Knowing ourselves can prove challenging — our cognitive biases impede us, as does our ignorance of how our childhood experiences continue to shape and distort our self-understanding. Self-awareness can also become more difficult as you gain power and experience, possibly because you have fewer people around you able and willing to give you honest feedback.

To cultivate more self-awareness, ask yourself some probing questions. Challenge yourself to name several areas in which you are uniquely gifted. If you struggle to think of them, reflect on those activities that leave you feeling energized and that seem to come naturally to you. What underlying traits or competencies allow you to succeed in these areas? Alternately, think of the three to four adjectives that everyone who has known you professionally or personally would use to describe you. Take time as well to list the skills you've built so far as you construct your superpowers list.

As helpful as introspection is, it isn't perfect. As Eurich notes, "We simply do not have access to many of the unconscious thoughts, feelings, and motives we're searching for. And because so much is trapped outside of our conscious awareness, we tend to invent answers that *feel* true but are often wrong." To understand ourselves most fully, we'll want to complement our own internal efforts at self-discovery with feedback from others. When's the last time you solicited not only advice but honest feedback about your passions, personal attributes, and values? As Margaret's story suggests, we're so used to asking others to advise us that we forget to ask them to help *us* reflect on ourselves and our gifts. Compile a quick list of friends, family, and colleagues and ask these individuals if they can share their *insights into you as a person*. I'd be surprised if you don't hear them mention at least one or two trademark strengths and skills you never considered.

Back in grades eleven through thirteen (Canadian high schools ran for five years, not four when I was growing up), I learned a memorable lesson in self-awareness. Our local school had one of the only full television studios and TV arts programs in the province, and I was lucky enough to discover a new love for video production and moviemaking. Mr. Tufts, the laid-back and bespectacled teacher running the studio, not only encouraged me to pursue my passion; he assembled a small crew of us to film the school's first-ever video yearbook. The experience left me with dreams of pursuing a full-time career as a movie producer.

As graduation approached, I found that I had multiple and diverse career ideas. Like my friend Margaret, I felt a creative calling and entertained the thought of heading to university to study film or journalism. I thought it was important to build a "safe career," so I also applied to an undergraduate program in commercial studies. Needing letters of recommendation, I asked Mr. Tufts for his support. He wrote me a letter, sending it to me directly to include in the package.

I was excited to see the letter, imagining all the great things Mr. Tufts had written about my intellect, creativity, and ambition. But responding to a query about my greatest strengths, Mr. Tufts used a word I never expected: *empathy*. He went on to describe my ability to relate to other people and feel their circumstances authentically, presenting this as a quality worth celebrating. I had never before stopped to think about the value of this strength, nor had I considered its role in my life.

Since then, I've come to see how empathy has accelerated my path to career success. I have received consistent feedback from employees, peers, and bosses that I care deeply about company and overall employee success, and that my ability to be authentic and relatable with others is an asset. If anything, my energy as a leader often leads me to appear to care too *much* about work rather than too little. I've come to joke about my tendency to tear up with every team I've joined over the past decade, whether it's because I'm happy, touched, feeling someone's pain, or, yes, even angry. (I do try to reserve that last emotion for when I'm alone in my office and can take time to cool off.) Relating to others with real emotion has taken me much farther as a leadership strength than I ever imagined as a student.

Overall, my particular passions, superpowers, and values have played a huge role in determining my career successes, especially at the outset. For instance, as I struggled to find that perfect first job out of university, I questioned why I didn't "fit" with many of the prestigious and somewhat conservative companies where I interviewed. I also found it hard to fit in at OpenTV when I first arrived in Silicon Valley. Meanwhile, I felt immediately at home at Merrill Lynch and Sky. Both offered aggressive, hustle-oriented cultures that resonated with my own strengths and values. In these organizations, I didn't have to waste energy trying to navigate an environment that seemed endlessly challenging. I was free from the first day to do my best work. Similarly, at Junglee, Yodlee, and Google I found people who appreciated and needed my unique strengths in strategy, sales, and analysis, allowing me to expand these skills even further once I arrived, while learning new ones.

Our challenge isn't simply to factor in who we are when making our choices, but to have the courage to bet on our own, deeper knowledge when taking key risks instead of blindly following others' advice. I paid a particularly high price for not heeding this lesson myself early in my career. When I began working at Merrill Lynch, I not only built new analytical skills but acquired specialized knowledge about the financial services sector. Because I had to track and understand the detailed public metrics of all the banks and thrifts for work, I decided to take a small chance and bought my first stocks in the banking sector as well. I profited from these small bets and I recall being very proud of myself for using my newly acquired expertise to make some money.

But several years later, I ignored my own knowledge and blindly followed someone else's. Let me explain. Remember that windfall in Amazon stock I earned through the Junglee acquisition? Flush with success and riding the massive initial dot-com boom, I hired a stockbroker to help me invest the money. When Jack (not his real name) told me to cash out of my Amazon earnings and bet on a web-hosting provider called Digital Island, I blindly followed his lead, putting 90 percent of my windfall money into this company even though I knew nothing about it or the infrastructure sector. Not a year later, the dot-com bubble burst, dozens of large public tech companies completely collapsed, and Digital Island went bankrupt. Overnight, I also lost virtually all the money I had made, all because I made a bet relying solely on *someone else's advice* and without leveraging my *own* knowledge or insight. I had to start virtually all over again in building savings in 2002, but with this very expensive lesson burned deeply into my psyche. Luckily, I was young, single, and living in a place with longer-term, massive tailwinds. But imagine if I wasn't.

WELCOME IN THE KRYPTONITE

It might feel awkward to hear about your superpowers from others, but we'll at least come away from these conversations feeling warm and fuzzy. Hearing about our weaknesses or shortcomings, on the other hand, feels much scarier. These elements — I call them our kryptonite — often turn out to be shadow sides of our trademark strengths, the painful and unintended side effects of what makes us so great. As tempting as it might be to ignore our weaknesses, confronting them directly allows us to make better choices, lowering the risks that we'll undermine our success through our own less productive actions.

As someone who has received dozens of performance reviews, not to mention taking personality tests like Myers Briggs or the Eneagram, I know firsthand that receiving developmental feedback never feels fun. That said, it does get easier with repetition. I still brace myself just a little upon receiving a 360-degree review, but I'm less scared than I used to be since I know I'll hear familiar themes. I've also learned to share negative feedback about myself with others (originally through team coaching sessions) and now tend to do so early and proactively. In fact, when interviewing folks who I may work closely with, I want to share these developmental areas to make sure others know where my style will likely prove challenging, and I will also probe to find my complement. I've consistently found that others respond well to self-awareness and humility about our developmental areas. It puts them at ease, often prompting them to graciously accept my imperfections alongside their own. I find that kryptonite loses its power to wound us if we face it repeatedly, internalize it as our ongoing leadership work as much as our strengths, and acknowledge it to others authentically.

Humbly acknowledging our weaknesses alongside our strengths need not wreck our confidence and self-esteem. When it comes to risk-taking, habituating ourselves to true feelings and being visibly imperfect actually *help* us behave more boldly by reducing the threat we face from ego risk. When we feel less pressure to appear perfect, we tend to obsess less about looking foolish if we fail, and we may feel empowered to consider a greater array of potential opportunities to discover, learn, or achieve an outsize goal.

Welcoming in our kryptonite affords us another benefit, the ability to mitigate unproductive behavior that might lower our odds of success. If we aspire to become a CEO but know we are introverted and struggle to sell well, we can consciously work on our salesmanship and surround ourselves with outgoing, charismatic leaders who complement us. If we tend to make decisions emotionally, we can adopt habits that help us behave more rationally, like slowing down a process enough for us to cool down, or talking to a level-headed mentor before making a move. Like our natural strengths, our developmental areas follow us wherever we go. Ideally, we'll put ourselves in situations that mostly allow us to thrive via our superpowers, but we should always seek out opportunities to mitigate our more difficult tendencies or help fill in our own gaps.

LEARNING YOU AS YOU GO

I began this chapter with my friend Margaret, the grad student who decided to become a writer and editor. Now let's spend a few moments with a writer who went on to become a successful Facebook executive, and who did so by being in touch with — and trusting — his inner strengths and values.

During his undergraduate years at Pomona College, Nick Grudin interned at Time, Inc., and was, he says, "really kind of inspired by the idea of being a journalist." Upon graduating in 2001, he applied to dozens of newspapers across the country, eventually landing a job as a beat reporter at the *Lodi News-Sentinel* in Lodi, California, a small town south of Sacramento. For the better part of a year he wrote up a storm, covering local crime. After that, eager to live in a larger city, he found a job at the *Los Angeles Daily News* and stayed for a couple of years.

Although Nick enjoyed his journalism work as a local reporter, he felt an itch to learn and perhaps position himself for a bigger job covering national news. In 2004, he enrolled at Harvard's Kennedy School of Government. There, he took an internship at the *Washington Post*, working not as a journalist but on the business side, helping the newspaper figure out a new business model to help it survive financially in the digital age. Nick discovered he not only loved working at the intersection of journalism, technology, and business, but he was good at it. Although he wasn't primarily using his writing skills, he found that he had developed some underlying analytical, problem-solving, and collaboration skills that he could now apply in a business setting.

As his time at Harvard wrapped up, Nick decided not to apply to big media outlets as he'd planned, but to try for jobs in strategy consulting. He snagged a position at Boston Consulting Group and spent the next two years working on an array of projects with clients in the mobile, travel, and music industries. Here, he honed his business skills, including strategic planning, organizational development, client management, and quantitative analysis. Afterward, he took a leadership role at *Newsweek*, helping the venerable media outlet develop a strategy for thriving in the digital world. Putting his newer business skills to work as well as his longstanding passion for journalism, he wound up managing all of *Newsweek*'s partnerships with tech companies, including Twitter, YouTube, and Amazon. He also developed new editorial franchises, such as *Newsweek*'s annual Green Rankings of Fortune 500 companies.

In 2010, anticipating that *Newsweek*'s corporate owner (the *Washington Post*) would soon sell it, he sought out a new opportunity. He didn't know exactly where he wanted to go, but he did know he wanted to follow his passions for media, technology, and business. He hadn't started his career with these interests in mind — they'd developed over the course of time. "It took those experiences in journalism, at the Kennedy School, the *Washington Post,* BCG, and *Newsweek*" to teach him what precisely he loved to do, and what he was also good at. "I also knew at that point how much I cared about the teams that I work with. I wanted to find a place where I would be challenged and kind of enriched by the people around me. I knew I wanted to be at a fast-paced, rapidly changing environment."

Nick wound up at Facebook in a role that would put him on the other side of the table, negotiating deals between the social media network and big traditional media outlets. As of 2020, he had been at the company for a decade, overseeing an expanding portfolio of responsi-

bilities that included entertainment, sports, news, social good partnerships with nonprofits, Instagram partnerships, video partnerships, original content production, education partnerships, health partnerships,
and more. Small at first, his team now numbers several hundred people around the world and is responsible for the development of video
on Facebook's platform, including Facebook Watch. As he notes, he has
stayed at Facebook because "every year it feels like something really new
is happening or we're iterating or adapting in some meaningful way that
forces me to grow again, as if I had a new job."

By this point in his career, Grudin well understands the importance
of taking risks to grow. But he also knows a thing or two about our
ability to learn more about ourselves through the risks we take. Whenever we make a new choice, our smartest move is to bet on choices that
play to our own natural strengths and values. That's what Nick did:
He was in touch with his strengths and values, and that has led him
throughout his career. But of course, the act of choosing possibility
also thrusts us into novel situations, revealing previously hidden facets
of our personalities and things we might be great at once we try them.
With every choice we make, we come to know ourselves just a little bit
better, ensuring that any future bets we make on ourselves will be even
more rewarding.

Choosing possibility also offers another powerful benefit when it
comes to self-development: As I've suggested, it allows us to build our
agility, flexibility, and resiliency. Many people assume that risk-taking
ability itself is innate, but risk-taking is a practice that can be mastered
with repetition, also. As we take chances, encounter unforeseen challenges, and occasionally fail, we learn to become more adept at adjusting, at making do with what we have, at developing creative solutions,
and at dusting ourselves off and trying again. By regarding risk-taking
as a growth process that unfolds over time, we can pursue careers that
not only play to our natural strengths but that boost our specific capabilities to flex and respond with agility regardless of how our choices
work out.

POSSIBILITY POINTERS

- Smarter risk-taking requires that we look inward as well, aligning our choices not just with our ambitions but also with who we are at our core.
- Build your self-awareness "sandwich," taking stock of your passions, superpowers, and values.
- Knowing our own kryptonite helps loosen its power over us as we seek to make choices and also execute better.

9 | BIGGER LEAPS

Would you forgo a senior executive role and a large paycheck to lead an early-stage startup? That's the anxiety-producing choice I contemplated back in 2008. I'd been at Google for over five years and in many respects had reached the pinnacle of my career. I had been fortunate enough to ride massive tailwinds, take on an increasing amount of responsibility in a supportive environment, broaden my areas of expertise, and build significant leadership skills. After helping to launch Google Maps and Local, I took over our international operations outside of Europe, helping to build our Asia Pacific and Latin America region into a multibillion-dollar business. My reputation and stature grew as well. I was now one of Google's most senior executives, and one of its most senior women, as well.

Yet despite this success, I was getting itchy. Google had grown into a much larger organization since I'd arrived, its headcount mushrooming from 1,200 to almost 40,000 (including contractors), and I was weary of the added bureaucracy. All too often, I found myself spending more time playing politics with other senior leaders than building new services or leading eager teams. It also became clear that a nontechnical leader such as myself would never become Google's CEO. My impressive business peers such as Sheryl Sandberg (now COO of Facebook) and Tim Armstrong (who went on to become AOL's CEO) started to peel off one by one, and I knew I'd need to leave as well in order to get the top job.

For my next move, I really yearned to take on a CEO role where I could grow a company using all the skills I'd developed. I had opportunities at my fingertips; exciting startups had approached me wondering if I'd join their teams and spearhead their growth. But FOF (fear of failure) and FOMO (fear of missing out) were battling it out in my head. I'd only get to "leave Google once" — I knew deep down that my choice of what to do next would be a big one. Personal considerations were also a big factor in all of this, too. I had arrived at Google when I was in my early thirties, single, and able to devote all of my time to work or to fun. Now I was nearly forty, married to a fellow Canadian in the Bay Area, and a parent of two (my stepson, Ryan, and my daughter, Kenya) with a third on the way. The argument for remaining at a large, highly stable company that knew and trusted me and offered incredible benefits was a strong one.

All of us face big, risky decisions, moments that represent true inflection points in our lives. At these times, the potential opportunities are eye-catching, but they also entail a variety of risks. How can we navigate our way to even greater success? As we discussed earlier, one important step is to *take small risks first* for the purpose of discovery, what I've called pipelining in parallel. I did this toward the end of my time at Google, taking recruiter calls many months before I left the company. But the ultimate decision, what to do next, required much more thought and analysis. So how exactly did I go about my own next big career jump, and how should you approach bigger moves in your own life?

YOUR ROUGH GUIDE TO BIGGER BETS

To help with smaller choices, it's enough to apply the risk-taking tips described in preceding chapters, thinking of them as variables to consider in straightforward assessments. With bigger goals, though, where the stakes are higher and multiple motivations and considerations come into play, we'll want to bring all of the variables together and assess them simultaneously. Winston Churchill once exhorted that we should "let our advance worrying become advance thinking and planning," and when it comes to bigger goals, I wholeheartedly agree.

We can combine the variables we've discussed together into a simple Five Factors Framework to help us take smart career risks (Figure 7). This framework can help us not only assess individual choices but compare and score them across multiple dimensions using what I call a Possibility Scorecard.

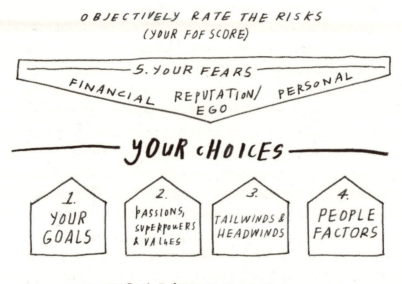

Figure 7

Let's start by listing the choices we're broadly considering, including "doing nothing" or "status quo" as possible choices. Our job is to first evaluate each choice under consideration against the four key variables that enable us to take smarter risks for more upside.

Let's begin by identifying our first variable, our larger goal(s), which after all are the reasons we're taking a risk in the first place. Often when making career moves, we pursue multiple goals at once, tangible ones (like achieving a certain amount of wealth or level of leadership responsibility) and less tangible ones (like achieving a larger business impact or finding a role that makes us happy). Learning may be its own goal as we seek to accelerate our skills and knowledge now for future opportunity. Mindful of your ultimate dreams, try to articulate your specific goals over the next two-to-five-year time frame, even if you're not yet sure what will come afterward. Also, prioritize these goals relative to one another if you can.

Second, let's outline our passions, superpowers, and values. Jot down these elements on a notepad or screen, remembering that you'll want each of your choices to leverage these elements while also affording you the opportunity to acquire new skills. Once we've jotted down these elements, we can begin to assess how well each choice under consideration aligns with our ambitions and who we are.

Next, we'll want to rate our choices against the two big external factors that can affect results: tailwinds/headwinds and "people fit." As we've seen, it's well worth researching the people with or for whom we'll work and the macro conditions (in a team, org, company, or industry) that surround any choice and may bolster or hinder our efforts. External forces will likely vary depending on the choices under consideration, making for more or less opportunity.

Bringing these four factors together, we can rate each of our choices against these variables. I personally like to rate quantitatively, using a scale of 1 to 5. Think of this as rating our upside opportunities for "great" choices. Laying all of this out on a simple spreadsheet (Figure 8), we can create an Opportunity Scorecard that helps us understand each choice and articulate which we're most excited about and why. A sheet like this can and should get our FOMO going.

Of course, taking bigger risks is as much about reducing our fear of failure as it is about maximizing our excitement about future possibilities. Given that bigger choices are inherently uncertain, it's time to address the fifth factor — our fears — and rate the potential downsides we face in pursuing every alternative. While we're at it, we should also visualize our choice(s)-after-the-choice and factor in our present state and "room to fail." Confronting our fears head-on is a pivotal and often neglected step in any decision-making process.

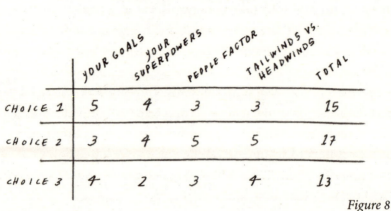

FOMO/OPPORTUNITY SCORE
(LOW TO HIGH 1-5)

	YOUR GOALS	YOUR SUPERPOWERS	PEOPLE FACTOR	TAILWINDS VS. HEADWINDS	TOTAL
CHOICE 1	5	4	3	3	15
CHOICE 2	3	4	5	5	17
CHOICE 3	4	2	3	4	13

Figure 8

In evaluating each choice, we can create a *risk-rating score* right alongside our Opportunity Scorecard. Do this by creating a second, similar worksheet and rating the level of potential downside we face in pursuing each choice. Individually rate each choice against the fears that most often confront us — financial, personal, and reputation/ego — on a similar 1–5 scale (with low scores representing the smallest risks). Use the fourth column to brainstorm choices-after-the-choice (our ideas for how we might recover in case of failure). I have found that listing all the actions we can take to mitigate bad outcomes after a risk goes awry helps to ease our anxiety and allows us to accurately rate our negative risks.

Remember also to assess the size of downside losses we face (small, medium, or large) relative to our present position and where we'll end up should we fail. As an example, if our financial position is already solid and a given choice open to us (say, to accept a certain job offer) would lower our earnings just a little while yielding future benefits, we're taking only a small risk. If we might easily find another job with a similar-size paycheck should this one not work out, that risk becomes even smaller. On the other hand, if we drop our entire savings into starting a new venture that winds up failing, the financial risk is at least medium but likely large, depending on our confidence that we can find a job afterward and rebuild our nest egg in a reasonable time period.

We should take care to separate out the personal and ego risks we'd take, weighing them individually. These risks might increase with our financial risks, or they might actually decline. In a place like Silicon Valley, for example, serving as a founder at least once in your career actually often enhances your reputation in the minds of prospective employers, even if your startup fails. And for all of us who have dreamed of becoming entrepreneurs, the rewards that come with learning how to innovate offer entirely new and powerful skill-building upside, independent of financial risk.

You should now have a risk-rating score for every choice you're considering also. It might look something like this (Figure 9):

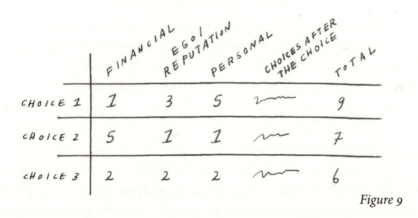

Figure 9

With both of these scores in hand, we have more realistically assessed our FOMO and FOF for every possibility we're examining and can compare them with one another. Check out what your final Possibility Scorecard might look like below (Figure 10):

FINAL POSSIBILITY SCORE

	FOMO/ OPPORTUNITY	FOF/ RISK RATING	TOTAL	OTHER ITEMS ON YOUR MIND
CHOICE 1	15	9	15 - 9 = 6	
CHOICE 2	17	7	17 - 7 = 10	
CHOICE 3	13	6	13 - 6 = 7	

Figure 10

Quantitatively assessing choices when making an emotional decision might seem normal to some of us, or overkill to others. Why should we bother ratcheting up our usual practice of assessing pros and cons to this level? What happens if many choices score closely to one another? I find that articulating and comparing choices more rigorously using a Possibility Scorecard helps us tease out why we feel excited about specific choices and also the true nature of the downside scenarios we fear. When I performed a roughly similar exercise with my sister Nicky, working with her to assess all of her options, she found it enlightening to outline her choices on paper quantitatively, both the risks they represented and the extent to which they served her financial and personal goals. It was the first time she had truly compared risks and rewards side by side in any numerical way.

In my experience, nothing clarifies our situations as much as the act of comparison. When I make any major decision, I try to articulate at least two viable options in addition to sticking with the status quo, clarifying my own highest goal and the risks I'm willing to take in hopes of achieving them. I also register the tradeoffs I'll likely have to tackle — financial versus personal, personal versus reputational, and so on — in making choices.

In deciding to leave British Sky Broadcasting and move to California, I traded off a steady job (financial risk) against the chance to pursue a more fulfilling career as an entrepreneur (personal satisfaction). When I contemplated leaving Amazon for the chance to cofound Yodlee, I dreamed I'd reap more financial rewards from that decision than from staying where I was. I also thought I'd find the life of entrepreneurship tremendously satisfying, and judged that the risk to my personal lifestyle was minimal given that I was single and mobile.

In making big decisions, we most often compare real options (an opportunity that is imminent, including staying with the status quo) with theoretical ones (opportunities we might be able to secure with some uncertain future effort). Only when we use frameworks like a Possibility Scorecard can we truly understand if moving now is best or if we would be better off extending our discovery period by some fixed amount of time. If it turns out that choices currently available to us don't get us very far toward our goals, we are at least prompted to identify theoretical options that might bear more potential and to get in motion, putting ourselves in a position to obtain more information quickly. Or, we can decide to move right now if we find that an actual opportunity puts us on the path to an ideal one fastest and will likely open up new, incrementally better options as we go. Before committing to a big choice, knowing as much as we can about all choices, real and imagined, is incredibly useful.

Bear in mind, whether you use my framework or devise one of your own, the magic is *not* in the final way you score the choices you outlined as much as it is in the *process* of scoring. When we can apply a methodology to name our possibilities and face our fears, we understand our decision-making criteria better and make smarter big bets.

GUT-DATA-GUT

Even with a great framework in our pockets, we might still find it hard to make a decision. What then? Is it time to "listen to our gut"? Successful risk-takers often harken back to that magical moment when they responded against all odds to their intuitions and the risk paid off. On the other hand, other experts tell us to listen to the objective data and follow it wherever it leads, observing that "good data never lies." As I've found, there's merit to both sets of signals, so long as you follow a specific progression that I call Gut-Data-Gut.

Going with our gut pretty much amounts to making a quick judgment with origins that remain somewhat mysterious to us. But such mystery doesn't mean we can't understand the inner workings of these judgments. As the German social psychologist Gerd Gigerenzer notes, gut thinking tends to involve the use of very basic "rules of thumb" that allow us to come to conclusions based on "simple cues in the environment." When we go with our gut, we're pushing away the wealth of other information that might be coming at us and zooming in on these cues. We do this subconsciously and also much more quickly than we perform rational calculations, often allowing us to obtain better results.

For example, in his own research, Gigerenzer found that people who use simple rules or heuristics to pick stocks often do better than the markets as a whole. The "intuitive wisdom of the semi-ignorant outperformed the calculations of the experts." But Gigerenzer also observes that "gut" instincts can fail us badly. After 9/11, people instinctively felt unsafe flying and wanted to drive instead, even though highway fatalities far outnumber air fatalities. Some 1,500 more people died on highways during the year after 9/11 than had died the year before.

Gigerenzer notes that as a scientist, he heeds both hunches and data. "I can't explain always why I think a certain path is the right way, but I need to trust it and go ahead. I also have the ability to check these hunches and find out what they are about." The Gut-Data-Gut principle operates much the same way. If you find yourself intuitively excited or fearful about a certain choice relative to others, explore why by identifying and rating the variables in the risk-taking equation. Quite likely, you'll connect your inner hunch with one of these variables and the rating you provide.

If after assessing your choices you still can't identify the variable that has you most excited or that is giving you pause, take one further action. Reflect on those experiences that you and others around you have had and consider whether your knowledge of any of them might be triggering an unconscious "pattern match" in your head. It's very possible your gut will be twitching because a given choice will remind you of a similar situation or several from your past that turned out differently from how you expected, either positively or negatively, and you don't want to be "surprised" again this time.

As my own career has progressed, I've found that my gut instincts have grown stronger, not weaker. I've compiled my own mental library of past experiences, and certain current situations trigger feelings in me when I sense they're starting to resemble something I've seen earlier. This instinctive pattern often tells me that some feature of a particular choice at hand might be more important or persuasive than the data alone would indicate. I want to listen to my intuitions based on real experience while also being mindful of unwarranted biases. By creating an Opportunity Scorecard and mapping out the risks, I can put all the facts on the table, including my fears, ensuring that I've given credence to everything in the analysis. In the end, I will honor the feelings triggered by the data as well as the gut reactions I'm having on top of the data, but I do want to do my best to name them. I'd also worry about making a potentially momentous decision based solely on vague positive or negative feelings I had without probing what element was specifically triggering them.

In general, the best decisions we can make in high-stakes situations account for both instinct *and* data, using our quick judgments and feelings in full concert with analysis. In the immortal words of Coach Taylor, from one of my favorite TV series of all time, *Friday Night Lights*, "Clear eyes, full hearts, can't lose."

FIND YOUR PROFESSIONAL PRIESTS

Even after running through a Gut-Data-Gut process, we might still remain torn about what to do. In these situations, it's easy to get stuck and not do anything at all, unwittingly subjecting ourselves to the even-greater risks that might come with inaction. To free ourselves from this trap, it helps to turn to those around us and talk the decision out, often several times. Those of us who are "auditory" or social learners advance our thinking through conversations with others more quickly than we can on our own. For people who tend to learn in more solitary ways, sharing our logic and analysis at least allows us to test their soundness. In general, the clarity of our thinking grows if we leverage the perspectives of others while retaining ultimate control over our own decisions.

Although many of us routinely approach our closest friends, family, and peers for advice, it's important to note we often fail to ask all the *right* questions. Simply asking the most trusted people in our lives to tell us what *they* would do can yield advice that reflects their *own* particular biases. For this reason, we would do better to ask for feedback about *ourselves* from our closest circle first and then share our own first assessment of our choices, asking our confidants to comment based on *what they know of us.* But again, we should expect that their responses will likely reflect their own preferences or feelings about how a choice of ours might affect them personally.

Another word of caution: Relying on spouses or family members as confidants also risks draining energy from our deepest relationships by saddling them with the weight of our work obsessions. In successful emotional relationships, each of us expects to give and receive joy and support in more or less equal measure overall (recognizing that someone might give or get more at any point in time). Injecting our work issues continuously into our partner conversations over long periods can drain our loved ones dry.

We might ease the burden on those closest to us and rely instead on a set of confidants whom I call our "professional priests" (Figure 11). These are select individuals who know us well from workplace settings and perhaps also personally: former bosses, peers, professional acquaintances, mentors, close or more distant friends, and even professional coaches we might hire. At the same time, these individuals are a bit more distanced from us personally than our spouses or closest family members.

For this reason, they harbor less bias — our decisions won't personally affect them. And since many of these individuals will likely be professional contacts, they'll probably feel less put out by endless work-related conversations, and they might also have a wider knowledge of professional opportunities that builds on our own. Take note, the "brainstorming buddies" I described earlier might or might not also serve as our professional priests. A few people in our lives might play all roles — confidant, creative brainstormer, and advisor — whereas others can fill only certain of them.

PERSONAL TRIBE
(PARTNER, family, close friend)

PROFESSIONAL TRIBE
(bosses, pEERS, EXTERNAL PARTNERS, MENTORS)

PROFESSIONAL PRIESTS
INVESTED IN OUR SUCCESS, UNBIASED HOW WE ACHIEVE IT

Figure 11

When I began pondering my transition out of Google more than a year before my departure, I needed help talking through all my options and navigating my own path. My husband had been incredibly supportive as my career at Google accelerated, but I understood I could easily drive him crazy with my constant work talk, and taxing him daily with every obsessive career-related musing was a quick path to a not-so-great marriage. So, I turned outward, joining a group called the Young Presidents' Organization (YPO) to find work peers and coaching.

Through YPO, I met my executive coach, David Lesser, and decided to work with him individually (on a paid basis), given how much time I was spending contemplating my transition. With his understated and compassionate style, David served as a trusted "professional partner" to me, someone with whom I could share my highest hopes and also deepest vulnerabilities as a person and leader. Session after session, I told David about my desires for both an impactful professional life and a satisfying personal one, and he helped me talk through and then balance the inevitable tensions.

In this way, David became a critically important professional priest to me, and we continue to work together to this day. But others around me helped navigate my way out of Google as well. At around the time I met David, I began investing in my friendships with women who were at similar work and life stages and who could easily identify with my specific challenges. This group became an inner circle with whom I could freely discuss career issues in a safe space. Although I might not see them as often as I do my closest friends, we continue to call one another even to this day, counting on each other for help when making large professional decisions and also some personal ones.

To find professional priests of your own, think of people in your network who know you well but who need not belong to your innermost personal circle. Current or past workplace colleagues and bosses are an obvious choice. One person I know relies on a longtime therapist who serves him a bit in the way of an executive coach, and also on a family friend with experience in business. Additionally, you might also join a professional community or an alumni group to make contact with potential professional priests. Try to find people whose experiences or personality traits complement yours. You might also consider people who've seen or counseled others navigating similar situations — maybe it's a senior manager in your group, the head of HR, or an old friend who happens to have experience managing others. Even if we can't assemble our own, enduring "professional cabinet," we can still benefit from talking through our choices with a few empathic and knowledgeable people in our outer circles when making any big move.

MAXVC AND MINVC

After evaluating our options, listening to our guts, and consulting with our professional priests, it's now time to make a decision. For some of us, using a risk-taking framework to evaluate the big variables is all we need to push us into making a new "stretch" decision. We might feel excited to embark on this new choice, but also nervous contemplating what we have to learn and the size of the challenge to which we've just agreed. We'll likely also suffer a bit from "impostor syndrome," the notion that we are unqualified and inadequate to the task at hand. Such insecurities never go away and usually indicate that we're just beginning a new learning cycle.

If you're feeling jittery, it's likely that you're making a truly big move — what I call a Maximum Viable Choice (MaxVC) — in order to change your career trajectory. A MaxVC usually entails undertaking fully one of the bigger choices on your Possibility Scorecard. Perhaps you're stepping into a stretch role for which you're not sure you're qualified, taking on a new job in a new industry, or quitting your stable job to launch a startup.

If your fears run so strong that they're paralyzing you and preventing you from deciding, remember that putting ourselves into motion is what matters most of all. If your analysis justifies the merits of a single, bigger action and yet you still feel unable to move ahead, try to make what I call the Minimum Viable Choice (MinVC). That is, identify the smallest and safest step available to you that moves you incrementally toward your desired full choice.

As I began contemplating my career after Google, but well before I felt ready or equipped to make a big leap, I took the MinVC of taking calls from recruiters and meeting with potential employers. In fact, as you'll see, I made at least three iterative moves (starting to pipeline and listen, leaving Google, joining Accel) before eventually making my "big choice" of accepting a job as a private company CEO in early 2010. With each step I added more knowledge about potential choices to my own Opportunity Scorecard without committing myself to a final decision. This process of successively choosing possibility enabled me to take one of the biggest risks of my professional career. I got started with a small action and stayed in thoughtful motion until I had completed a large career pivot.

This wasn't the first time that I stepped my way into a bigger action: I did it early in my career as well when I moved from Sky in London to OpenTV in California. We can all begin to iterate toward a major change at any stage of our lives. During our twenties, we might find that our first job delivers a paycheck but little fulfillment, and as a result, we dream of doing something different. We can plot our choices, from going back to school and earning an entirely new degree to quitting our jobs and moving to another field or industry that our intuition tells us might fit us better. We might take action straight away (MaxVC) if we know enough to confidently choose, or we might make the MinVC of discovering more about other career paths, perhaps by doing informational interviews or taking a part-time course. If we feel convinced that we need to make a big leap in our career, let's at least commit right now to taking the first step, no matter how small, so that the process of choosing possibility can begin.

Whether we make a MaxVC or a MinVC, our ability to undertake at least some movement mitigates one of the biggest risks we face: the risk of missing an opportunity altogether. We might keep uncovering new possibilities only to find that many of these choices expire as we wait to make a move, subject as they are to conditions and forces outside of our control. If we endlessly dither, we might lose options that we counted on in our deliberations, and we also prevent ourselves from learning and growing through action. Time waits for no person, not least the ponderers among us.

MY BIG JUMP

After listening to others pitch me a few different job opportunities while still at Google in 2008, it became clear to me that I would make a better decision if I could fully explore the larger landscape of new companies emerging in Silicon Valley. I had spent the last several years focusing on Google's business outside the U.S., and I honestly felt out of touch with the startup world. Beyond my goal of becoming a CEO of my own company, I actually had two other ambitions. I wanted to help build a great consumer service that would delight people (potentially in e-commerce), and I also wanted to build further wealth for myself and my family.

To better evaluate my options, I made the decision to quit Google first and find a way to study the wider ecosystem of companies before choosing where to go. Resolved to give myself a "blank slate" before making a final choice, I left Google when I was three months pregnant and joined Accel Partners, a top Silicon Valley venture capital firm and an investor in my previous startup, in a temporary role as CEO-in-residence.

In the months that followed, I helped Accel evaluate investment opportunities across a wide variety of digital sectors, with a particular focus on e-commerce, taking the opportunity to study those companies I might join or think of starting from scratch. One of Accel's key partners, Theresia Gouw, helped me brainstorm, joining my own cadre of professional priests. We had known each other for over a decade (I originally met her as a young founder at Yodlee) and were at similar stages of our careers, so I knew she could identify personally with my career quandaries. Like me, Theresia was pregnant with her next child and at a similar life stage — yet another commonality.

While at Accel, I spent a disproportional amount of time testing my macro thesis that online shopping was about to explode in new ways. I had seen the rise of e-tailers at Google (many of these companies, such as eBay and Amazon, were Google's largest advertisers at the time) but many of the leading e-commerce sites like Amazon and Zappos still had a utilitarian feel to them. Meanwhile, new fashion and décor e-commerce sites such as Rent the Runway, Gilt, Houzz, Wayfair, and One Kings Lane were popping up everywhere and growing rapidly. These sites sought to tap into a more aspirational and entertainment-oriented kind of shopping experience and move it online. Expert investors like Accel and others were funding them, and my own observations suggested that this area would yield another big wave of online consumer growth. These lifestyle categories of shopping also appealed to me personally; I was the target customer for many of them.

I started to work on an idea of my own for a new e-commerce service, a luxury version of eBay, while listening to the pitches of every e-commerce company that was looking for funding and talking to several that needed early-stage CEOs. I continued to listen to non-e-commerce pitches as well, simply to give myself a point of reference for evaluating online shopping opportunities.

At Yodlee and Google, I had been lucky enough to work with incredibly smart and talented people who shared my values, and I wanted to do the same at my next venture. I wanted to work with great investors, too, and fortunately I had the ability either to work with Accel-funded companies, start my own, or leverage other investor relationships I'd developed. I spent time with multiple company founders to try to discern who they were as leaders, in addition to what they were working on.

By this point in my career, I had a pretty clear idea of my own superpowers and values, so I looked to find companies that could make the most of my unique gifts and whose founders or senior leaders had strengths complementary to mine. Specifically, I hoped to join a company with a very strong engineering and product management culture that needed a CEO with strategy, vision, business development, fundraising, and team-building expertise. Applying these criteria, I turned down several opportunities at companies whose founders had skill sets too similar to mine, reasoning that this overlap might lead to conflict if I ever became CEO.

Finally, I used my time at Accel to think long and hard about the risks I would take in becoming a startup CEO and whether or not I could afford to fail. My biggest risk by far was ego- and reputation-related. Mindful of how precarious early-state startups are, I truly feared that I would leave a successful role as a global executive only to suffer a very large and visible failure. But the more I thought about this, I faced this ego risk head-on and concluded that my reputation as an executive from Google would hopefully be strong enough to survive one failure if it came to that.

The personal risks of taking on a startup CEO role felt different but not greater than those associated with my job at Google. While I knew that serving as a first-time CEO while having another newborn at home (my son Kieran) would be immensely stressful, I would likely benefit from no longer traveling around the world for days and weeks on end and working across multiple time zones, as I had previously. Last, I evaluated the financial risks of potential moves. Although my startup equity would have very uncertain value for a long time, I judged this a risk worth taking, given how excited I'd feel to have more impact and responsibility as CEO. While I lost a large financial package in choosing to leave Google and switching to a startup salary, I could pay the bills at home while digging into my savings only slightly. Under these conditions, I was prepared to make the leap.

In early 2010, almost a year after I left Google, I finally found the right opportunity and decided to join fashion technology startup Polyvore as its full-time CEO. A precursor to Pinterest, Polyvore was based on the idea that women could "clip" online images to create fashion and décor idea boards digitally that were instantly "shoppable." Millions of young women (including influencers) were already using the service and loved it. The founding team was led by a rock star engineer, Pasha Sadri, along with three other product and technology folks he recruited from the likes of Yahoo and Google.

Pasha was known for his intelligence, and we had connected informally over the years for coffee, each time having great discussions about business strategy. In fact, Polyvore twice before had tried to recruit me to become its CEO, once when I was at Google and again at the time of my departure from that company in 2008. Back then, I'd spent a productive afternoon with the founding team, helping them think through their business model. I also knew Peter Fenton, one of Silicon Valley's most successful investors and a leading funder of the company. Peter was the one who first introduced me to Polyvore and who continued afterward to passively court me.

Having spent so much time exploring my options from multiple angles, I was now poised to make a great decision. I felt convinced that e-commerce was starting its next wave of growth, and felt excited to be part of it. Within that vision, Polyvore was among the companies best positioned to succeed, and I knew I could contribute in significant ways to building a service that would delight millions. I was impressed with the strengths of Polyvore's founder and investors and anticipated that I would be able to complement their efforts nicely. Recognizing that my success as a startup CEO hinged on my relationships with the founder and board, I had also invested time to get to know them.

Meanwhile, I had faced my fear demons, taking financial risk but negotiating my offer aggressively to account for downside scenarios I imagined, and coming to grips with my ego risk. With all this work in place, I finally jumped. After managing a multibillion-dollar profit and loss (P&L) and leading a two-thousand-person team at Google, I became the newly minted CEO of a ten-person fashion startup in February 2010.

As we tee up the bigger choices in our careers, we all face critical moments of decision. No choice we make will be perfect, and all the frameworks in the world won't eliminate risk entirely. But we don't need perfection or freedom from risk. We just need to take the next step. By choosing thoughtfully, using all the tools at our disposal to maximize our upside and anticipate our downside, we can grasp the opportunities available to us while equipping ourselves to handle whatever challenges reality throws our way.

POSSIBILITY POINTERS

- We can make bigger calculated leaps by evaluating our choices across five key factors: our ambition, our personal qualities, our "people fit," external headwinds and tailwinds, and our fears.
- The Gut-Data-Gut principle can help you make smarter decisions, as can finding your professional priests.
- If your MaxVC seems too scary, start with your MinVC. Make any choice that gets you moving.

PART III

Get Rewarded

The highest reward for a person's toil is not what
they get for it, but what they become by it.
— JOHN RUSKIN

No matter how seasoned or experienced we become in our professional careers, risk remains our constant partner. We can perform all the due diligence and advance planning in the world but we'll still never eliminate risk entirely. The case in point for me: Polyvore. When I joined the company, I was thrilled, excited, and ready to go in my first CEO role. Unfortunately, just six months later, I left the company, sustaining one of the biggest failures of my professional career.

Before I agreed to join Polyvore, my coach, David, and I discussed the biggest factors that would inform my success or failure once I was on the job (my "execution" risks). The first and most critical one, we decided, was still likely to be the people factor. Despite my diligence during the job search, it was possible that once I was in the CEO seat, I wouldn't work as well with Polyvore's founder (and its CEO right before me) as we both hoped.

In most Silicon Valley companies, founders serve as starting CEOs even if they lack the management experience and skills required to scale a business. As companies evolve, founders can gain the skills they need, or their boards might suggest bringing in a professional CEO (like me in this case). Having been a founder myself at Yodlee and having recruited and worked closely with a professional CEO, I understood the tension that exists between the founder's financial ownership, vision, and moral authority and that of an ambitious CEO brought in from the outside. A founder-CEO relationship is like a marriage: Both partners must want it to work, and they must both be willing to do the work. Like a marriage, this relationship also has at best a fifty-fifty chance of succeeding.

Polyvore's founder, Pasha, and I had developed rapport with each other, having spoken several times before I came on as CEO. I now wanted to build on that rapport and establish a trusted and productive relationship between us. We possessed complementary strengths but very different leadership styles, and I hoped they would prove compatible. We set up a regular coffee date, and I committed myself to spending more time during my first three months listening to his ideas than expressing my own. I wanted him to become comfortable with me, and me with him.

Relatedly, I worked hard early to establish a productive relationship with the board. Although I had known one of the key investors, Peter, for many years, I understood that startup boards often feel a strong allegiance to their founders (and rightly so), and that this might influence the dynamic among myself, Pasha, and the board members. I committed myself to checking in regularly with the board early on and informally, soliciting their views both on my performance and Pasha's attitudes toward the leadership change.

My third key focus on the job was the work I needed to do to help build the company. Here, I was quite comfortable, as the main requirements — building business models, selling and business development, hustling, and attracting strong talent — were superpowers of mine. Nonetheless, I got to work helping the company increase its revenues and hiring a great team. During my first five months, we doubled our workforce to twenty people, attracting some killer talent that included Katrina Lake (who a year later would go on to found the multibillion-dollar online personal styling service Stitch Fix), Jennifer Skyler (who would go on to become director of consumer communications at Facebook and chief corporate affairs officer at American Express), and Philip Inglebrecht (an ex-Googler, serial entrepreneur, and cofounder of the music service Shazaam, among other accomplishments). I hit the road ambitiously to meet key advertising partners and help to raise Polyvore's public profile. The board complimented my work, with one venture capitalist commenting that I was off to the strongest start of any CEO they'd seen in their portfolio.

But taking proactive steps to identify and mitigate known risk doesn't guarantee that you'll avoid it. Despite my best efforts, tension started to mount between Pasha and me. By month four of my tenure, I began to express my opinions more openly, and I sensed that Pasha often had different ideas. While he and I kept meeting, I also talked to the board and my coach about how best to handle any potential conflict between us, understanding that our very different leadership styles might exacerbate it. The root of the problem soon became apparent: Two people wanted to run the company two different ways — its current CEO and its former one.

The situation burst out into the open at the six-month mark and soon proved untenable. Over the course of ten days, the board had to (re)decide which of us would run the company. Anguished, I convened my professional priests: my coach, David; my mentor and former boss Venky; my close friend Bud Colligan (ex-CEO of Macromedia and a Yodlee board member); and my employment attorney. I also cried on the shoulders of my husband, mother, and sisters as I tried to chart a way forward.

Although the board acknowledged the challenges I'd faced and assured me that I bore no blame, it picked Pasha to return to the CEO role over me. I thought of fighting to retain the CEO seat, but my mentors strongly advised against it. Harkening back to the key issue of values fit, they noted that my style and the culture of the company under its previous founder were diametrically opposed, and that the conflict had eroded trust between all parties. At the end of September 2010, my nightmare scenario came to pass. I went from being a first-time, ambitious CEO to utterly dejected and out of a job.

I felt humiliated, betrayed, heartbroken, and ashamed — it was the biggest reputational and personal failure I'd ever suffered. Although publicly we announced that the company and I had "mutually agreed" to part ways, I anticipated that my business peers would judge me harshly.

In my own eyes, I deserved their disdain. Despite my due diligence, I had made a terrible mistake in failing to understand the size of the values mismatch between me and the founder. Did I really have what it took to become a successful CEO? I was no longer quite so sure.

Yet amazingly, there were some unexpected silver linings in my unsuccessful career move. As painful as the Polyvore debacle was for me personally, my fears that it would scuttle my career really didn't materialize. My previous track record still remained relatively intact despite this incident. In terms of financial risk, Polyvore actually turned out to be a significant win. Knowing that relationship difficulties often arise between founders and CEOs within startups, I'd aggressively negotiated financial protections to cover me in case I was ousted for anything besides my performance. As a result, I owned a good amount of equity in Polyvore upon my departure. The company continued to grow, riding bigger tailwinds as Pinterest launched and grew rapidly, making shoppable inspiration boards online a mainstream concept.

Within a year of my leaving, Pasha was moved out of the CEO role again, replaced by another of the company's founders, who in turn helped the company thrive. In 2015, Yahoo agreed to acquire the company for over $200 million, seeing its service as a way to enhance its growth at a time that the dot-com giant continued to struggle. All of a sudden, my ownership stake in the company was worth a lot of money. As a Polyvore board member said to me many years later, "Think of that as your hazard pay for stepping into that challenging situation"—and indeed it was.

The move to Polyvore worked out in other ways, too. I took a risk not just on a company but on a new role and industry (being a CEO and entering e-commerce), and the passage of time revealed these choices to be good ones. I loved being in the top job, bearing both the joy and burden of handling everything from strategy to team-building to product development to P&L management. My thesis that e-commerce would explode into new inspirational/lifestyle categories like fashion and décor also proved correct. Over the decade since, I've built on my initial industry experience at Polyvore and immersed myself fully in e-commerce, becoming a successful angel investor, board member, founder, and CEO again.

The truth is, *none of this would have happened without my original choice to take a huge personal risk to leave Google* and my subsequent choices to become a CEO, enter a new industry, and join a promising startup in the category.

I recount this story to make a simple but important point: Even when we carefully analyze and map our choices in advance, taking a big risk in hopes of earning a big reward, reality is usually messy. The risks we take don't always yield the direct rewards we envisioned right away, and assuming larger risks doesn't necessarily mean we'll realize bigger rewards right away. Life is more complicated than any simple framework. Each significant choice we make carries multiple consequences that in turn often take time to unfold. So, what's the precise relationship between risk and reward in the real world? Once we take action, will our gutsy leaps actually pay off?

THE MYTH OF RISK AND REWARD

Let's be clear: Although frameworks can't guarantee us ultimate success, we do still need them. In the case of Polyvore, I assessed the key Five Factors thoroughly, trying to make a smart career decision. This rough framework helped me identify trends and roles I wanted to pursue, articulate and confront my fears, and feel more comfortable making the jump. Using the model to organize my thinking, I decided to pursue my career ambition of being a CEO, selected e-commerce based on my sense of both the tailwinds at play and my interests, and chose Polyvore after assessing both my own skills and the people involved. I understood well the financial, ego, and personal risks I was taking and put a thoughtful plan in place to mitigate them, including people-related strategies, ongoing professional support, and those all-too-important financial protections. The thoroughness of my analysis in turn allowed me to act with conviction. True, seven months after I joined Polyvore, this move seemed like a failure on many levels. But a decade later, it looked much more successful given the many rewards I've received and career highs I've notched since.

If the rewards of risk-taking as illustrated by this story seem indirect or unclear, perhaps it's time we adjust further our ingrained model of risk. Similar to the Myth of the Single Choice, popular culture teaches us to expect a straightforward, linear relationship between risk and reward: The bigger the chance we take, the bigger the payoff. We might also presume that we'll be able to clearly spot the results of any big risk we take in a relatively short, fixed time period — a year, say, or two. Believing that the world operates linearly helps us wrap our head around the idea of risk and reward and make sense of it. The more orderly and rule-bound the world seems to be, the better.

It's no mystery why we tend to regard risk and reward as proportional and linear — we perceive growth in general that way. As children, we proceed from grade to grade, progressing step by step, expending more effort to achieve bigger goals until we reach our objective: graduation from high school. If we go on to college, we embark on a similar process. Within particular courses of study, we proceed serially, mastering a set of concepts or skills, taking a test to document our proficiency, tackling more difficult concepts or skills, taking another test, and so on. For much of the twentieth century, corporate life has unfolded similarly. Hierarchically organized companies offered clear, logical career ladders. Professions such as law or medicine offered clearly defined job paths after graduation. Résumés today still capture this orderly view of careers, listing jobs in order from most recent to earliest, followed by educational credentials. Even the video games we play are linear, with players graduating from level to level as their mastery of the game improves. Each assumption of risk leads naturally to a reward as well as yet another, stepwise assumption of risk.

Deep cultural and biological factors incline us toward notions of linear growth trajectories. As scholars have observed, "Decades of research in cognitive psychology show that the human mind struggles to understand nonlinear relationships. Our brain wants to make simple straight lines." Western societies in particular seem to emphasize linear thinking, whereas thought processes in Eastern cultures tend to be more holistic and less logical. As the psychologist Nick Hobson describes it, we in the West are "analytic thinkers, meaning we see the world in a linear fashion, carving out separate events and peering at them through a lens of cause and effect. We are rule-bound and systems-oriented and we are drawn in by focal events."

In truth, the connection between risk and reward is often not so neat and tidy. We take risks for multiple reasons, often pursuing several goals at once and notching results against these goals at different times and in different ways. The results of our choices can unfold over months or even years as we keep pivoting in response to the results we've obtained so far, iterating our way to the next possibility. Once in motion, we persist, and our road ends up being more winding than we originally imagine. We can try to correlate a single move to a single result, and the size of any effort to the size of the return. Sometimes we'll find that these elements do align nicely as predicted, but more often than not we find ourselves charting an unstable, shifting course.

If we plot individual outcomes in our lives, we find that they look less like straight lines and more like scatter charts. In my case, some small risks I've taken have yielded outsize outcomes, and some outsize risks have yielded small outcomes. Choices that initially seemed low risk blossomed into meaningful successes, and some surface-level successes were personal failures.

Accepting the cofounder job at Yodlee constituted a big financial risk compared to staying at Amazon, and while I made money, in relative financial terms it represented a failed outcome. Yet it was also a positive outcome overall for the company and one of the most positive emotional and reputational events of my career. Creating an innovative company from the ground up that had a large and enduring impact in its industry was incredibly satisfying, as was building and leading a team of incredibly smart people, many of whom shared my values and became part of my lifelong and deep professional network.

Conversely, moving to Google was one of the least risky moves of my career, as the company was already profitable and growing fast. Nonetheless, this small risk yielded some of the largest financial wins of my career, and it gave me a chance to learn and grow as a leader at an unprecedented rate. Note that Google made me an offer almost entirely because of my achievements at Yodlee, which of course owed to a riskier choice I made in leaving Amazon.

If I were to limit my analysis to any specific time period, decisions I made might look like raging positives, raging negatives, or "to be determined." But what most jumps out is the *multiple number of moves* it took for me to unlock an outsize career reward, as well as the "tacking" required to get there. Overall, my career grew enormously between the mid-1990s and 2010. I rose from an analyst at Merrill and British Sky Broadcasting to become president of a multibillion-dollar business and then a startup CEO, and the overall trajectory is compelling. But that upward trajectory unfolded over time and many choices, and the individual moves I made defied that governing logic. The relationship between risk and real reward is anything but linear when it comes to measuring individual decisions and results. Take heart in knowing that even if the initial results of a certain decision you've made don't work out immediately, over time and multiple moves, they may resolve in your favor, so long as you're prepared to keep choosing the next possibility and to learn from the current one.

MULTIPLE MOVES REALLY DO YIELD MORE

It seems counterintuitive, but if we're willing to take many risks and keep taking them even after we fail, we're far more likely to achieve outsize rewards over the long term than if we focus on taking sporadic, individual big risks. Conversely, if we don't make risk-taking a habit, our ability to forecast, assess probabilities, or even understand our gut feelings will suffer, and with it our ability to make smarter choices and advance our careers. Bear in mind, my own career pathway is not all that unusual. These days, taking multiple risks to gain larger rewards overall is increasingly common. Let me give you another example.

When Corey Thomas, chairman and CEO of the publicly traded security firm Rapid7, first started out on a business career, he dreamed of one day having an important impact as a leader and building a large business. He's achieved that dream, but as he told me, his success came in a somewhat circuitous fashion through the threading together of multiple risks over a number of years. After getting his MBA, Thomas took a leap akin to the one I made by joining Polyvore: He left a comfortable job at Microsoft and took a 30 percent pay cut to work as a marketing executive at the Seattle-based tech startup Parallels. His parents thought he was crazy to sacrifice a portion of his compensation, but Thomas was eager to experience a more entrepreneurial environment and was lured to Parallels by the chance to learn from its smart, aggressive, and highly successful founder (see chapter 6 on choosing people over passion).

After he had spent two successful years at the company, Parallels merged with another firm and Thomas wasn't thrilled by the new job the organization offered him. Although he retained a strong network of professional sponsors from his time at Microsoft and could have easily found a job at a large company, he opted again to take a 20 percent pay cut and move clear across the country to serve as chief marketing officer at Rapid7, then a Boston-based startup. The lure again was the people — a former boss of his was running the company, and he liked its founder — but also the chance to start a company of his own (Rapid7's backer Bain Capital promised to fund an entrepreneurial venture of his in a few years if he performed well at the company).

After four years at Rapid7, the company had grown to about $20 million in revenues and two hundred employees, and Thomas was ready to leave in order to begin an entrepreneurial venture. But it was not to be. Shortly before Rapid7 was to go public, its CEO left the company. Although Thomas had no experience in the CEO role, much less in taking a company public, Bain Capital asked him to take it, arguing that he could quickly learn the necessary executive skills while transitioning into the job. Thomas had no illusions about how risky it was to step into a job for which he wasn't yet qualified, and he also knew that some board members didn't fully support this move. But he decided to accept the CEO position anyway. He wound up taking yet another big risk once in the job, pushing hard for controversial changes to the company's strategy. His plans ultimately succeeded, and in 2015 he led the company through a successful IPO.

Since then, Thomas has helped Rapid7 grow quickly (as of this writing in 2020, the company's annual revenues stand at about $350 million). He had achieved his objective of leading growth and making an impact, and as CEO of a public company, no less. This never would have happened had he not made a series of choices that looked risky at the time, with the positive results not immediately clear. Each move he made since leaving Microsoft helped him gain experience in the startup world and build relationships. In the end, these moves put him in a position to benefit from serendipity and step into a CEO role.

"Sometimes life twists everything in convoluted ways," Thomas says. There is a "creative exploratory aspect of risk-taking. As you go along, you actually lead through your hypotheses, learn, make adjustments, and redirect and move in ways that you didn't expect when you actually started." Thomas is right. Successful risk-taking is a process of choosing possibility, a series of steps whose logic and direction only become clear when viewed in retrospect. Take a risk, and you might get a reward right away. But you will much more likely simply get another opportunity to take a risk, and another, and another, only eventually getting where you want to go.

POSSIBILITY POINTERS

- The Myth of Risk and Reward leads us to believe that any reward occurs directly after, and in equal proportion to, the risk we originally take.

- In reality, this relationship is more complicated. A combination of moves big and small over different time periods unlock bigger rewards.
- Risk-taking unfolds through a process of hypothesizing, learning, making adjustments, and redirecting in ways you didn't originally expect.

've tried to put failure into perspective, but let's face it: Failing big is *hard.* Adding to the pain of disappointment is the relentless self-punishment we administer by chastising ourselves for our own perceived mistakes. After Polyvore, I initially felt sorry for myself, so I hid out from my peers in the Valley and spent time with my family. It didn't matter that I was nearly twenty years into a largely positive career. I still felt battered and bruised.

Deep down, I felt that I'd emerge from the disaster and eventually choose my next possibility. To help me get there, my coach, David, and I discussed what had happened so I could process it, take away the key learnings, and move on. David gave me perhaps the best advice I received, encouraging me to stay "open." I had succeeded, he noted, in large part because I was an authentic and energizing person who generally saw the world and people as full of possibility. It would be easy to become jaded, close myself off from others, and grow paranoid after such a painful episode, but if I did, I'd diminish my own superpowers. Along with David, my family helped me retain my sense of self amid my career trouble. My husband and I decided to take a short ski trip as a family. Doing something we loved with each other and our kids for a couple weeks was a much-needed distraction and a way for me to get out of the Valley and lick my wounds.

Within a month or two, after the initial shock had dissipated, I began to consider what to do next, taking into account what I'd learned. Two distinct paths attracted me: working again as a professional CEO in e-commerce, or founding my own company. I loved being in the top job and working in the online shopping category, specifically the lifestyle-oriented subcategory of goods and services, which offered consumers delight and inspiration. I considered joining a larger company where I could leverage my leadership skills to the fullest, where a founder had long ago moved out of the role, and where the financial risk was pretty low. If I were to pursue the second option (less likely, in my view), I resolved that, given the high risk inherent in early-stage ventures, I would only want to run a company that I had started, where I would own the majority of the upside, and where I could establish my own culture and team.

Sure enough, as David had predicted, recruiters began calling, and I listened with an open mind to the jobs they offered. I also found myself haunted by an e-commerce idea of my own that had first come to me within a few weeks of leaving Polyvore. I knew consumers wanted access to "shoppable" content like inspiration boards to find great picks in fashion, beauty, and home. I also knew that brands wanted to sell products this way, as they feared commoditization by Amazon. Thinking back to my last years at Google, I remembered how YouTube "haulers" had emerged on the platform, becoming style and beauty influencers by sharing videos of items they'd gone out and bought. Yet video commerce (in other words, shoppable videos) hadn't yet become a major trend online. QVC and HSN continued to dominate in this space, their large audiences of older female consumers addicted to shopping on broadcast television. Instinctively, I felt I had spotted an opportunity to create the Internet's first real video shopping channel focused on fashion, beauty, and home products. There was big money to be made here: QVC and HSN were multibillion-dollar enterprises, and an online video shopping channel could be too.

As I researched the idea, I became even more intrigued. My FOMO was raging. At the same time, I wasn't sure I wanted to start another company from scratch. After Polyvore, the possibility of sustaining a big failure again petrified me. I was genuinely torn about what to do. I began working on a prototype of a video commerce website and shot several videos with a local influencer featuring fashion and beauty products. I showed these videos to twelve female friends in my living room to gauge their reaction. Meanwhile, putting my tactic of pipelining in parallel to work, I kept interviewing for the bigger CEO jobs that came my way.

By January 2011, about five months after I left Polyvore, it was decision time. I was the top contender for the CEO job at a large online travel e-commerce brand (one you would recognize). Meanwhile, the early feedback coming in from my shoppable video tests was very positive. The travel CEO opportunity was far less risky and certainly more prestigious, but the brand was struggling to grow in a commoditized industry. Despite my mixed emotions about being at an early-stage company, I really did think video commerce would emerge as a massive trend in the coming years, and I was excited about the idea of creating the first service like this from scratch. Ultimately, that excitement won out. I found myself making my second "higher risk" decision within two years of leaving Google, starting Joyus, a pioneering online video shopping platform for women.

I certainly had no illusions about the entrepreneurial journey on which I was embarking. After Yodlee, I knew that getting any new venture off the ground would be a long and winding road, particularly a company trying to create a new market and catch a new trend or tailwind at just the right moment. Five or six years might pass before I would even know if Joyus would survive long term (in other words, if consumers would adopt it easily, if we could scale it, and if we could get to profitability after several rounds of venture funding). I was certainly dreaming of building a large company and reaping the rewards, but that potential payback was far off. In starting Joyus, I faced the same challenge that many of us face when beginning a long journey: How would I get started and then find energy, fulfillment, and success over a long period until I reached my dream destination?

SUCCESS STARTS WITH OUTCOMES

The answer, of course, was to aim for real and tangible milestones on the way to my larger goal. Whether we're aspiring triathletes, entrepreneurs, or chefs, we all know that iterating in smaller increments over time allows us to realize larger ambitions. Milestones motivate us, allowing us to pursue smaller goals and celebrate their accomplishment on our way to something bigger. Practically speaking, it's also almost impossible to achieve outsize results in one fell swoop. We must deliver smaller outcomes first and then make the most of the momentum they create to advance our progress (Figure 12). Any entrepreneur or leader of a multifaceted business division will tell you that success comes from solving one, and then two, and then multiple problems, often in sequence. At some point, these solutions unlock compounding benefits for us, and our progress begins to accelerate with each next problem we tackle.

Have you ever worked through a really challenging jigsaw puzzle with many hundreds of pieces? Some folks (like me) want to build the border first. Others like to begin by joining together pieces of similar color. We can assemble different portions of the puzzle separately, but once enough sections are complete, our progress then mushrooms as we link them together and gain a sense of the whole puzzle. While we can certainly build sections of a puzzle and never complete the whole, we can't finish a puzzle without first completing some constituent sections. Likewise, in our careers we can keep delivering meaningful results without achieving the ultimate success we imagined, but it's virtually impossible to succeed at something large without first delivering many smaller outcomes. The key to unlocking long-term returns always starts with short-term impact.

Many people think their job is essentially done once they've made a bigger choice, but in fact, it's just beginning. You now have to execute in increments to capitalize on the opportunity.

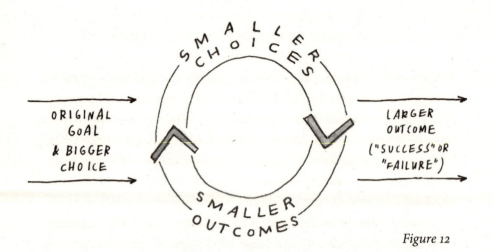

Figure 12

ALL OUTCOMES HAVE IMPACT

Impact has a neutral definition — as a result or "a significant or major effect." When we execute iteratively toward a goal, not every result we notch will be a micro-success on our way to the biggest one. Results can be positive (the achievement we expected) or negative (a "failure" relative to our expectations). While we've been trained in our careers to value only positive results, the truth is that negative outcomes often advance us toward our goals as well, and deliver impact, too, by helping us to see which actions of ours worked and which didn't.

If we're lucky, all of our actions will yield positive results the first time we try something, but we each know how unrealistic that sounds. When we're trying to innovate, we usually make progress by using insights from a current action to inform and execute the next one until we get to a positive outcome. In the tech sector, entrepreneurial teams *expect* their first attempts at a product feature to fail to delight consumers, and they use iterative cycles of feedback over time to deliver positive growth. In scientific research, expectations of iterative failures run even higher. If you're developing a breakthrough cancer drug, you know you're liable to see negative outcomes many times over before you eventually see some glimmer of success.

No one knows more about building a successful career by piling up smaller impacts, including thousands of little failures, than my old tennis partner, Mathai Mammen. Mathai now serves as the global head of all Research and Development for Janssen, the pharmaceutical division of Johnson & Johnson. Earlier in his career, he was an SVP at Merck, and before that he started the biotech companies Theravance and Inoviva. Throughout his career, Mathai has focused on producing breakthrough outcomes by taking a variety of risks, big and small. As he told me, the lengthy process of developing new drugs entails proceeding down a risk-taking funnel. At first, you take a larger number of small, inexpensive bets on ideas or technologies that are relatively unlikely to succeed but that will yield life-changing medicines if they do. From there, you progressively take fewer but bigger risks. By the end of the funnel, when you're deciding which drug candidate to submit for regulatory approval (with all of the expensive testing that requires), you bet a great deal on a single medicine.

I asked Mathai how he could stay happy and fulfilled as a scientist during the decade (or more) it might take to proceed all the way down the funnel. A big part of it, he said, had to do with remembering the ultimate purpose: helping keep people alive, healthier, and happier. "You know every day that the destination you're aiming for is really important. When you alleviate a disease burden, you help not only the patient, but also the family and community. The impact is huge and that helps you stay in the game." Mathai also emphasized the importance of working toward milestones along the way and celebrating them when you reach them. "We have to celebrate heartily the little wins along the way to the big win." These milestones might include understanding the mechanism by which a disease unfolds in the body, discover a drug agent to address that mechanism, and validate that the drug actually works in real patients.

Mathai's ability to stay focused on achieving small impacts has not only yielded great success; it has positioned him to do some of the most important work of his career. In 2020, Mathai and his team were among the teams racing to find a workable vaccine for the Sars-CoV-2 virus, which causes COVID-19. Because of years of painstaking work creating vaccines for HIV, ebola, and other viruses, Mathai's team had assembled technology, people, and processes it thought it could mobilize to create a successful COVID-19 vaccine and successfully produce it at scale. Joining the race was a tremendous bet, but it came as a result of a career built on hundreds or even thousands of smaller bets. Mathai and his team had focused on impact all along, and now it was on the verge of paying off in a way that was both massive and unexpected. In 2020, Johnson & Johnson became one of three top firms around the world to put a vaccine into clinical trials. In early 2021, the company was the first to deliver a single-dose vaccine to the FDA for approval. While other vaccines required storage at super-cold temperatures, Johnson & Johnson's could be maintained using regular refrigeration.

As we aim to deliver against short-term micro-goals, we often create derivative outcomes we didn't expect. This happens all the time in technology: Scientists or engineers are looking to solve problem A, but they find a bigger solution to problem B instead. Sometimes derivative impacts we realize while pursuing a large goal give us joy and satisfaction in ways we couldn't anticipate. We might find that in the process of executing we've been able to build a happy and successful team, that we've uncovered a superpower we didn't know we had, or that we created a new, enduring process that benefits everyone. As these outcomes emerge, we can stack up multiple types of impacts that become the building blocks for our future pursuits, with most but not all also contributing directly to our current goal.

AIMING FOR IMPACT LIFTS ALL BOATS

Focusing on impact means continuously directing and redirecting our daily and weekly efforts, taking actions that are more likely to deliver tangible results in the short and of course long term. That said, aiming for impact isn't some self-obsessed pursuit. Almost any milestone we pursue hinges not just on our own efforts but on those of colleagues and teammates with whom we share work goals. Indeed, much of the joy and satisfaction we achieve from striving toward goals comes from the feeling that we're contributing to something larger than ourselves and that we're helping others have impact too.

To reach our milestone goals, we must stay focused on our own ability to deliver individual results while also accelerating the results of the teams of which we're a part. When we ignore others and only focus on our personal outcomes, we can make some progress but will struggle to achieve larger success. Early in my career, I tended to pursue ambitions that were narrow and objective: I sought to build a company or service of a certain size and achieve rewards like money or a prestigious title. As the years progressed and I matured, I built teams and felt fulfilled as they notched successes, realizing bigger personal rewards in the process. Today I frame my career choices in line with two equal and enduring passions: helping build services that delight or empower millions of users (as a digital leader), and helping others accelerate their own career success.

SEVEN MOVES FOR MORE IMPACT

What separates the more "impactful" among us from those who deliver results far less consistently? It isn't personality or innate intelligence but rather how they approach execution. More impactful people choose to take smaller risks more often and in very specific ways to out-execute and achieve outcomes repeatedly. Here are my *top seven strategies* for taking small risks on the job, no matter what journey you are on (Figure 13).

1. *Put Passion into Your Work, Even When the Work Isn't Passion-Inducing*

When Simon Chen applied to work at Joyus in 2015, he was struggling to find his first full-time job despite having graduated from an elite university (UC Berkeley) with stellar grades. Simon probably didn't think he'd be considering an entry-level administration position upon graduating,

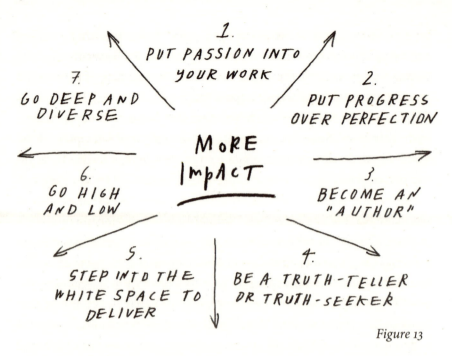

Figure 13

but that's the job he enthusiastically sought with us: as an executive assistant serving the CEO (me) and David, our company's chief merchandising officer.

Since I had no time to interview Simon (I was constantly on the road meeting with customers, investors, and others), I let David handle it. He called me one day raving about Simon and expressing his eagerness to hire him. I wasn't so sure: I preferred to hire a career executive assistant who would hit the ground running rather than hiring a new grad who might have complaints about how much work the job entailed. Nevertheless, I deferred to David.

Simon started off strong, showing himself to be an extremely hard worker. But more than his work ethic, what impressed and delighted me was his enthusiasm to learn about all aspects of his job as well as our company. Many of the day-to-day tasks assigned to him were mundane and repetitive: managing my calendar, ordering groceries to keep the company's fridges stocked full for employees, and so on. But Simon still performed these duties with real passion, figuring out how to automate some of the more boring tasks while still seeing to the details, and personally handling the most important work, such as setting up board meetings or handling communications with high-level executives. At all times, Simon seemed eager to figure out all the aspects of his job, not just the occasionally glamorous parts, and to do them well. He also took full advantage of the access he had to the CEO, constantly peppering me with questions about the meetings I was having and why, picking my brain about the company as a whole, and seeking out feedback on his performance.

Reflecting on his experience at Joyus, Simon relates that he did indeed go into the job determined to learn. He saw performing his basic duties well as an "entry ticket" that would allow him to explore the inner workings of a startup to gain experience and see which parts resonated with him. "Right out of college, it wasn't about chasing a fancy title. It's about what can I learn and who can I learn from," he says. Simon also tried to seek out meaning in his job, even when it came to mundane tasks. Taking the example of an employee assigned to buy snacks for the office, "One person's point of view can be, 'This is such a boring job, an office manager.' The other person's point of view can be, 'Hey. I actually get to affect employee morale by the things I purchase.'" By seeking out meaning, Simon could motivate himself to put everything he had into his job and into learning.

Was pouring himself into his entry-level position a serious risk for Simon? Perhaps. But by bringing a positive and fresh attitude and approach, he transformed his job into a much bigger career opportunity for himself.

Within just a few months, Simon had mastered his role and distinguished himself as one of the best EA's I've had in my career. By saving me time, he enhanced the impact I could have in my own job. Within a year, we promoted him into our Planning and Analysis group, where he had been moonlighting while working for me. Years later when we sold Joyus, Simon applied to his dream job at Facebook. When a Facebook recruiter called to ask me for my assessment of Simon, I told them that they should have hired him yesterday, and what was more, that Simon would probably turn out to be one of the best people they'd ever hire. "He'll be a CEO someday," I said, "and I'll be lining up to be on his board."

To excel at a job, performing it with high levels of quality (effectiveness) and speed (efficiency), you can't simply work hard on only the parts you like. You have to risk your time and energy and seek to master *all* aspects of the job, including the boring parts. When I worked for Hank the Crank at Merrill, I put together great pitch books by sweating every last detail, down to the fonts and whether the decimal points in the figures were in the right places. I also showed curiosity, putting myself out there and asking Hank endless questions about the savings and loan sector. I used that knowledge to do an even better job on the pitch books, thus freeing up time that he could use on his more important work. As I showed that I could master my job responsibilities and was hungry for knowledge, Hank gave me more responsibility, which in turn allowed me to develop more new skills and have greater impact. Thus it was that I outperformed my peers, achieving top ratings in my first year, and landing a plum assignment my second year in London.

2. *Put Progress over Perfection*

If many of us become paralyzed when making our next big choice, getting bogged down in endlessly analyzing our options, something similar often happens once we're in motion. As we execute, we can overplan in our attempts to make every smaller choice or action we take absolutely perfect. Perfection, as we've seen, is an illusion. By spending more of our time simply executing, we obtain more and better data about what works in the real world. This insight in turn helps us more than any abstract plan we might create in our heads. Scientific discovery works this way as well. As the statistician George E. P. Box once observed, progress didn't come from endless theorizing or the piling on of data, but "motivated *iteration* between theory and practice." By spending too much time planning out each and every action (the "theory"), we don't gain as much practical insight, and we slow our delivery of impact.

In other words, by waiting and procrastinating until you have everything just perfect in any planning cycle, you delay obtaining valuable knowledge that might help you achieve a desirable outcome with your next move. You must have the courage to plan roughly and efficiently and then to move ahead as best as you can, even if you know that you don't have the perfect solution just yet.

As Harvard's Leonard A. Schlesinger and his coauthors have noted, small business owners may actually be more susceptible than they think to this tendency; they tend to follow "prediction reasoning," which entails going heavy on the planning and thinking before taking real action. Although this approach can prove fruitful, Schlesinger and team argue that small business owners can make more progress by leading with action (an approach that, I'd note, might feel riskier at first) and applying their learning to build toward results, not least because it's often impossible to predict future conditions. At an extreme, we might overplan because we're overthinking in general, obsessively worrying about the future and factors beyond our control. As one expert observes, overthinking might lead us to "get stuck in potential consequences that may not even happen, just worrying about certain outcomes, and that can paralyze us or freeze us from taking an action."

At every company I've joined, whether it was Yodlee, Google, or Joyus, I've seen the everyday tension that exists between "getting it right" and acting fast, particularly as teams create and implement quarterly OKRs (objective and key results). When it comes time to set goals for the coming ninety days, some teams spend weeks producing ten-page decks outlining their precise goals, while others spend an hour producing a single slide. But if we devote two to three weeks out of a twelve-week period to planning, we lose a great deal of time executing and learning. As teams start to realize this for themselves, they tend to shrink the process of devising OKRs, setting goals more effectively by getting to the essence of a problem and identifying the key tasks required to execute. When they can let go of perfect planning in favor of getting into motion and pivoting their plan as they go, the real impact and learning happens sooner.

Perfect planning is also troublesome for another reason: It presumes that time we lose to "planning" doesn't cost overall efforts very much.

But as we've noted before, the conditions around us keep changing, and the time we spend dithering might have greater repercussions than we realize. We shouldn't just feel motivated to get learning and impacts faster by getting into action; a healthy dose of paranoia also helps, as we realize that favorable conditions might dissipate the longer we wait.

3. Become an "Author"

Authoring, as I define it, entails having an original idea about how to accomplish a task or goal and putting that idea out into the world to accelerate progress and to move forward. Many people view authorship as the preserve of founders, inventors, artists, and other bigger risk-takers, associating it with extraordinary originality or inventiveness. In truth, all of us have original thoughts. Authoring can be as small as throwing out an idea you haven't heard anyone voice yet in a planning session, or as large as spending your time trying to launch a new product, service, or process and roping others into joining you. Whatever the case, we can exercise authorship and magnify our impact if we're willing to take a small risk, let go of our fear of looking stupid (what we've described as ego risk), and have the courage to speak up.

As I think you'll find, the benefits of speaking up far outweigh the potential costs.

Authors help us all advance more quickly toward our goals, pushing themselves and others around them to try new tactics and to learn from the results. Whenever we're willing to try something new, we encourage others to try their hands at authoring as well, and any learnings become building blocks for an entire team's next set of efforts. It's more likely that others will acknowledge us for our talents and contributions as well.

4. Be a Truth-Teller or Truth-Seeker

Even when we lack original ideas for tackling a problem, we might still harbor important observations and opinions that help advance a goal. If we're willing to play the role of truth-tellers and speak frankly about our thoughts, we can increase our odds of identifying actions that will truly yield beneficial outcomes. Further, our candor can rouse our colleagues to do the same, leading our teams to identify the real impediments to their collective goals.

Like authoring, speaking a truth out loud entails taking a small risk to our egos and careers. It also carries a small amount of personal risk, as speaking openly can feel uncomfortable at first. We fear looking inept, offending someone unknowingly with a comment, or having a boss scold us publicly. But staying quiet also carries risks of its own, as we might fail to uncover or share diverse perspectives, thus limiting our team's effectiveness. On the whole, speaking the truth carries a potentially large upside in its ability to accelerate impact, and has a comparatively small downside (at least in settings where we feel a strong sense of trust and underlying values fit). At worst, others might think less of us, but more likely we'll advance our collective progress and even give others a license to speak more candidly as well. Of course, you'll want to be sure to present your thoughts and feedback in a polite and civil manner so as not to alienate or anger your colleagues.

Another way to accelerate our impact is to actively seek out the truth, asking thoughtful questions in order to solicit honest feedback or thinking from others. The best truth-seekers strive to make it safe for people to give voice to their true opinions for the team's benefit, without experiencing any negative consequences.

Some of the most impactful individuals I've ever worked with have been both truth-seekers and truth-tellers. They not only share their own views but help others do so as well. Orit Ziv, an ex–Israeli military officer who now serves as chief human resources officer at Sony Playstation, is gifted with this superpower. I worked with Orit after Joyus when I became the leader of the ticketing marketplace StubHub (more on that soon) and she was the company's chief human resources officer. I met her when I first interviewed for my job, and as I distinctly remember, I couldn't help but feel a little intimidated by her friendly yet probing questions. Once I started in my position, Orit was one of the few people willing to give me direct feedback on my effectiveness as a CEO, treating me as a respected peer instead of trying to be overly deferential. Orit also drove new insights by asking the right questions of me and other managers and leaders at the company, helping us each uncover our truths, opinions, and vulnerabilities.

When I asked Orit for the best advice she can give others on being a truth-teller or truth-seeker to help accelerate progress, she emphasized how important it is to speak the truth in ways that others can hear it, especially when you're dealing with a boss or someone in a position of power. She makes sure to ask permission of others before speaking candidly, and she also takes steps to ease people's fears about what they might hear. "I tell them that we can argue and disagree and have tough conversations behind closed doors, and once we leave the room, I will always represent the decision that they made." As for being a truth-seeker, she notes that she tries to put people at ease, having them articulate their fears about speaking the truth and then helping them to see that the risks might not be as great as they perceive them. She also tries to show curiosity, asking questions to draw people out and gain context rather than confronting people with assumptions or beliefs and having them react.

5. Step into the White Space to Deliver

A couple of months after Simon Chen started at Joyus, the company experienced a sudden bump in customer service queries. We didn't have enough staff to handle them all in an expeditious way. Simon had never worked in customer service before, but he was eager to learn and to help out the team. On his own initiative, he went in on the weekends to help respond to some customer service tickets and then to help us manage the rush of requests we fielded over the holidays. Customer service was by no means part of his job, but he saw an important need and didn't hesitate to fill it, taking a small risk of his incremental time and energy to learn and contribute.

When attempting to drive impact, we all focus on delivering results within the formal confines of our roles. At the same time, we depend on others to execute their responsibilities well, too. When others don't do "their fair share," or we spot a gap that no one is filling, our frustration can mount. We rush to blame the other person or team when we miss our collective goal, pointing to the items that others missed. To maximize our impact, we must set aside the notion that some areas are "not our problem." To deliver results, we must often step into the white space that no one else is willing to own, even if this feels uncomfortable or personally risky.

As I began building Joyus, I managed to recruit strong leaders who had a "hustle" mindset. Alongside my cofounder, Diana, I brought in one of Yodlee's early engineers, Sin-Mei Tsai, to become our chief technology officer. We began building the company and delivering results as a small team. As we started to scale, execution became more complex, and it became easier for each specialized function to blame others when a project didn't get delivered well. Everyone thought success meant delivering only on their piece of the puzzle, but according to this logic everyone would claim success even if we missed our collective goal.

Our leadership team struggled to explain to employees the importance of feeling a broader sense of ownership, one that didn't just extend to tasks within their direct control. It was ultimately Sin-Mei who, at an all-hands meeting, delivered one of the best analogies I've ever heard about ownership. "Each of us has individual roles in the company," she observed. "Imagine your own role and draw a circle around it. This is what you own directly. Now let's imagine each of us lining up our circles next to one another's, and you'll see that there are gaps between the circles. True owners don't just own what's in the circle. They also own everything that falls in the gaps."

Sin-Mei was right. People who disproportionately drive outcomes concern themselves with the white space in a task or project—a piece that they may not officially own but that nobody else is stepping up to do either. No matter where we are in the organizational pyramid, this is often where we can add the most value in any project. Not only do people who think like "owners" deliver more often; others also turn to them more often as goals and roles become bigger or more complex.

6. Go High and Low

As a related point, we can increase our impact by occupying ourselves with both the small details *and* the "big picture" of what we're trying to accomplish. When we increase what I call our "operating range," zooming out to see and address the big-picture issues and also zooming in to see and address the minute details, we position ourselves and others to execute more effectively than we would if we were only willing to "be strategic" or "stay in the weeds." People attuned to putting their "heads up" can cue in to changing external conditions that disproportionately influence our ongoing success. But when they also know how to put their heads down and identify smaller details of a project that effect progress, they can help drive total success. Most people think that excelling at a job means working incredibly hard — and it does. But to deliver results, you also have to work *smart*, understanding the full picture and applying yourself to solving the right problems and taking the right risks at any level of a project — the forest or the trees.

Let me give you an example to illustrate. In 2004, Google asked me to leave my role running the teams responsible for businesses such as Google Maps, Local, Scholar, and Shopping and move to a new job building our operations in the Asia Pacific and Latin American regions. The challenge felt daunting to me at first. I knew nothing about these geographies, and the managerial situation was complex, with many people across the company spending only part of their time supporting these different countries. I quickly realized that I would need to find the most talented people in the company already working part-time on the international business and centralize them into a single full-time team dedicated to Asia Pacific and Latin American operations (APLA). This is how I met a shrewd executive of Mexican and Canadian descent named Daniel Alegre.

Daniel joined Google before I did and had been hard at work forging business development partnerships with international companies seeking to integrate Google's search and ads services into their own sites.

Within five minutes of meeting Daniel, I knew I wanted him on my team. Luckily for me, he agreed to join, and during the years that followed we went on to build these geographies into a multibillion-dollar business for Google.

What made Daniel so indispensable was his incredible operating range. Trained as a lawyer, he managed every aspect of our business development relationships, from the loftiest strategies to the most detailed redlining and negotiating of contract details. I trusted him to go in and meet with an international CEO, identify the biggest strategic issues, manage a sales pipeline, and worry about the minute details as well. Because I trusted his work, I gave him the autonomy he needed to drive outcomes, and I think he felt fulfilled in his own job as a result.

Within the first several months of my job, it became clear that Google needed to decide whether to operate in China. If it sought to enter that market, it also needed to identify a strategy for doing so (remember, this was back in 2003, when people hoped that business engagement with China would lead to the country opening up societally as well). Alongside our global engineering leader, Alan Eustace (the skydiver from chapter 5), I argued that Google couldn't afford to stay out of the Chinese market. As challenging as it might be, we had to enter China and offer our services to Chinese consumers and small businesses, helping them to access more information than Chinese-owned search companies such as Baidu could. Working with Google's founders, board, and employees, Alan and I tried to get them comfortable with an engagement strategy.

When we finally won support for entering China in early 2004, our team then had to figure out how to actually do it, given that none of us had worked in China before. The process was complex, but it began with a lot of legwork, including finding an office in Beijing, hiring our first people there, setting up a WOFE (wholly owned foreign entity), and obtaining the necessary approvals. When I asked members of my team if they wanted to go to China to make all this happen, Daniel was quick to raise his hand. In addition to running business development for all of our APLA countries, he deployed to China personally and became our first leader on the ground there, handling everything required to get us up and running.

As Daniel recalls, this move was a real career risk for him. "I could have certainly failed and tarnished my reputation at Google and in the industry," he says. But the upside was quite compelling. "Back in 2005, there were very few foreigners outside of banking living in China. I had been to China a few times for short business trips and I could tell back then that the economy, and the Internet economy in particular, were going through a tremendous boom. Although I had limited exposure to the country and didn't speak a word of Mandarin, the opportunity to help build a company like Google in China from the ground up was really unique—a chance to learn and stretch my capabilities. I disregarded any potential blind spots or fears and took the plunge."

Daniel flew high, flew low—wherever he needed to (literally!) make things happen in the APLA business. Our relationship became one of the most fulfilling of my professional career, and Daniel also earned the respect of our international management team and Google's executive leadership team. When I left Google, Daniel was my top pick to succeed me in my job running the business, and he won the job. He stayed at Google in a variety of leadership roles, leaving in 2020 to become the president and COO at Activision. Given our busy schedules, we don't see each other much, but we remain close, in large part because of the trust we built while working together to accelerate impact so many years ago.

7. Go Deep and Diverse

As we discussed earlier, we can take smarter risks by putting ourselves in roles that take advantage of our unique capabilities. These capabilities don't include just innate strengths we have by virtue of our personalities, but also the deep skills and knowledge we might have amassed by virtue of our experiences. Companies spend billions hiring programmers, marketers, salespeople, consultants, and professionals of every stripe, precisely because they hope to take advantage of their deep and demonstrated expertise. Of course, specialized knowledge can allow us to drive results better and more efficiently than if we were novices starting from scratch.

We likely won't have specialized knowledge early in our careers, but not to worry: Companies will hire us on account of our potential, looking at our superpowers and skills we've demonstrated in our academic or limited work endeavors. As we establish ourselves, we can start to develop deeper expertise that enhances and complements our superpowers. As we take on new assignments and goals, we'll want to take advantage of our deepening knowledge to drive results faster. A great deal of research has linked achievement to deeper and deeper specialization. This includes the work described in Malcolm Gladwell's bestseller *Outliers,* which would have us put in our 10,000 hours to achieve expert level success.

Building knowledge in our careers has other advantages. Most of us will develop one or two specialized areas in which we deliver impact, develop our reputations, and receive promotion — for me it was business development and financial analysis. But in my experience, the top jobs in business increasingly go to individuals who consistently put themselves in roles where they gain expertise in additional areas. In a large study analyzing the career choices of approximately 459,000 members, the professional networking site LinkedIn found that taking on additional job functions helped individuals propel themselves into the executive ranks. A new job function delivered the same career boost as three years of work experience. So how do we reconcile the promise of specialization with the learning we gain from diversifying our skills?

The answer, I believe, is to follow a path we might describe as "broad-narrow-broad." As we graduate college, almost all of us lack deep functional expertise or even know where our strengths and passions lie. We can go broad-based in choosing a job or role and count on building deeper skills, impact, and self-awareness as we go. As we look to accelerate our impact at work, choosing to specialize in a function or industry helps us become more efficient, effective, and happy in any role, taking us into our "zone of deeper impact."

Within this zone, we should push to keep expanding our knowledge within our field while also taking new, small risks to further master our craft and contribute. At a certain point in our careers, our ability to learn nonlinearly and have even more impact will decline; almost every leadership role today requires us to navigate multiple functions and fields and to operate in situations we've never seen before. At that point, the very same aptitudes that allowed us to have impact in the past will impede us from having impact going forward, so we should seek to broaden our scope. What today's companies really seek is deep expertise *and* a breadth of perspective. As business conditions become ever more dynamic and complex, we should strive to develop deep specialization as well as a set of diversified experiences in which we broadly apply what we know and keep learning to adapt and expand our knowledge further.

Early in my career, I possessed a basic knowledge of sales as well as some financial literacy skills I had picked up while attending undergraduate business school. Choosing to become a financial analyst first and then a business development manager, I further developed skills in both areas, eventually realizing my full potential as someone who could drive partnerships, sales, and revenue. I've tested and expanded that expertise across a number of different industries, company stages, business models, and geographies.

I'm proud to say that I've never really been specifically qualified for any job I've ever had upon first taking it. Throughout the first half of my career, I always took risks to learn something new and different while deepening and broadening my core expertise. Luckily, I convinced each hiring manager to bet on my prior specialization as a starting point while challenging myself to take on roles that would require me to apply my expertise in new ways, and sometimes learn entirely new fields. Of course, becoming an entrepreneur at a young age also gave me a crash course in this regard. But as a result of pursuing depth and breadth in different stages of my career, more and more choices have opened to me as my career has progressed, including the opportunity to be a general manager and then a CEO.

A NEW VIRTUOUS CYCLE

Here's a scenario for you, one that's similar to many I've witnessed during my career. Senior leaders at a major bank asked Ann, a high-performing manager, to run a new division that would launch and market a new personal finance product for younger consumers. Her goal: build it and hit the business plan of $100 million in annual revenues within four years. At first, Ann wondered if she should take on the assignment, as it amounted to a scary career risk. A failure, she suspected, would tank her career. But Ann moved ahead and said yes, pushing herself to choose possibility.

Ann worked hard for the next four years, taking many small risks to produce successive outcomes, but ultimately failed to achieve the larger goal. She did, however, deliver a number of positive outcomes. She built a high-performing team, was highly regarded as a manager, launched a new business model, and achieved $50 million in annualized revenues (half of the original goal, so a failure). In addition, for the first time in her career, she learned online user design principles (on account of managing the rollout of an online app related to the personal finance product). She felt deeply disappointed but also pretty resilient, given she had also tried six different experiments with her team to grow customers faster. To return to a metaphor we developed earlier, Ann had failed to assemble the entire puzzle and reach her goal, but she had assembled several sections of the puzzle — thanks to the impacts she had generated and the new superpowers she acquired.

Two years later, the company shut the division down because it wasn't big enough to sustain the investment required. Ann returned to her former job and continued to excel there, managing an established business again. Some months later, a headhunter called about an opportunity to become CEO of a new startup in the fintech field. Ann now recognized all the ways that the impact and outcomes she'd created while running her company's new division had set her up for this kind of opportunity. The startup's founders saw this too and offered her the role, choosing her over several other well-qualified candidates who, like her, ran big businesses.

My point is, we tend to conceive of the results of risk-taking as binary. Either build the full puzzle (achieving our original overarching goal) or we're left with nothing to show for our efforts, just a scattering of parts. In truth, the sections of the puzzle we put together along the way have value in and of themselves, allowing us to assemble entirely new and often unforeseen puzzles in the future. Think of all the professional outcomes we attain and the personal superpowers we build (including the attributes of agility, resilience, and confidence) while iterating as the most valuable, enduring, and reconfigurable parts of our careers we'll ever assemble (Figure 14). Whether we succeed or fail in our initial ambitions, we retain the rewards we've acquired in the process of risk-taking, and they will turbocharge our overall career success.

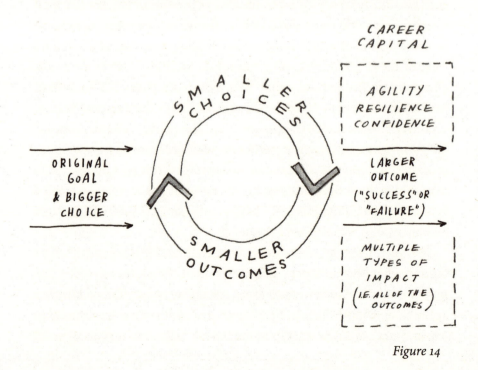

Figure 14

By making iterative choices, taking smaller risks in execution, and delivering multiple types of impact, we build a kind of "career capital" that pays us back not just once but many times over. Ultimately, as we keep choosing possibility when executing, we might well attain the original goal or ambition we imagined when we took our first bigger risk. Or we might miss and find ourselves in an entirely different place, while still realizing these rewards. Whatever happens, we *always* gain career capital by building more impact and enhancing or adding to our superpowers. Every time we iterate, our track record of impact, agility, resiliency, and confidence grows, and with it our chances of enjoying a more successful career over the long term.

POSSIBILITY POINTERS

- To achieve a larger success later, focus first on delivering shorter-term outcomes and impact.
- Seven key choices in your day-to-day execution can help you drive more impact.
- The outcomes you create along with the superpowers you build are the real rewards of any risk-taking journey, whether or not you achieve your original goal. This "career capital" continues to accumulate through successes and failures.

As we continue to choose possibility toward a bigger ambition, it's inevitable that we'll fail at times, encountering problems that elude our repeated attempts to solve them. When we feel unhappy or unproductive while executing without quite knowing why, we might also be experiencing what I call an "impact fail." Such fails can make all the difference between attaining our original goals or not. For this reason, learning how to diagnose the problems when they arise so that we can adjust our approach becomes vitally important. We must also know when to keep trying and when to let go of a bigger risk we've taken and embrace an entirely new ambition — a lesson I learned as a result of building and running Joyus.

The six years I spent at the company (2011–17) were as fun, fulfilling, incredible, frustrating, and painful as any pure startup experience can be. I helped attract an amazing team, secured millions of dollars in several rounds of venture capital, and built patented new technology to enable real-time commerce through a video player.

My team and I authored a new business model for monetizing online videos via shopping, ran Joyus studios (which created beautiful videos with lifestyle experts and killer products), and forged online distribution partnerships with large companies like Time Inc., AOL, and more. We doubled our revenues every year, growing from zero to $17 million in annual sales and tens of thousands of customers by the end of 2016.

At the same time, I began angel investing in other e-commerce start-ups using the industry expertise I was building, becoming the first investor and a board member at Stitch Fix and taking stakes in other successful companies like the RealReal, Reformation, and Sun Basket. I also joined boards at larger companies such as TripAdvisor, Ericsson, and Urban Outfitters that sought to benefit from my knowledge and that gave me a chance to expand my executive skills.

Yet despite the significant outcomes we produced at Joyus, I didn't create the category-winning video e-commerce company I'd hoped for. If I had to diagnose why, using the same Five Factors Framework discussed earlier, I attribute it to the headwinds we encountered (consumers weren't yet ready for e-commerce, nor were video platforms used for that purpose) as well as a number of specific choices we made. I'd taken a risk to become an innovator once again, spotting an opportunity to pursue a new business model that could capitalize on online video's high growth. For most of Joyus's existence, however, shoppable videos still seemed foreign to most users. At the time, the only large video platform in existence — YouTube — was still dominated by young audiences and focused on music and gaming, and had a brand-advertising business model. We had a hard time luring large new audiences to video commerce and doing so profitably. Video platforms like Facebook Video, Instagram Video, Snapchat, and TikTok had not yet emerged; once they did, people did not commonly use them for shopping. All told, we had to spend a great deal of money on online marketing and bespoke partnerships to find audiences of women who would want to watch *and* buy unique lifestyle products.

This challenge led to a second one as the years ticked by: how to balance multiple competing objectives — including high growth, a great customer experience, and profitability — in our drive to become a large, viable, stand-alone company. I wanted to create an offering that was different from YouTube or Amazon, but the choices we made to maintain our own studios and exclusive products in inventory, in addition to our marketing costs, had repercussions. Six years in, we had a loyal customer base but were struggling to grow the business in a cost-effective way.

During 2016 and 2017, we took many steps to make Joyus viable over the longer term, reducing our staff, moving to a zero-inventory model, and more. None of this proved to be the winning combination we needed, as customers still cost us more to acquire than they were worth. Thus it was in 2017 that Joyus sold its brand, audience, and technology to another private company, StackCommerce, for a very small sum (StackCommerce continues to operate Joyus today).

In 2020, about a decade after Joyus's launch, a large crop of new start-ups in the U.S. received funding to enter the video commerce space. Each pursued the same dream we had, hoping to leverage the massive tailwinds now provided by large and growing video audiences on Instagram, Facebook, and TikTok, all of whom now had shoppable video features themselves. In China, meanwhile, Pinduoduo emerged as a multibillion-dollar video shopping platform serving millions with entertainment and group discounts.

For me, the Joyus journey was bittersweet. Unlike Polyvore and OpenTV, where my failures, however painful, occurred over a short period of time, this one unfolded after years of effort and despite the generation of multiple outcomes. As a result, the disappointment I felt was much deeper. That said, the results we achieved as a pioneer and startup and my personal growth as a CEO and e-commerce expert gave me a stronger feeling of confidence and personal capability than I had as a successful big company executive.

As difficult as it might seem, continually diagnosing our misses is also part of the practice of choosing possibility. Embracing our smaller-impact fails throughout any journey, including at its end, powers us to more risk-taking success. Neglect these fails when executing, and we won't adjust our actions in real time to influence our upcoming results. If we neglect to diagnose our bigger failures, we squander the chance to turn a miss in this chapter into a win in the next one. We also won't know when to keep tweaking our own performance and when to cut our losses and move on to our next big choice.

THE ENEMIES OF IMPACT WE CONTROL

Before we examine the external forces that contribute to our negative results, we should look first at ourselves and how we might inadvertently thwart our own advancement. Over the course of my career, I've identified a number of quite common "impact fails" — the choices we *fail* to make — that can trip up the best of us when executing (Figure 15). Let's take a look.

Impact Fail #1: Too Much Peanut Butter

In 2006, an acquaintance of mine, Brad Garlinghouse, wrote a now famous memo to Yahoo's senior leadership called the Peanut Butter Manifesto. A senior vice president at the time, Brad felt frustrated to see Yahoo, a once great Silicon Valley giant, floundering in its attempt to turn itself around. As he saw it, Yahoo had tremendous talent to draw on but was trying to do too many things moderately well instead of pursuing one to two things and excelling. The problem of spreading ourselves too thin turns up all the time on the individual level, as well. We can all relate to the problems we create when we pursue too many goals at once and fail to make much headway on any of them.

At the same time, it's unrealistic to think that within large pursuit we won't have to balance two goals and optimize between them. When your boss asks you to build a new product or service at work, he or she will probably also want you to do it while constraining the resources you use. At Joyus, making any shoppable video highly successful was a balancing act between the price point of an item and how many video views it would likely require (at a rising cost to us) in order to generate a single purchase.

If we want to produce meaningful results, we must rein in the complexity and limit our focus at any given time to just one or two key goals, considering the likely tradeoffs between them.

Impact Fail #2: Mistaking Motion for Impact

When we're in motion and always busy, it might feel like we're making tangible progress. But if we focus on the urgent over the important and treat our activities as accomplishments in their own right, we can fail to channel our efforts toward meaningful results.

I often see people excessively fixated on staying in motion when I review résumés and hold job interviews. Candidates focused on delivering impact might describe their previous positions on their résumés with phrases like "I helped create . . . ," "I developed a new product or process," or "I boosted sales by 25 percent." Most résumés I see don't use language like this. Applicants might list impressive past employers only to divulge that they "worked on" a particular product at a past job or that they were "responsible" for doing X or Y or that they were "on the team" that handled a particular product. Such descriptions might well be accurate, but they fail to identify what tangible results people created with their activities. How was their team or organization better off because of their own unique efforts? If your résumé comes loaded down with language describing *activities* rather than *outcomes,* you might not be as oriented as you think to delivering impact.

In job interviews, I also find it revealing how people respond when asked about their past failures. Do they talk about them lightly, giving a "non-fail" fail? ("My boss said I was working *too* hard and feeling *too* passionate about our team's success.") Do they talk only about the external factors that caused a plan to go sideways, absolving themselves of responsibility? Or do they give a heartfelt, thoughtful answer, outlining precisely what they did that didn't produce the result they imagined, and what they would likely adjust going forward? Individuals focused on *motion* rather than *impact* struggle to discuss their failures in any meaningful way. They also can't talk about what they learned in concrete terms and tend to conflate success with mere busy-ness. They presume that employers want "perfect," and as a result they're afraid to acknowledge any flaws they might have. They think acknowledging their flaws lowers their chances of getting hired, when in fact it *increases* them.

Impact Fail #3: Keeping Your Fingernails Clean

Wouldn't it be wonderful to just waltz into new environments that are waiting for us to put our imprint on them and then start creating positive results? Wouldn't it also be fun to only work on the things we love to do and avoid the rest? Sadly, reality doesn't work that way. If we wish to have an impact in any given area, we'll usually find ourselves entering existing situations and dealing with people dynamics, previous failed attempts, and other challenges. We'll find ourselves working on the "exciting" stuff, but also having to deal with hidden undercurrents. Many of us will shy away from the less-than-ideal situations we encounter when executing, fearing discomfort or a tarnishing of our reputations. We would do far better to *lean into* these situations, figuring out what needs solving and tackling it.

I've described my role running Google's international operations in Asia Pacific and Latin America as incredibly positive, and it certainly was. But in taking on this assignment, I also inherited some of Google's most challenging markets. Many countries were emerging markets, with much lower per capita income, lower online penetration, and smaller online advertising budgets than the developed markets managed by my peers. On top of that, we had challenging regulatory environments in China, Brazil, India, and most of Southeast Asia. We also had three markets where Google was losing (China, Japan, and Korea), a much different situation than existed in the U.S. or Western Europe. Every country in our business had its own "messiness" and my team was dealing with all of them at once across a massive geography. At the same time, we always had to make the case for adequate resources, often competing with markets that were bigger, easier, and already moneymakers for the company. While scrappiness, hustle, and dealing with different messes was the "normal" state of our team, we had our share of frustrations as well in managing these situations.

At the time, the legendary executive coach Bill Campbell was spending a lot of time internally at Google, coaching senior leaders including me. You might have heard of Bill: A former football coach, he made a name for himself as the "trillion dollar coach" counseling iconic leaders such as Steve Jobs, Eric Schmidt, and others. One day, while I was describing my current frustrations to Bill, he looked at me gruffly and told me to be proud of having the team at Google with "dirt under our fingernails." We were taking on tough problems and solving them — not an easy task, but a vitally important one. Dirty fingernails are the sign that you're having impact, and it's hard to imagine how you can produce results without them.

Impact Fail #4: FTF (Failing to Take Feedback)

We talked earlier about incorporating feedback from others so that we can know both our superpowers and our kryptonite and join the right teams. Once we're in motion, we need others' perspectives to help us decrease execution-related risks, whether associated with our own unproductive behaviors or other factors. Most of us dread receiving personal feedback, and we often feel defensive hearing any kind of commentary. Arrogance also prevents us from listening to others. When we presume we know better than everyone else, we signal to colleagues and partners that we care more about sustaining our own egos than generating results. Such a stance tends to repel high performers who might otherwise wish to collaborate with us. Our chances of success improve dramatically if we can drop the arrogance and insecurity and invite others' feedback about our effectiveness or our approach to our work.

1. PURSUING TOO MANY GOALS @ ONCE

IMPACT FAILS

4. FAILING TO TAKE FEEDBACK

2. MISTAKING MOTION FOR IMPACT

3. KEEPING YOUR FINGERNAILS CLEAN

OTHER ENEMIES OF IMPACT

1. HEADWINDS

2. "PEOPLE FIT" ISSUES

3. BIAS & DISCRIMINATION

Figure 15

THE EXTERNAL ENEMIES OF IMPACT

We can and should diagnose and address our own impact fails, but our analysis of our challenges isn't complete without taking into account external forces that make it more difficult to produce our desired results. Larger headwinds and tailwinds along with poor "people fit" aren't just issues we assess when we make a big choice. They are signals we must continually read and to which we must continually respond when executing. Some of these forces might only hamper our short-term performance, but others might threaten our ultimate goals. Further, some forces might be so powerful that any adjustment we might make to try to circumvent them will prove futile. How do we know when to keep fighting the good fight in the face of external conditions, and when to throw up our hands and head elsewhere?

As we've seen, both headwinds or tailwinds in an industry or company might afford us excellent opportunities for career growth. The prospect of strong, damaging headwinds might tempt us to go elsewhere, but sticking around to drive results might allow us a chance to take on new responsibilities and challenges and to feel a sense of purpose and meaning in our work. When headwinds place so many constraints on us that they severely hamper our day-to-day productivity over an extended period, we might well be better off looking elsewhere for better conditions in which to operate, or even consider whether to change our bigger ambitions.

Likewise, when we find ourselves working on unproductive teams, we likely struggle to execute well too. In these situations, we must determine where precisely the gap is and whether we can fix it. When we work with people whose strengths complement our own and who share our values, we can feel pretty good about taking a small risk and openly sharing our concerns; candor and constructive discussion can go a long way toward helping us find a solution. But if team members (ourselves included) lack self-awareness or a commitment to improve, or worse yet, if our team members don't share our deeper values, it's hard for us to trust them to resolve disputes fairly. This holds doubly true if the team members we distrust wield power over us. If one of us is more "at risk" in a situation, and we aren't all equally incented to find common ground, sharing our concerns might not lead to the positive change we seek.

My painful choices to leave OpenTV and Polyvore both reflected my deep distrust and perception of a values mismatch. In each case, I felt more exposed sharing my concerns because I felt a power imbalance (with my direct boss in one situation, and with a founder who owned a lot of the company and was on the board in the other). In each case, I left the organization, choosing to pursue the same goal but in an entirely new environment. In both situations, I feel quite confident that I made the right call.

THE MOST HARMFUL ENEMY OF ALL

All of us form preconceived notions about people or groups as a result of our experiences or environment. In recent years, organizations and executive coaches have focused on helping people to overcome these biases so that they don't inform our decisions and action. Sometimes these biases only have subtle effects, which are bad enough. But when bias rises to the level of discrimination and harassment, it fundamentally threatens the ability of a person or group to feel productive and drive impact, while giving others privileged access to possibilities. In these situations, identifying bias, discrimination, or harassment is essential, although it also carries important risks of its own.

Like many people from diverse backgrounds, I've encountered some bias personally, but my sensitivity has grown as I've seen even more disturbing acts directed at others. I grew up as one of the few Sikhs in a small town in Ontario, and our family was visibly different; my father wore a turban throughout his life, as did many of our relatives. I recall frequent catcalls at the local shopping malls, hostility as we drove through certain states on a family trip to Disney World, and occasional ethnic slurs directed at my sisters and me on our school bus. Mostly, though, I escaped overt discrimination and accessed more than enough possibility over time in the schools, companies, and cultures of which I was a part.

As I progressed in my career as a female professional, a number of people welcomed my naturally intense style, and I was able to succeed. At least once during my early career, at OpenTV, I found myself typecast for my perceived aggressiveness. As I became an entrepreneur and CEO, I enjoyed increasing amounts of possibility, but I also came to notice more micro-biases. As the only woman in an all-male boardroom, I would hear others "mansplain" my opinions, and on at least one occasion while I was serving as CEO I felt reasonably sure that a male investor was shrinking from confronting an urgent and difficult issue with me because he feared my "female emotion." As frustrating as such experiences have been, they pale in comparison to stories I've heard about from others.

In a courageous June 2020 blog posting, Ade, the successful founder and CEO of Formstack with whom I worked many years back, shared his own experiences with discrimination, as well as the many ways he's had to alter his actions and movements:

> I don't tell you about all the ways I live my life differently than you do. How I think about it nearly every day, and it's suffocating. How it comes up in things you might not expect, like when I trained for a half marathon. How I never ran after dark. How I chose clothes to try to make it clear to everyone that I was just a runner, not a black man running away from something. How I'd sometimes cross the street if I was coming up on someone too fast. . . . I don't tell you how it's not just those with hate in their hearts that I've come to fear. That I fear more the system that might not protect me.

Another woman I've gotten to know in recent years, Susan Fowler, shared publicly the shocking experiences that led her to quit while also calling attention to the harassment, discrimination, and corporate resistance she faced at Uber in 2017. After arriving at the company and joining her new group, her new manager messaged her about his quest to find new sexual partners. When Susan reported the situation to HR, her career prospects suffered while the manager in question escaped larger consequences, even though he had apparently perpetrated offenses against other women. After a chaotic year that saw continued challenges with HR and potential retaliation for having spoken up, Susan quit but courageously wrote a powerful blog post at the same time. Reading it is painful and absurd, and the underlying behavior and original corporate response is hard to fathom. But such episodes occur far more often than we realize. In fact, at least one other woman, a Latina engineer named Ingrid Avendaño, courageously came forward and sued Uber with similar allegations of an intolerable work environment, including harassment and discrimination.

Facing any form of bias in the workplace and especially discrimination and harassment can make it extremely difficult for us to operate, let alone achieve impact. When these situations involve our managers or people wielding direct power over us, it's even harder. Some of the most challenging career choices we'll ever face include how to react when suffering such harms — whether we should speak up, stick around and say nothing, or leave.

If we are part of companies, cultures, and groups that align well with our values and that have demonstrated a willingness to take and act on feedback at all levels (including the leadership level), we might well be able to speak up for ourselves, change our situation, and go on to grow our careers. Successfully handling bias requires that both the individual exhibiting bias and the organization overall are open to confronting the feedback early. By the time we've experienced several cycles in which we've experienced bias, spoken up, and encountered resistance, we likely won't want to stay where we are and will seek a career change to achieve our goals.

When we witness or experience bias directly that harms not just an individual but a larger group of people, preventing them from achieving impact at work, the decision about how to proceed remains equally difficult. Calling out these acts of harm can deliver larger and bigger impact, but sometimes not in the way we envisioned. Succeeding with this kind of personal and reputational risk requires real courage on our part as well as on the part of our company and its leaders. All too often, employees doubt whether leaders are truly receptive to whistleblowing and truth-telling, and so they decline to speak up. One British study of 1,400 employees found that more than half had witnessed acts of racism, but less than 20 percent reported what they'd seen. Of those that remained quiet, 40 percent cited a fear of the consequences as the cause.

Such fears drive many of us to perceive whistleblowing as a "one-way door" type of risk. We deem it unlikely that we'll be able to remain on the job and thrive after speaking out, since we'll experience retaliation. Still, the possible impact is immense. Susan Fowler's blog post created systemic change not only at Uber but arguably within the entire tech industry. Another whistleblower, Nicole Birden at UCLA Hospital in Santa Monica, was fired and successfully sued for damages due to hostile work environment afterward, raising public awareness about the problem in healthcare.

More options today exist for us to speak up and help eradicate bias —the choice between speaking out and remaining silent often need not be either/or. For example, we can leave employee reviews in online forums or comment anonymously about our companies on news websites. Within companies, we can also organize others in an attempt to bring about positive change. If you love where you work but want to see it improve its track record, you might find a way to create impact by organizing with your colleagues, using the power of the collective to mitigate your own personal risk. Companies such as Amazon, Facebook, and Microsoft have all spawned large cohorts of current employee activists, people who love their companies' ideals and environments but who also boldly call out opportunities for improvement.

CHOOSING OUR NEXT ACT

If our efforts fail to bear fruit, how do we know when it's time to leave? We might wish for neat, tidy, and successful conclusions to all of our big chapters of effort and execution, and often this happens—we achieve a big goal and naturally begin contemplating our next ambition. I found myself in this situation at Google, where I'd risen to the seniormost levels of leadership and dreamed of becoming a CEO. Other times we fail, but even here we can accept a conclusion and move on when we have pursued impacts, outcomes, and learnings to the fullest, as I did at Joyus. More difficult are the in-between times, when we're executing and having some success but aren't sure if we should make a bigger change.

Remember the process of choosing possibility: We take a small or large risk in hopes of more discovery, learning, or achievement. We begin executing iteratively to produce outcomes, making choices for more upside. When we feel like our learning or impact has flatlined while executing and we can't identify how to fire it up again in our current role or company, it may be time to pursue new career goals. I tapped out of Yodlee, for instance, at year five, because I had performed virtually every role in the company. I doubted the CEO job would become available, and I knew the company wasn't growing fast enough to spawn new and bigger opportunities for me over the coming twelve to twenty-four months. Since I was eager to further my knowledge and reach new levels of professional success, it was time for me to move on.

In other instances, we might find that we're achieving outcomes and learning yet lack a sense of satisfaction over extended periods. This is often a telltale signal that it may be time to make a new choice also. We all want our day-to-day efforts to not just succeed but bring us joy and a sense of purpose. So long as our work, our original ambitions, and who we are remain largely aligned, building impact, perseverance, and agility with our actions can feel good, even when times are tough. But when short-term impact and learning feels unfulfilling or our larger goal no longer seems relevant, we can feel as if our careers are drifting.

That's when it's time to pull out the Five Factors Framework and use it to (re)examine our goals, our strengths, interests, and values, analyzing how our current choice serves both these needs. We also should probably start taking small new risks again to discover what other possibilities exist that might help us become more satisfied with our careers.

As my time at Joyus concluded, I had a chance to reflect on what I'd learned and on where I might take my career from there. While I felt satisfied with the risk I'd taken to become a startup founder six years earlier, I found myself craving a chance to combine my entrepreneurial hustle with my larger company executive leadership skills in my next career chapter. Thus it was that at the end of 2017 I set my sights on becoming the professional CEO of a big e-commerce company.

NAIL THE TRANSITION

Once you've decided to make a career move, you also have to execute the transition well. We can maximize impact on our way out of any situation by staying in the game mentally, timing our departures right, and leaving in ways that allow others who stay to maximize their impact, too.

1. Don't Leave Before You Leave

While she worked at Google, my friend and former colleague Sheryl Sandberg offered some great advice to her female colleagues, cautioning them to be careful not to "leave before they leave." She was referring to the tendency of mid-career women to start planning for motherhood and even decide to leave well before their pregnancies materialized. I would extend her advice to everyone, urging all of us to give our best and fullest efforts to our current endeavors until we actually depart. It's tempting to downshift our efforts once we've decided to move on, dreaming of what's next while shortchanging our current goals. But finishing well means completing what you've started and making good on your promises to your team or company. Not only is this the right thing to do; it furthers your career. How you leave will help determine how people remember you. Putting in maximum effort until the day you leave protects your reputation as well as the impact you've worked so hard to achieve. You'll reap the rewards the next time you need a reference from a boss or colleague at your current job.

2. Beware the Cost of Lingering

Although you should keep your mind in the game, don't drag out your departure for too long. The last thing you want to do is exit with a whimper, hanging around without much work to do. You risk seeming marginal to your team's efforts and leaving that unhelpful impression in your colleagues' minds. If you've performed well and are trying to hit a short-term milestone (staying until the first of the next month to get COBRA benefits or for another sixty days until your stock options are vested, for instance), your colleagues will probably understand why you chose to stick around. But if you don't know what to do next and have checked out mentally for an indefinite period while still collecting a paycheck, people will notice. If at all possible, stay busy, focused, and productive until the very end.

3. Leave More Opportunity in Your Wake

In the course of departing, we can help the colleagues we're leaving behind to have more impact. First, we can build our team members' skills and competencies by creating new opportunities for them to deliver results while we're still at the company and able to provide support. In particular, we can identify high-potential candidates who might lack the skills required to do our jobs but who could blossom if given the chance. We can help these colleagues acquire new skills, grooming them to take on our roles after we leave. This is as easy as having colleagues help out with our projects, giving them time and space to try out new things, make mistakes, and learn. Helping to train our successors not only benefits them; it helps us build our own legacy of impact.

We can also advocate early within our organizations for high performers, creating formal transition plans that allow us to get our successors up and running before we leave. While so-called battlefield promotions (in which a company gives someone a large jump in responsibility after someone else unexpectedly quits) are great, we can increase the odds that others will succeed in our role if we can help orchestrate our own transitions and provide support.

Finally, we can maximize others' impact by leaving behind a well-functioning team and situation. This means doing the mundane and often thankless work of tying up the more difficult loose ends in our jobs instead of selfishly dumping them onto someone else's lap. On the way out of any organization, I've tried to take care of the worst outstanding issues — a lingering dispute with a partner, an unfinished negotiation with an important vendor, or a team member who is behaving in toxic ways — so that the person coming in can have the best start possible in their new role. In all cases, when we leave, whom we leave behind, and how clean a slate we leave all bear heavily on our cumulative impact.

4. *Middle Steps Before Big Steps*

Maximizing our impact until the very end can tire us out during a transition period. At the same time, we might feel pressured to make our next choice—an uncomfortable position if we lack clarity. I've seen many people rushing to extract themselves from a bad situation who make their next choice too hastily just so that they can have something in hand.

If you can afford to take some time off before starting a new job or venture—what I call a "middle step"—consider doing so. It's rare to spend weeks, months, or even longer accountable to no one but ourselves, able to explore choices freely. If you have this opportunity, make the most of it. As I've recounted, I've chosen to "go to nothing" for brief periods during most of my career transitions, confident that I would always find a job and wanting a chance to explore new options full-time. A middle step might feel daunting depending on your finances, or you might fear leaving weeks or months unaccounted for on your résumé. If you feel hesitant to stop and pause, taking even a short vacation between big goals—just a week or two—can help you recharge and start strong in your new position.

When we don't know what to do next, we might have little choice but to take a middle step. If we spend this time contemplating our past successes and failures and learning from them, we might come away with just the insight we need to realize our next big success. My friend Adam Zbar took a middle step in 2013 when he faced a large turning point in his career. Previously, he'd succeeded as a management consultant, had started and sold two venture-backed startups to the founders of YouTube, and had built a reputation for creating award-winning, innovative products.

When I met Adam in 2011, he had just started a mobile local product search company, serving up inventory from local stores. It sounded great on paper, but executing on it proved more difficult than expected. Renaming the mobile application, Adam decided to offer a fun set of initial products—wine, spirits, and snacks—that would differentiate his offering from fast-moving on-demand food apps. While Lasso worked better than its previous iteration, the unit economics didn't work out, putting Adam at a crossroads.

Instead of quitting, he decided to take an entrepreneurial inventory of what he'd done right and wrong both at Lasso and his previous start-ups. Adam realized he'd consistently had strong visions, identifying early markets with large, untapped needs and creating innovative solutions to meet them. He'd built up many of the skills necessary to be a successful Silicon Valley CEO, including the ability to raise venture capital, build teams, and develop award-winning products. What was missing, however, had been a great business model. Adam hadn't ever taken the time to think through his business ventures closely enough.

Despite pressure from investors to quickly pivot to another idea, Adam forced himself to think more deeply about his next product. He stayed up late trying to come up with a new product idea that met three big criteria: He had to feel passionately about the idea; the idea had to meet a major unmet need; and it had to lead to a great business model. During the challenging period in which Adam was deeply disappointed at Lasso's limited success, he surprised himself by coming up with the idea of selling personalized, healthy meal kits online. As he tells it, the idea popped into his head right after he'd sat down in the middle of a hiking path and, in the throes of frustration, proclaimed to his then girl-friend (now wife) that he was "done" with his life as an entrepreneur.

The idea of an online, personalized healthy meal kit service imme-diately met Adam's first criteria. As the son of a scientist and psycholo-gist, he deeply cared about health. He knew a lot about healthy meal kits since he'd recently transformed his eating habits and his life by craft-ing healthier meals for himself. But before rushing into the idea, Adam resolved to work out the basics of the business, including market size, an understanding of the customer, the unit economics, and a plan for scaling. Like many entrepreneurs, he had previously designed his busi-ness model with the goal of getting to the first million dollars in reve-nue. While that remained important, this time he worked out a business model that would get him to $100 million in less than three years.

Adam named the new product Sun Basket after doing a "sun run" (he and his friend Tyler tried to race to the top of the mountain before the sun came up). Adam and Tyler realized it was the perfect name for the new product, since all delicious, healthy food grew under the sun. Adam wanted to put the sun (figuratively speaking), real organic ingredients, and recipe cards into a box and ship it to customers so they could make healthy, delicious meals at home. Before he could get started, he needed to recruit a new team, since his prior one had left. Following his focus on creating great products, Adam brought on board as cofounders a top San Francisco restaurant entrepreneur, an award-winning San Francisco chef, and a longtime creative collaborator.

Sun Basket finally nailed it. Customers loved the product and ordered in droves. The business model worked better than Adam had projected, and revenues grew explosively from the moment the product was launched in 2015. By 2019, Sun Basket was doing $300 million in annual business and employed more than a thousand people. As the company turned from a food tech company into more of a food company, Adam transitioned from CEO to executive chairman. In 2020, when COVID hit, the company experienced its own massive tailwind as virtually the entire country turned to online grocery and food delivery to get family meals on the table.

Adam was proud of all he accomplished at Sun Basket. However, he was not done yet as an entrepreneur. In mid-2020, he started a new venture, HamsaPay. He knew now that what he loved most about business was the process of starting new companies itself. It was time to do it all once again.

POSSIBILITY POINTERS

- Continually diagnosing our misses so we can keep adjusting our next choices and actions is essential to the practice of choosing possibility.

- Beware the most common impact fails in our own control: too much peanut butter, mistaking motion for impact, trying to keep our fingernails clean, and failing to take feedback.
- Beyond external headwinds and poor "people fit" factors, bias and prejudice are the greatest external enemies of impact, preventing individuals or groups from accessing possibility equitably.

After leaving Joyus, I took several months off to evaluate different opportunities to lead a larger company, hopefully in e-commerce. As disappointed as I was that we couldn't make Joyus a large success, I felt optimistic about my prospects, thanks to my overall track record as an effective and resilient executive, entrepreneur, investor, and board member. As such, I was thrilled when the role of president at the global ticketing marketplace StubHub became available and I got a call to discuss it. StubHub was a brand I knew and loved. And after my years-long risk at Joyus, I was ready to jump into leading a successful and well-established consumer service and help it to grow even more.

The more I learned about StubHub, the more excited I became. The Stubbers (our name for StubHub employees) I met shared my values, and all shared a passion for live music and sports. I would have a full mandate to lead the company operationally, to further shape its culture, and to frame its strategies within the context of its parent company, eBay, which had owned StubHub for close to a decade. StubHub's business was sizable, posting over $1 billion in annual revenues and close to $5 billion in annual ticket sales volume. As president, I would be asked to help StubHub grow in new areas even as it improved its customer experience and delivered steady profits for eBay. Evaluating all of these factors, I agreed to join the company. I expected the job to be challenging and anticipated risks to my professional success related to my leadership execution, competition, and changing priorities from our corporate parent. In this regard I was right; but major unforeseen risks would also unfold on my journey.

During my first months on the job, my team and I worked hard, restructuring parts of the business to improve its efficiency, as well as beginning to invest in new products and services. I recruited a number of new leaders whose capabilities and principles were strongly aligned and who were equally energized by what we could build together. Prior to accepting my role, I had come to believe that the ticketing industry would need to consolidate through mergers and acquisitions, and that StubHub could play a key role in this evolution. I was now even more convinced of this strategy, and lobbied eBay's CEO to allow us to acquire other ticketing companies so that we could compete more effectively against our main rival, Ticketmaster/LiveNation.

StubHub did end up achieving industry consolidation during my tenure, but not in the way I envisioned. Two big events changed our journey, one of them a "subway" (an occurrence we could potentially anticipate), the other a "coconut" (a freakish, truly unexpected event). In 2018 and 2019, eBay faced mounting pressure from shareholders. Its growth lagged that of rival Amazon, while its profit margins had eroded as well, thanks to rising marketing costs. I had closely considered these challenges (the subway) when I took the job, but concluded that I could still thrive and have impact as StubHub's leader. As I saw it, shareholder pressure might even open up new strategic possibilities, like spinning the company out into its own independent public entity. I was prepared to take on this type of corporate risk, which would directly impact my own ability to succeed in the job, although I took care to include protections in case of a company merger or acquisition when negotiating my employment contract.

Some market experts predicted that if eBay couldn't boost growth and profitability, activist shareholders would mount a challenge to the company, as Carl Icahn had done years earlier (resulting in the spinoff of Paypal as a separate company). Within nine months of my arrival at

StubHub, that's exactly what happened. In January of 2019, activists took a stake in eBay, joined the board, and petitioned it to sell StubHub in order to create more shareholder value. Instead of StubHub acquiring another player in live entertainment, as I had lobbied for, the board concluded that it was time for eBay to sell its non-core assets, including our business, to another player. *We* would be the company acquired, not the ones doing the acquiring. The implications for my own role at StubHub were uncertain. Depending on who acquired us, I might have the opportunity to lead the company post-sale, or I might not.

By my one-year anniversary, my team and I were preparing for the months-long process of selling StubHub. The months that followed were all out — we had to pitch the company to private equity firms and other ticketing companies seeking to acquire us, all while trying to keep employee morale high amid the uncertainty, and executing our operational game plan. Ultimately, the founder and CEO of Viagogo, a highly profitable international ticketing player about a quarter of StubHub's size, agreed to pay more than $4 billion for StubHub. Viagogo's founder also happened to be one of StubHub's original founders, a serial entrepreneur who had left the company under less-than-ideal terms in 2006. He was thrilled to be buying his old company back fourteen years after he'd left it.

The sale price was a record sum for eBay, making the deal a massive professional success for me and my team. Personally, though, I found it disappointing. Viagogo's CEO would want to run the combined company, leaving me out of the top job and unable to realize the bigger ambitions I'd had for the company. Since I had no interest in serving as StubHub's number two leader after the merger, he and I agreed amicably that I would depart shortly after the transaction closed. On February 13, 2020, the sale process concluded, and I began mentally preparing for my upcoming departure.

Then came the coconut, an event none of us could have predicted. On March 13, precisely one month after our company's sale, COVID-19 dealt the U.S. entertainment industry a body blow. Overnight, every sports league in the nation postponed its season, and promoters and venues canceled thousands of planned music events. Within a seven-day span, StubHub went from handling more than a billion dollars in ticket sales in any given quarter to almost nothing. This was not just big —it was unprecedented. What had initially been a relatively low-risk career move for me with mostly upside morphed into a high-risk situation, with the company now in unexpected peril. Somehow, I'd have to navigate us through it.

If a crisis like this had hit us earlier, we'd have been in better shape to weather it. We'd have had a massive public company like eBay behind us, with enormous amounts of cash reserves on which to draw. Now, as a newly private company owned by another private company also strongly affected by the pandemic, we had a much smaller balance sheet and faced an industry shutdown ruining our entire business. Instead of a smooth and happy departure, I now had to scramble to keep the company going for an indeterminate period of time until the live entertainment sector managed to recover.

During March and April 2020, our leadership team and I rapidly restructured multiple parts of StubHub and its operations. First, we adapted all of our previous policies to our new COVID reality, dealing with thousands of angry customers who wanted their cash back immediately for ticket purchases they'd made on now suspended events. We ourselves chased thousands of sellers who already held these same funds in their own bank accounts (since we remitted cash to sellers very quickly after any ticket sale in the course of normal operations). We did the best we could, offering a combination of 120 percent credits on the site toward future purchases and cash refunds in certain states, and trying to communicate transparently. Understandably, the situation remained difficult and challenging, with many still frustrated as we managed the tangled mess between sellers, buyers, leagues, venues, and more.

While all of this was going on, we were also forced to quickly restructure every part of our internal cost base. Among our most difficult decisions was the need to let go roughly two-thirds of our U.S. business's employees given our steep decline in business volume. Although we did our best to offer reasonable severance packages and other resources, there is no denying the dislocation and pain people experienced. We also delayed all nonessential initiatives, in essence creating an entirely new operating model for the company, designed to last as long as necessary.

As difficult as these changes were, we managed to set up a stable but much smaller base of operations that would allow us to endure the live events industry's indefinite stoppage. It was highly stressful work for everyone, conducted swiftly under a time crunch, but the entire company came together to help get it done, showing great flexibility, understanding, and resiliency, as well as a sense of urgency. By June, we had completed the majority of our restructuring, including the downsizing of most of our senior leadership team. It was now time for me to leave and begin my own next chapter, secure in the knowledge that I had completed the critical work of helping the company survive the immediate COVID crisis and stabilize for the longer term.

Although I couldn't have predicted the pandemic and its implications for StubHub, and the decisions at the end were excruciating to make, I look back on my time as StubHub's president as a success in terms of my ability to deliver outcomes and have impact. I had not expected to preside over a record sale of the company, to be out of a job within two short years, or to manage the extreme risk and volatility that unfolded during my tenure, but there it was. It was time for me to choose possibility once again.

REAL GROWTH HAPPENS IN CYCLES

If my later career journey sounds similar in some ways to my earlier experiences, it was. As we've seen, the risk-taking process doesn't unfold in a straight line from A to B. Each of our personal chapters follow their own circuitous path as we anticipate opportunities, make choices, drive results, learn, deal with expected and unexpected forces, and make new choices. As chaotic as choosing possibility iteratively might seem while we're moving through individual parts of the journey, over the course of a career we find a pattern emerging: We repeatedly cycle up, down, or through larger chapters of risk-taking. Most times we hope to be actively choosing the risks we're taking to pursue our ambitions, but inevitably new risks and uncertainty are thrust upon us along the way as well.

If we remain focused on delivering impact through each chapter, iterating to unlock results, we'll ultimately build to larger outcomes in our careers ("successes" or "failures"). Sometimes the career rewards we realize are exactly as we originally expected, and other times they differ. Regardless, as we come to a natural conclusion of any chapter of ambition, we have an opportunity to choose once again, whether we feel like we are on the top, the bottom, or somewhere in the middle in terms of our current career status. Career growth, it turns out, resembles a sine wave as we take risks, create successive impacts, respond to conditions, reach larger conclusions, and take risks again.

Consider my own career trajectory (Figure 16). I struggled out of college to get a great job (failure). I eventually landed at Merrill Lynch and then at the British broadcaster Sky, where I built a strong reputation and advanced (success). Eager to become an entrepreneur, I quit my job at Sky and moved to California. After an initial stint at OpenTV (failure), I had a successful outcome at one Silicon Valley startup, Junglee, and landed at Amazon before founding another startup, Yodlee. That eventually went public (a professional success, although not a financial one). Then, taking a tiny risk, I went to Google, where I helped build multibillion-dollar businesses and achieved outsize financial rewards (success). Afterward, I experienced my painful Polyvore exit (failure). Over the next decade, I immersed myself in e-commerce, becoming an entrepreneur at Joyus (failure) as well as an e-commerce investor and board member (success). As StubHub's CEO, I achieved my longstanding ambition of leading a large e-commerce company to an industry-transforming sale (success), while also weathering one of the greatest crises of my professional career. Today, as a result of propelling an ascending sine wave of career growth over time, I have more opportunities

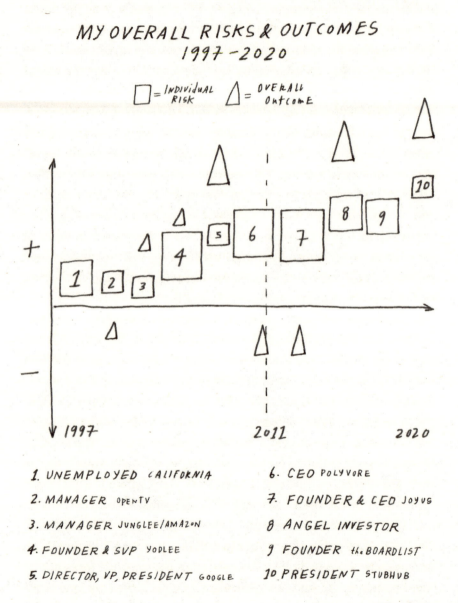

MY OVERALL RISKS & OUTCOMES
1997 - 2020

☐ = INDIVIDUAL RISK   △ = OVERALL OUTCOME

1997   2011   2020

1. UNEMPLOYED CALIFORNIA   6. CEO POLYVORE

2. MANAGER OPENTV   7. FOUNDER & CEO JOYUS

3. MANAGER JUNGLEE/AMAZON   8 ANGEL INVESTOR

4. FOUNDER & SVP YODLEE   9 FOUNDER th. BOARDLIST

5. DIRECTOR, VP, PRESIDENT GOOGLE 10 PRESIDENT STUBHUB

Figure 16

to lead, invest, and advise than I ever dreamed of, and I feel profoundly grateful.

Looking back on all of this, I enjoyed more cumulative rewards because I took more risks, but the path to these rewards as well as their nature and size almost always deviated from what I originally imagined, sometimes by a little and sometimes by a lot. A series of risks and choices unlocked compounding benefits as I built valuable career capital and created new inflection points in my career. Over time, with more practice, my intuition grew and I better anticipated the known risks I was taking. While I didn't mitigate them all perfectly, I put more effort into protecting myself against the downside than dreaming about the upside, and that paid off when problems arose. I also learned to conquer some of my own ego risk, not so much by succeeding as by managing through multiple failures. I became comfortable in the knowledge that I wouldn't always win through sheer desire alone, although I knew I could at a minimum count on delivering valuable impact if I took smart risks. I encountered at least one gigantic coconut that I wouldn't wish to go through again, but even there I emerged with more agility, resiliency, and confidence as a leader — in other words, better prepared to choose possibility again.

One can never entirely predict how any single choice will work out. Still, if we're willing to keep successively choosing, acting in ways that achieve impact, learning from our mistakes and the conditions around us, and allowing our hard-won wisdom to inform our next choices, we'll experience more and higher peaks in our careers. We'll also experience more troughs, decisions that will "fail" to deliver the outcome we hope for as a result of our own actions and the conditions around us. Even in these situations, we'll produce impact and reap incredible professional benefit. This is how career growth *really* happens (Figure 17).

What do you really have to lose? The management guru Peter Drucker observes, "People who don't take risk generally make about two big mistakes a year. And people who do take risk generally make about two big mistakes a year." I don't know about you, but I'd rather take the risks, make my two mistakes, *and* reap all the rewards.

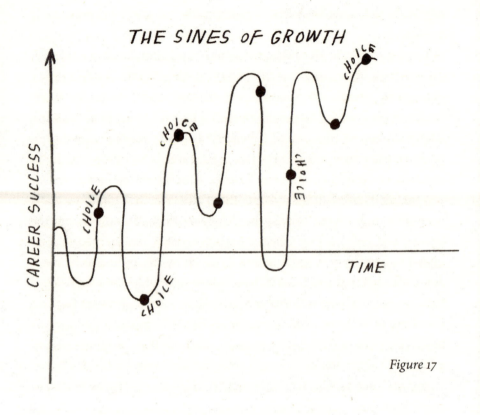

Figure 17

SINE WAVES EVERYWHERE

Once we recognize sine waves in our career trajectories, we start to notice them everywhere. Study any successful person's extended career, and you'll likely find they've experienced their own cycles up, down, and through difficulty, even though the wider world only registers their peak experiences. To help illustrate my point, let me return to the story of Stacy Brown-Philpot and her career sine wave.

Brown-Philpot is one of the tech world's most prominent female leaders and Black executives. Most recently, she served as CEO of the gig economy marketplace TaskRabbit. As Brown-Philpot relates, she grew up under very modest circumstances in Detroit, raised by a single mother and other relatives. Her first big risk was applying to the

University of Pennsylvania's Wharton School as an undergraduate, even though she already had a full scholarship to a local school and didn't know how she'd pay for Wharton. She got into Wharton and was able to pay for it through a combination of grants, scholarships, and part-time jobs (success).

Upon graduation, Brown-Philpot became a CPA at Pricewater-houseCoopers, pursuing her goal of eventually becoming a partner at a public accounting firm. After two years on the job, she realized she didn't want to become a career accountant after all. She worked for a year as a senior analyst at Goldman Sachs as part of a fellowship program and then enrolled at Stanford Business School to get her MBA. Upon graduating in 2002, she had a hard time finding a job. Instead of making the safe choice to return to Goldman Sachs, she took a risk and joined Google. That might not sound like much of a risk today, but back then the company only had about a thousand employees and was just one search engine among many. Further, Brown-Philpot's title was "senior financial analyst," below what her peers at Stanford were accepting.

But Brown-Philpot thrived at the company over the next several years. She took a moderate risk in 2007, moving from Finance to Operations (success), a change that took her off the track to become a future CFO. She then took a bigger professional and personal risk in 2009, accepting an opportunity to move to India and direct Google's sales and operations. Not only would she lead 1,000 people instead of just 200; she would have to manage a long-distance relationship with her husband, who would stay behind in California. "I'd had to take some personal risks along the way, but nothing like this. So, I made sure to negotiate with Google to ensure that my husband and I could see one another and I could mitigate the risk to our relationship." Living and working in India turned out to be a wonderful experience (success), both in terms of the business success Brown-Philpot achieved and her growth as a leader. As she recalls, "I learned I had to be more inspirational as a leader, as opposed to just methodical. [The India experience] really forced me to become a whole lot more vulnerable as a leader and to develop empathy, and to share more of who I was as a person."

After returning home and choosing to run another large team in operations, Brown-Philpot found herself feeling antsy. "I wasn't pushing myself enough," she says. "I wasn't learning. My learning curve was flattening." Determined to maintain her upward career trajectory, she took two risks in 2013 aiming at a goal of serving in a C-level executive role. First, she left her plum position as a senior executive at Google, which by now had become the "hot" company to work for. And second, she opted to join TaskRabbit as its COO. Although she was accepting an executive role, TaskRabbit was then a startup, which made it inherently risky. Further, people in the Valley didn't regard it as a high-flying startup on par with others. Brown-Philpot chose to go there anyway, as she loved the company's mission. Good thing: In 2016, after three years in her role, she became the company's CEO (success). And in 2017, Brown-Philpot successfully led the company to its acquisition by the global home retailer IKEA, helping this iconic brand transform itself digitally and adapt to the new gig economy. The following year, she was named a founding member of SB Opportunity Fund, a $100 million fund created by the Japanese conglomerate Softbank to invest in ventures undertaken by people of color.

Whether it's Stacy Brown-Philpot, Adam Zbar at Sun Basket, Alyssa Nakken at the San Francisco Giants, Reshma Saujani at Girls Who Code, Corey Thomas at Rapid7, Nick Grudin at Facebook, or any of the other dozens of leaders I've been privileged to know, you'll find the same pattern. Seen from the outside, their careers appear to neatly move from peak to peak. But look more closely and you find a messier picture. Between the peaks, these leaders experience troughs of different sizes and spanning different lengths of time. Although often painful at the time, these troughs play a vital role in their overall career ascents, and the leaders involved become conditioned to experiencing misses as well as wins. Look around you at the successful people you admire. If you closely scrutinize their careers, you'll spot their macro and micro cycles of success and failure as well.

THINK FREQUENCY

If careers boil down to a series of cycles, how can we ensure that we don't experience a series of successive failures that leave us flatlining over the long term, or even worse, careening downward? A big part of the answer is merely practice. We must be willing to keep choosing, following through by delivering outcomes and learning from each result. As we take more risks, bigger or smaller, we'll naturally get smarter, learning to recognize patterns in ourselves and our environments and anticipate opportunities and challenges. In risk-taking as in any other meaningful endeavor, practice yields proficiency, increasing the odds of overall success.

Figure 18 illustrates the power of frequent risk-taking, taking into account as well the size of the risks involved. If we make many choices of varying size (the upper-right box), we can sustain many more failures, small ones certainly but also at least one or two big ones, and still come out far ahead. Even if almost all of our risks are small but we take many of them (the upper-left box), we'll still see our career prospects soar. Conversely, many people stagnate in the lower-left box — they're afraid to move and take few, infrequent, and minuscule risks. If we find ourselves in the lower-right box, taking only one or two very large "one-way door" risks with few or no options for recovery in case of failure, we'll need one gigantic rocket ship of a success to propel us upward.

I don't know any elite operators in any field who count on this kind of luck. The vast majority of successful people take many risks, benefitting from the accumulation of small and large rewards. The world credits them only for the largest, but they and those closest to them know the truth.

YOUR WIN RATE MATTERS TOO

The frequency with which we take risks is one thing, but if we can notch a strong "win rate" as well (to borrow a term from financial trading),

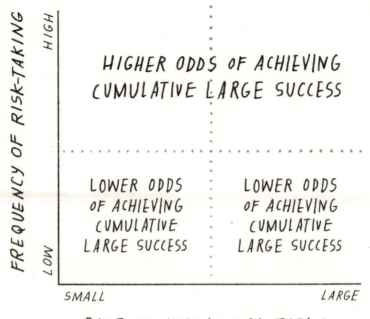

Figure 18

we'll likely put our careers on a positive trajectory. We want the total magnitude of career wins (accounting broadly for both the number of positive outcomes we achieve and their size) to exceed the total magnitude of our career misses (again taking into account both the amount and size of losses). Note that wins include not just the biggest goals we've consciously met but all of the tangible positive impacts we've achieved in our journey as well. Our losses are tangible negative outcomes we've manifested, including investments of our own (or others') money, time, or energy that failed to bear fruit over an extended period.

You might wonder just how high a win rate we would need to muster in order to build a solid track record of success and ultimately an impressive career. There is no standard answer — it varies by profession. A car salesperson might jump for joy with a win rate of 20 percent (since the average for the industry is about 12.5 percent), while a doctor performing spinal fusion surgery might need at least 80 percent and maybe more like 90 percent of her patients to feel happy about their procedures in order to think of herself as successful. In the NBA, top players make more than five out of ten of the shots they take. During the 2020 season, for instance, the top 100 players in the league for true shooting percentage (a measure that takes into account the different kinds of shots that players take) posted win rates between 56 percent and 72 percent. Yet in baseball, players headed to the Hall of Fame likely notch a batting average of between .300 and .400 over multiple seasons, meaning just three or four hits for every ten times they stand at the plate.

To put yourself on a trajectory toward a great career, choose repeatedly and deliver impact consistently, worrying less about whether you achieve success in any individual move. Over time, as we get smarter about choosing and achieving impact, we want to make sure that even if we don't achieve all our bigger ambitions, we can still generate more positive than negative outcomes and contributions over a large body of choices. This is the tangible career capital we keep accumulating that others can see, alongside the intangible superpowers we discussed earlier. If we keep choosing but fail to generate positive impacts consistently alongside our misses, we'll likely stay flat in our careers. We'll remain in our current roles, not liking them terribly much, or we'll move on to comparable or smaller roles, failing to achieve our full potential.

If you're just kicking off your career, take note: It's hard to measure your win rate when you've only made a few choices. Emerging disappointed from your first risk or two doesn't mean you're doing something terribly wrong or lagging behind. You must keep taking risks, having faith that over time you'll amass a sufficiently strong win rate, in part because you learn disproportionately from the negative ones. As we saw earlier, we don't even need to know our long-term goals upon first starting out — we can use risk-taking and the creation of outcomes as a means of discovering and clarifying them. Darren Gold, veteran executive coach, managing partner of the management consulting firm the Trium Group, and author of *Master Your Code,* remarks that risk-taking is a "recursive process, where you figure out your purpose and vision through experience." Without experiencing more successes and failures, it's hard to even get a sense of our goals, let alone put ourselves on a longer upward trajectory.

DIVERSIFY YOUR RISKS

As we've noted, the relationship between risk and reward is nonlinear at best. Sometimes small choices pay off in large and unexpected ways, and large risks hardly guarantee us large wins. Often it takes many different choices to lead to one larger success, or, to adopt a boxing metaphor, a combination of punches of unequal weight or force. When we find ourselves trying the same approach over and over again and not finding impact or larger success, it may be time to change up our own combination. Risk diversification is a smart strategy for all of us to consider over our multiple career choices.

I've diversified my own risk-taking in several different ways. Over the course of my career, I've chosen to learn and grow my experiences across multiple company growth stages (startup, private, public) and three different industries (e-commerce, media, and fintech). When I was taking large entrepreneurial risks, I also joined larger company boards so as to keep my "executive skills" current. After two successive startup experiences, Polyvore and Joyus, I decided to take my CEO experience back into a company with more size and scale, but one that needed my "diverse" entrepreneurial hustle in the top job. By seeking out a variety of risks rather than taking the same one over and over, we can maximize our win rates, agility, and future prospects, too.

BE A CHOOSER

There really is only one obstacle to a career that blossoms over the long term, and it isn't failure. It's *inaction* — staying in that lower-left box in Figure 18, where we opt out of choosing as a routine practice. The process of taking smart risks to achieve our ambitions, breaking our bigger goal down into smaller ones, driving results, responding in an agile way to what happens, and making a next move is what allows us to realize any possibility we seek and new ones we didn't. As our impact, agility, resiliency, and confidence mount, including through failures, we reap more rewards, although not how we perfectly imagined them. All we need to do is keep choosing and repeating the cycle. Failing to choose leaves us far more vulnerable than any single incorrect choice we might make. As the philosopher Seneca taught, "It's not because things are difficult that we dare not venture. It's because we dare not venture that they are difficult."

We should also note that the price of inaction mounts over time. Each month or year that we delay, we limit how far we might ultimately travel. And inaction doesn't allow us to stay roughly where we are. In our volatile world, where "subway" and "coconut" events proliferate, we'll keep encountering risk, whether we seek it out or not. Our careers will likely *decline* over time if we fail to anticipate, choose, and move. If we master the risk-taking process proactively, we gain more autonomy and control over our destinies even in uncertain environments. If we don't, we become beholden to other people's choices and the effects of changing macro conditions.

At the outset of our careers, we might resist taking risks because we fear failure. We might think that this fear diminishes over time, but in many cases it intensifies or changes. As we achieve more success through risk-taking, we might come to fear losing a comfortable lifestyle we've built thanks to a single big choice, or even more than that, we might come to fear a blow to the notion we've built of ourselves as "successful" or "established." We become paralyzed once again even though our possibilities have expanded.

If you feel yourself growing too comfortable or risk-averse, go back to your root principles. Remind yourself that we usually take risks in order to grow, and that if we fail, we'll likely find many possible choices-after-the-choice by which to make a recovery. Our ability to bounce back if we fail becomes even greater as we go, and we build increasingly strong career capital by delivering impact through all our choices.

"REBUILDING THE BEAST"

Continually choosing possibility over the long term gives us an opportunity to evolve and reinvent ourselves several times over. We can take the puzzle pieces of our career that we've acquired in the past and reassemble them to generate expanded new career opportunities. In the process, we don't just reinvent our careers, but ourselves. Today's website designer might become tomorrow's influencer, entrepreneur, or author. Today's sales associate might become tomorrow's e-sports agent, media executive, or CEO. Whether we're coming off a high or a low, choosing possibility is the process by which we continue to not just reimagine our careers in cycles, but expand who we are and what we're capable of.

Festus Ezeli, a professional basketball player who helped the Golden State Warriors win the 2015 NBA championship, uses a different metaphor to describe the process of managing cycles while reinventing ourselves. When he came to speak to us at StubHub, he described his own winding path through success and failure alike, noting that through his own chapters he is constantly reinventing himself. In each of these cycles, Festus is, as he puts it, "rebuilding the beast." Each of us has this opportunity in our own journey.

POSSIBILITY POINTERS

- Real growth isn't linear, but cyclical.
- By delivering impact through each larger chapter of ambition, iterating and taking smaller risks continually to create results faster, we'll build successful overall careers.
- Frequency of risk-taking and win rate are key to longer-term success, while our biggest threat remains inaction. We each can decide to become a chooser.

When I give talks to early-career professionals, they often ask: "Knowing what you now know, what is the most important piece of advice you'd give to your younger self?" I tell them, of course, about the importance of choosing possibility consistently. I also convey another point: Possibility and power are not a zero-sum game. There is more than enough to go around.

When we're just starting out, we tend to think of our careers as one giant competition for opportunity and success. If we land the best opportunities, we presume we'll achieve more. The more we achieve, the more financial rewards and power we'll obtain. As we become more powerful, we'll control our own destinies and exert greater influence on the events, environments, and people around us. But power, like possibility, seems to be in short supply, and the road to acquiring both seems narrow, long, arduous, and not for the faint of heart.

Our cultural context only serves to reinforce our notion of power's scarcity. We gaze from afar at the world's most successful businesspeople, politicians, and entertainers and regard them as powerful by virtue of their celebrity. As these individuals amass more followers, their influence and wealth grows and they appear even more distant from the rest of us. As a result, we often place power ever higher on a pedestal, aspiring to acquire it ourselves.

When I began my own journey. I believed there was only a fixed amount of possibility to go around, and that I needed to grab the "best bits" before others did. During those depressing months after I graduated, I spent countless hours comparing myself to my peers with glamorous jobs. That wasn't all bad: I harnessed competitive energy to hustle for opportunities. But my mindset of scarcity fueled unnecessary doubts and prompted me to question my self-worth. I assumed that if someone was more worthy of possibility, I surely must be less so.

These fears vanished as I began taking risks and growing my career, but new ones emerged. I continued to compare myself to my peers who had achieved similar success and felt anxious about keeping pace with their accomplishments and influence. What ultimately made me more confident was experiencing and surviving a number of small and large failures alongside success. As I kept choosing possibility, I came to feel a deeper sense of empowerment. I've come to realize that it isn't what we achieve that makes us powerful. It's our ability to keep taking risks, creating impact, and adapting as we go. We can feel and actually *be* powerful in any situation, even losing ones, simply by choosing possibility.

As the spiritual teacher Gary Zukav suggests, power comes when you see yourself not "as a victim who reacts to your circumstances," but "as a creator who chooses your response" to them. If we think of empowerment in this way, as taking risks and producing results to help shape our destinies, then the world doesn't need to bestow power on us, and neither can it take it away. We possess *innate* power, and we possess it in spades. We also generate more power for ourselves as we keep iterating. My sense of confidence has grown with every risk I've taken, outcome I've experienced, and lesson I've learned. Just like possibility, power isn't zero-sum. It's abundant.

Our freedom to keep choosing and making impact frees us from the unhealthy obsessions and jealousies that come if we think of possibility and power as scarce. These days, I care much less than I once did about whether others see me as powerful, because I see *myself* as able to choose, to respond in an agile manner, and to gain knowledge every time I move — and that's what counts. I obsess far more about how to achieve impact over the next day, week, month, quarter, or year, comparing my new attempts at impact to my previous ones.

Whereas I used to egotistically associate power with achievement, I now associate it with failure as well, which after all is part and parcel of risk-taking. Relatedly, I don't think of humility as the opposite of power, but its valuable companion. I'm reasonably sure I will fail many more times and succeed many more times. As skilled a risk-taker as I may be, my predictions of what will transpire and my own execution will never be perfect, so I need to stay truly open to learning as I go. As I watch others achieve, I'm reasonably sure they're riding their own sine waves of growth, and I'm happy to see them deliver successful outcomes after undoubtedly toiling with numerous challenges.

I don't know of any perfect journeys or perfect people. I only know of a process that allows us to keep choosing our way imperfectly and delivering impact. Over time, our accomplishments stack up enough that other people begin to notice. They tend to downplay or ignore our failures, label our accomplishments as "success," and label us as "powerful," observing that we wield influence over others. The truth is that we were powerful long before our biggest success, and we'll remain powerful long after our biggest failure. We'll keep working on creating possibility for ourselves, generating more power with every choice we make.

What would I say to my younger self? Choose a goal, then make a choice, however small, and start executing, aiming for impact every time. Then, keep choosing, because the more you do, the better you'll feel, and the higher your chances will be for succeeding across time. You don't need anyone or anything else to make you feel truly powerful. Sooner or later, your power will become obvious to the world around you.

POWERFLOW BEATS POWERFUL

Who, folks also wonder, is my hero? That's an easy one. My hero isn't a billionaire entrepreneur or a creative visionary who changed the world. It's a man who changed *my* world and that of everyone else he met. I'm talking about my father, easily the most powerful person I've ever known, a man who embodied and modeled the process of choosing possibility.

My father wasn't loud, boisterous, or openly opinionated. Yes, he was incredibly charismatic and a great storyteller, with a constant twinkle in his eye, but I remember him primarily as a gentle giant, a man with infinite patience, much more of a listener than a talker. He cared far more about learning and growing than what others thought of him. He was ambitious and open to every possibility, but he made his choices in a quiet, understated way. Over time, as he took smaller and bigger risks, his impact grew. He built a successful life for himself in Africa, then rebuilt that life in Canada, opening a medical practice and small business alongside my mother. He created wealth, built a great reputation, and notched numerous other accomplishments during a career that spanned five decades. Mostly he viewed the world around him as abundant with opportunity, and everything worth learning and trying.

My father did something else, too. As he strove to build a life for himself and his family, he also used much of his energy to helping others realize their own possibilities. My father generously gave his time, praise, optimism, and warmth to people around him — his patients, friends, members of his church community, just about anyone he encountered. As a result, people sought him out, hoping to spend a minute or an hour with him. They left feeling energized, full, and alive to their own potential. This was my father's greatest gift: to bestow on others *a sense of what they might become.* My father wasn't just powerful in how he held himself. He served as a source of power for others.

At my father's funeral in 2000, I was fortunate to hear many stories of how he had passed possibility along to others, both in large and small ways. An old family friend named Bobby came up to see me and share his tale. Bobby's father had been one of my father's dearest friends from Africa and sadly had passed away when Bobby was younger. Bobby came over to Canada from England for part of his summer vacation one year, staying at our home and getting to know us all well.

Now a doctor, Bobby told me about a brief episode he had with my father when he was applying to university and considering medicine as a profession. Uncertain whether he should pursue this ambition, he asked my father for some parental advice. As always, my dad's response was simple. He took Bobby's hands in his own, turned them up and turned them down, and then looked Bobby squarely in the eye, smiling. "Bobby," he said, "these are most certainly the hands of a surgeon." In that single moment of kindness and generosity, Bobby received the encouragement he needed to choose this possibility for himself.

Have you ever known someone who seems abundant or full of possibility and who gives you energy whenever you're around them? People like this are everywhere. They come in every shape and size and from every walk of life. They may be a boss, a neighbor, an aunt, a nephew, a barista, or more. When we know or meet these people, we want to get a little closer. We all recognize and benefit from having others around us who breathe possibility and life into their surroundings and ours.

I like to think of any individual's power as a renewable energy, somewhat like solar or wind power. Many of us grew up believing that oil and gas were the world's most precious resources because they were scarce. Today, we prize solar and wind precisely because they are both abundant and regenerative. Personal power is endlessly renewable too. We can constantly produce power for ourselves as we actively choose possibility. And the more power we generate, the easier it is for us to distribute and share it. Solar panels on our homes feed power not just back to us, but to an entire city's power grid. Likewise, those who amass the most impact don't hoard power to themselves. They let power *flow out* to others to create bigger benefits, while continuing to generate more themselves. Such *powerflow* was the secret to my father's lifelong success, long before I truly recognized it for what it was (Figure 19).

The concept of power as a flow might seem daunting or overly idealistic. But while we're choosing possibility for ourselves, we can easily make small choices to help others realize their own possibilities and generate power. We can share ideas to benefit everyone in a meeting, acknowledge someone else's terrific idea publicly, say yes to a coffee when someone asks for our advice, volunteer to write a blurb for someone's website, or if we can, write a check to encourage someone else's dream. When we accelerate possibility for others alongside ourselves, the impact we might generate multiplies many times over.

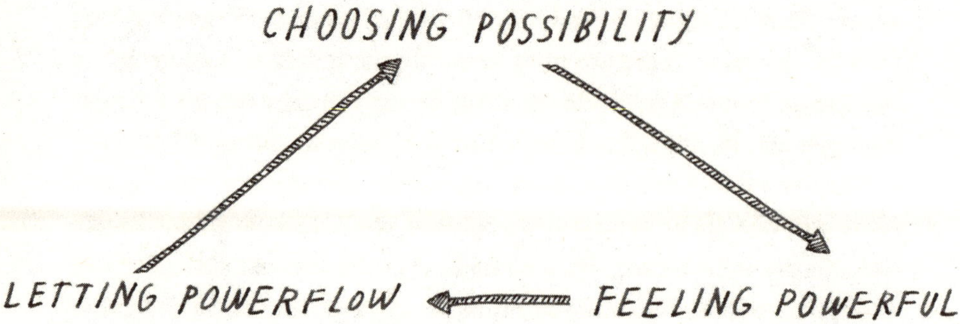

Figure 19

UNLOCK POWERFLOW BY CHANGING THE SYSTEM

If an abundance of power lies within each of us just waiting to be unleashed, why do so many people have a hard time paying their rent at the end of the month, much less achieving their dreams? Why do we see so much inequality and *lack* of opportunity?

As we've discussed, the first step in our journeys is to start our own practice of making choices and taking risks so that we can have real impact and produce meaningful, positive rewards. But we've also seen that larger forces exist that can thwart our efforts, no matter how diligent, smart, or well-intentioned we might be. Whether it's a pandemic or technological disruption, changes come at us from the outside world that leave some groups of people reaping benefits and others disproportionately bearing the costs. Alongside these macro shifts, systemic biases have created unequal distribution of possibility, even as each of us seeks to choose and shape our destiny as much as we can. As we generate possibility for ourselves and share power with others, we must take it even further, seeking opportunities in our teams, companies, or industries to fix underlying systemic causes of inequity.

When I was working at Joyus, I became increasingly attuned to systemic gender inequities, specifically in the tech industry of which I was a part. I felt immensely grateful for the opportunities I had found in Silicon Valley, but I knew the stories of discrimination, pay inequity, harassment, and more from women entrepreneurs and CEOs were very real. I also remembered my first tech job and the negative comments I received about my perceived aggressiveness. I noticed that the plight of women in tech was becoming a bigger topic in the news media, with many observers decrying the widely held notion that our industry was a place of possibility for all.

At around this time, I received a group email from Keval Desai, my lead investor at Joyus. Addressing himself to me and several other successful female founders and CEOs in whom he'd invested, Keval wondered out loud whether one of us might use our own voice to share our unique experiences. Feeling that women leaders' voices were largely missing from the conversation, I volunteered to speak out. In an op-ed the following month called "Tech Women Choose Possibility," cosigned by dozens of other female founders and CEOs and published in the tech industry journal *Recode* and on Medium, I shared results of a survey I'd performed of almost one hundred women leaders in tech.

A staggering 84 percent said that they would recommend that their daughters become entrepreneurs. At the same time, an almost equal percentage — 86 percent — saw unconscious bias at work within tech, as evidenced by a tendency to critique women for being "aggressive" or to expect or require them to be "likable." About two-thirds of women witnessed what they perceived as bias firsthand, and one-third had been sexually harassed.

Based on this data, I observed that women in the tech industry were thriving as entrepreneurs because they chose possibility every day. Nevertheless, women weren't able to contribute fully to the tech industry, because they had to contend with significant bias. Women could and would continue to build amazing companies, but the tech industry needed to take bias seriously and take decisive action to address it for every woman to be able to thrive.

The response to this op-ed was immediate and overwhelmingly positive, and it prompted me to think more seriously about some of my own ideas for leveraging technology to bring about change in Silicon Valley. In particular, I felt convinced that we could have a large, untapped, and immediate impact by focusing on boardrooms. Although Silicon Valley boasted many talented female executives (some engineers, some not), very few women sat on the boards of startups and established tech companies. If we could harness the power of the Valley's great and diverse female talent, getting these people into the boardroom faster and more often, I believed we'd see better company performance and better company cultures, starting from the top. When asked why more women didn't occupy board positions, too many male CEOs commented that the pipeline of female talent didn't exist. There weren't enough great women leaders, they claimed, and CEOs didn't know how to find them. I felt pretty sure that technology could help correct this inaccurate perception in short order.

Within sixty days of the "Choose Possibility" op-ed, I had pulled together the most basic of websites and launched my third company, called theBoardlist. Based on ample evidence that companies drive better performance when they have diverse leadership, theBoardlist was a simple "talent marketplace" that allowed experienced leaders to recommend and discover diverse talent for any company's board, and allowed great women leaders to access more board opportunities. To kick us off, I opened my Rolodex and asked thirty experienced CEOs and entrepreneurs I knew if they would send me names of great women leaders they knew to serve on boards. Every single one said yes, and just like that we crowdsourced more than six hundred women for theBoardlist. Meanwhile we promoted theBoardlist to companies as a single, trusted source of highly recommended, diverse leaders for their board openings.

During the years that followed, theBoardlist (my side hustle, where today I remain founder and chairman) built a small and mighty full-time team and a community of leaders who cared deeply about solving board diversity. By 2020, theBoardlist had grown to about 16,000 members, including CEOs who recommended and searched for board talent, and women nominated for and receiving board opportunities.

The company had also facilitated almost two thousand company board searches and become an authoritative voice on building diverse boards and solving inequity in the leadership ranks. In 2020, we also expanded the platform to help great leaders of color access more board opportunity, and we raised our first venture capital round. Every time I watch leaders recommend others and share new board searches on the platform, I see powerflow in action and am encouraged to keep going.

But back when I first wrote that op-ed, did it feel risky to me? Certainly. I had built my reputation as business leader first and woman second; what would happen to people's perceptions of me if started being stereotyped under a "gender lens" myself? Today, I am branded that way sometimes, but the confidence I've gained through repetitive risk-taking has taught me that my track record is also with me wherever I go. As important, having used my voice to try to level the playing field of possibility has been far more personally rewarding than professionally costly.

I can't predict what theBoardlist will ultimately become, any more than I could have predicted the future of other companies I've started. That's okay — I'm content to focus on impacting iteratively and have stopped trying to project what will happen over the long term. But more than any other company I've created, theBoardlist has the potential to truly change the distribution of opportunity and power systemically, and to everyone's benefit. It's certainly the most meaningful and ambitious pursuit of my career so far.

A FINAL STORY ON CHOOSING POSSIBILITY

If you'd like to learn about unleashing your own power and helping others do the same in parallel, then you'd do well to visit Big House Beans Cafe in Brentwood, California, and ask for the owner, John Krause. I met John myself in early 2020 when a local nonprofit I'm involved with granted him an entrepreneurship award. While most successful entrepreneurs have a compelling story to tell, John's is exceptional.

When John was four, his father died right in front of him — the two were on a motorcycle that crashed. His mother was a severe alcoholic and drug addict who lived on the streets of Richmond, California. John was fortunate to have a loving grandmother who raised him, but as a child he struggled to deal with the trauma he experienced. Every so often he'd find his mother drunk and beat up in an abandoned building or huddled with other transients outside a liquor store. She was so out of it that she didn't even recognize him. John didn't know how to handle the anger that he felt — he had nowhere to turn and had trouble fitting in at school. "It was hard for me," he said, "because as kids you feel like people are talking about your mama in the schoolyard or your daddy, and it never feels good."

At the age of twelve, John began getting drunk with other neighborhood kids who hailed from broken homes. From there, he graduated to smoking pot and rolling with a gang. "My main mission and focus wasn't academics," he said. "It was what are we going to smoke between periods at school." At the age of fourteen, he became addicted to meth, and that's when his encounters with the law began. For the next sixteen years, until he reached the age of thirty, he was in and out of juvenile hall, jail, or prison for drug possession, theft, and other offenses. When he wasn't incarcerated, he would stay sober and work for short stints, but he then resumed his addiction, committed crimes, and wound up back in the "big house." All told, he spent about a dozen years out of these sixteen behind bars, including almost a full year in solitary confinement.

The turning point came in 2009, during John's last year in prison. His grandmother, who had until then always been the anchor in his life, passed away. For the first time in his life, he had absolutely nobody to fall back on. He had become religious not long before, and for days on end he cried in his cell and prayed to God. When he was released, he knew he had to make a decision, either to stop trying and give himself over to drugs and alcohol, or to finally stay sober and build a life for himself. Either to stay trapped in old patterns, or to try something new. Either to stagnate, or to choose possibility.

He chose possibility.

In 2011, with the help of friends he'd met at a local church, he got a job recycling waste cooking oil from restaurants. It was dirty work and it didn't pay well, but it was at least something. About a year later, he and a partner took a risk and started their own oil collection company. John and his partner had to put a business plan together, present it to investors, and convince them that they could make the business work. "One thing I'd say," John recalled, "is I was given the gift of desperation, and I was willing to do whatever it took to be successful . . . One of my mentors taught me to be persistent. He taught me so many things, but one of them was it's okay to get a no, because that just means you're one step closer to a yes, and what did you learn from that experience?" This lesson was especially important, John noted, because if you don't take the time to reflect and learn from your mistakes, "how can you go back out and be willing to take another risk?"

John's risk-taking paid off. Within a year and a half, his business was a success, booking more than a half-million dollars in sales. This in turn gave him a measure of stability that had eluded him all of his life. He was earning a six-figure income, had full health coverage, had gotten married, and had even been able to obtain custody of three children he'd fathered during his years in and out of prison. But his risk-taking wasn't over — it was just beginning.

Despite their success, John and his business partner weren't getting along. Realizing that their partnership wouldn't work over the long term, John decided he had to make a change. He had come to love fresh roasted coffee and had a vague idea that he might start his own coffee roaster, but he had no specific plans and he knew nothing about the coffee business. Still, despite the risk, he finally decided: He would sell out to his partner, walk away, and go off on his own.

Overnight, his income went to zero. His wife was completely "freaked out." John himself felt stressed, but not despondent. He had learned so much from starting his first business — everything from how to do a cash flow projection to how to sell — and had accomplished something impressive, building it up from scratch. This gave him the confidence that he could succeed on his own. He scrambled to put a business plan together and raise capital. John had a vision of a coffee-roasting business that wouldn't simply grow and allow him to support his family, but that would help others like him get a start in life. "My dream was to use the company as a platform to share my story, to bring people together and build a community, to create jobs for people with barriers to employment, and of course, to make as much money as I could. That was my dream."

John bought a $40,000 roaster and taught himself how to use it. In 2014, Big House Beans was born, selling coffee under the tagline "Coffee with Purpose." John did everything himself — roasting coffee, bagging it, delivering it, selling it. The business struggled at first, but eventually John got a big break, landing an account at Airbnb's corporate cafeteria. By 2019, he had grown the business to $1 million in sales, opened a café, and had plans to open three more.

John decided early on to staff Big House Beans cafés with men and women who had formerly been incarcerated. While striving to realize possibilities himself, John was equally determined to help others do the same. As the Big House Beans website explains, the company hires "the 'least desirable' yet hard working women and men," mentoring them and teaching them job skills they can use to improve their lives. The company is both a second chance for John and is dedicated to giving second chances to others, "birthing potential through highlighting diversity." Its "main goal" is to "empower individuals through unconditional love and opportunities."

John's story is extreme, but instructive. John started from nothing. In fact, he started off much worse — in a prison cell. As he chose possibility, he unleashed a power inside him that he didn't know he had. One choice begat a second begat many, some succeeding and others failing. Through a virtuous cycle of choice, impact, learning, and more choice, John moved in the direction of his dreams, which was to enjoy a stable, successful, happy life. Quite naturally, as his ability to make choices and influence his own destiny swelled, he felt moved to help others do the same. No, possibility isn't scarce, and neither is power. If we start reaching for one, we'll surely find the other. All we need to do is take that first chance to *choose possibility*.

POSSIBILITY POINTERS

- Possibility and power are abundant, not scarce. When we choose possibility consistently, we don't need others to make us powerful. We generate power for ourselves.
- The most powerful people are those who help power flow to others.
- We all have an opportunity to generate possibility for others in the process of generating it for ourselves. We can choose to multiply our impact too.

ACKNOWLEDGMENTS

As daunting as it is to write a book, ensuring that you've thanked everyone who made it possible is even more so. I'll try my best here.

To my husband, Simon, and my kids, Ryan, Kenya, and Kieran: Thank you for always being incredibly supportive of who I am, including my professional dreams. I know that my ambition and passion for work often puts pressure on our family life. I couldn't have asked for a better life partner and a more wonderful set of children. Whenever I feel work intensity take over, just being with you helps me quickly put life in perspective again. I love you immensely and feel insanely grateful for our family.

To my late father, my incredible mother, and my two sisters, Nicky and Neeta: Thanks for encouraging me every day of my life. Ever since my dad's passing, my parents' dear friend and our church leader, Bhai Mohinder Singh, has served as an important father figure to me. It's hard to convey the fundamental sense of security and support I have felt since I was born, which has made choosing possibility so very *possible* in my life. While my father passed on to me a special set of lessons, my mother quietly demonstrated to all her daughters that we need not be what the world expects us to be. By any measure, my mother pioneered her own path professionally, bucking tradition in 1950s India to delay marriage and motherhood until her thirties and become a doctor first. Both my parents also taught me that our work, passion, and purpose in life don't need to be distinct from one another. It is possible for what we do, who we authentically are, and our desire for impact to come together in careers that truly create fulfillment every day.

To all the educators, empowering leaders, and professional mentors who throughout my life allowed me to "run," I can't tell you how much I appreciate you. So many people gave me space to "do more and be more," and that was exactly what I needed to thrive. While I could only share stories of some of you in the book, I feel grateful to all of you.

To all of my professional peers, colleagues, and teams: Thanks for putting up with my intensity and tremendous imperfections as we came together to make things happen, in companies big and small. Throughout my career, I've been privileged to work with tribes of incredibly talented people who also are really good humans. Who can ask for more than that when they go to work every day?

I have had the benefit of having an amazing set of friends, both lifelong and more recent, who have always made me feel supported in both my personal and professional life. Thank you all for your friendship and love. I want to especially thank a few people whose longstanding support and friendship have helped guide many of my professional choices, including the decision to write this book. To Anh Lu — my very best friend for over thirty-three years (how is that even possible!): I appreciate that you are always, always there to listen to anything and everything I've ever had to say, across one time zone, or all of them. To David Lesser, my executive coach over the past ten years: Thanks for always being there to help me navigate my way to the next possibility, in great times and more challenging ones. To Shea Kelly, an incredibly talented HR boss and insightful and empathetic friend: Thanks for taking a chance on me twenty-plus years ago and always lending an ear when I've needed it since. And to my more recent partner and friend, Orit: I love both your truth-telling and your encouragement! I will always remember the plane trip when I shared my secret ambition to write this book after selling StubHub; your telling me to go for it kick-started this new journey.

So many people played a role in the creation, publication, and promotion of this book. Many thanks to Kim Scott, Scott Galloway, and Magdalena Yesil for your critical introductions into the world of publishing. To the amazing Jim Levine, one of the world's best agents, I so appreciate your taking my first call and making time to hear my story. I will never forget how quickly you grasped my father's uniqueness and his influence on me during our very first meeting. Right then and there, I knew I'd found the right partner for this book.

To Seth Schulman, the incredible writer who agreed to write this entire book with me in less than six months, despite the many other amazing potential authors he could have chosen to work with: It was an absolute delight. You could have written this whole book yourself and it would likely have been more eloquent and a more efficient process. Yet you helped structure a process that allowed me to authentically write this book with my own voice, while also injecting your expertise to shape, structure, and edit it, making it so much better. Your patient and giving nature shone through the entire process, and if I ever write a book again, I'd beg you to write it with me.

To Christie Young and Monika Verma: Thank you for helping me to tell my story in pictures. Your ability to capture what was in my head and effectively translate it into illustrations in quick cycles has made this book much more useful for readers.

To Rick Wolff, Olivia Bartz, and Deb Brody: Thank you for believing in the idea for this book from the day I first pitched it to you. Rick, your involvement in every chapter as we wrote it is something I now know to be both rare and exceptional. Olivia, you applied care and diligence to the step-by-step shepherding of this book from draft manuscript to its final launch. Heather and Alison, thanks for painstakingly copyediting this book and getting it into production. To Lisa McAuliffe, Taryn Roeder, and Andrea DeWerd, I love the energy you put into marketing this book and making its messages as relevant and appealing as possible for readers. And to Mark Fortier and the entire PR team who worked on successfully launching *Choose Possibility* and helping it find its moments among a myriad of messages, thank you.

To Robin Harvie and the whole team at Pan McMillan, thank you for believing in the potential of *Choose Possibility* globally. I'm particularly proud that we were able to take its messages to the corners of the globe to which I feel personally connected, and also where it can have bigger impact. And to Kalyan Krisnamurthy of Flipkart, thanks for lending your influential voice to launching this book in India, the country of my roots.

To all the leaders whom I approached individually and asked to share their stories in the book, thank you for agreeing to be a part of it. While I've had the privilege of knowing many of you, in other cases you simply took our cold outreach in stride and graciously agreed to participate. Nicky, Alyssa, Reshma, Stacy, Ade, Adam, Corey, Nick, Simon, Orit, David, Shea, Alan, Simon, Darren, Daniel, Mathai, Ashvin, Festus, John, John, and Deb: I appreciate your generosity of time and spirit immensely.

To Shea Kelly, Kim Scott, and Stoyan Stoyanov: Thank you for the valuable feedback you provided as readers of this book. While I wished I could have surveyed the whole world in real time while writing it, it was comforting to know I had the benefit of your valuable and diverse perspectives. To Jonathan Rosenberg, my former colleague from Google and an amazing author in his own right: Thanks for sharing all your wisdom on how to actually launch and market a successful book. And to Alex Dacks and Jean-Christophe Pope: Thanks for being my creative partners and helping me create and execute a holistic content strategy around *Choose Possibility* that would help amplify its messages across every channel.

Finally, I would be remiss if I didn't look upward with gratitude as my parents taught me to do. I was raised to believe that we are all part of something bigger, and that I have someone bigger to thank for all that we have been given. My parents prayed every day in appreciation, and to this day my mom reminds me to feel grateful to God for every possibility I've experienced.

Don't worry, Mom — I remember.

Sincerely,
Sukhinder

NOTES

INTRODUCTION

page

xvii   *"possibility of loss"*: *Merriam-Webster Online*, s.v. "risk," accessed November 5, 2020, https://www.merriam-webster.com/dictionary/risk.

      "Life is either a daring adventure": "With the Light Inside, This Kerala Girl Challenges Limitations with Determination," *New Indian Express*, July 19, 2020, https://www.newindianexpress.com/good-news/2020/jul/19/with-the-light-inside-this-kerala-girl-challenges-limitations-with-determination-2171729.html.

xix   *"All life is an experiment"*: Ralph Waldo Emerson, *The Heart of Emerson's Journals*, ed. Bliss Perry (New York: Dover Publications, 1995), 189.

xxi   *"locus of control"*: Melody Wilding, "Successful People Have a Strong 'Locus of Control.' Do You?" *Forbes*, March 2, 2020, https://www.forbes.com/sites/melodywilding/2020/03/02/successful-people-have-a-strong-locus-of-control-do-you/#45e76ebb7af3; Paul E. Spector et al., "Locus of Control and Well-Being at Work: How Generalizable Are Western Findings?" *Academy of Management* 45, no. 2 (November 30, 2017): 453–66, https://doi.org/10.5465/3069359.

      "Freedom and autonomy are critical": Barry Schwartz, *The Paradox of Choice: Why More Is Less* (New York: HarperCollins, 2004), 99.

CHAPTER 1: DITCH THE HERO'S JOURNEY

5   *"Throughout the inhabited world"*: Joseph Campbell, *The Hero with a Thousand Faces* (Princeton University Press, 1973), 3, 30.

6   *"Uncertainty acts like rocket fuel for worry"*: Markham Heid, "Science Ex-

plains Why Uncertainty Is So Hard on Our Brain," *Elemental,* March 19, 2020, https://elemental.medium.com/science-explains-why-uncertainty-is-so-hard-on-our-brain-6ac75938662.

"one fear to rule them all": R. Nicholas Carleton, "Fear of the Unknown: One Fear to Rule them All?" *Journal of Anxiety Disorders* 41 (June 2016): 5–21, https://doi.org/10.1016/j.janxdis.2016.03.011.

uncertainty ruffles us: Dylan Walsh, "People Don't Like to Take Risks Because They Just Don't Want to Deal with Uncertainty," *Quartz,* July 11, 2017, https://qz.com/1022250/uncertainty-makes-us-less-likely-to-take-risks-due-to-a-strange-quirk-of-human-psychology.

7 *our fear of losing what we already have:* Rose McDermott, "Prospect Theory," Britannica.com, https://www.britannica.com/topic/prospect-theory; Daniel Kahneman and Amos Tversky, "Prospect Theory: An Analysis of Decision Under Risk," *Econometrica* 47, no. 2 (March, 1979): 263–92, https://doi.org/10.2307/1914185.

9 *crafting individualized, nontraditional career paths:* See Elaine Pofeldt, "Full-time Freelancing Lures More Americans," *Forbes,* October 5, 2019, https://www.forbes.com/sites/elainepofeldt/2019/10/05/full-time-freelancing-lures-more-americans/#341b4fe57259 and "Alternative Routes to the Top: The Rise of Non-Traditional Career Paths," *Tempo,* November 8, 2018, https://www.heytempo.com/blog/non-traditional-career-paths.

In one study of female business leaders: Avery Blank, "Female Leaders Take Non-Traditional Career Paths, Study Says: How You Can, Too," *Forbes,* April 28, 2019, https://www.forbes.com/sites/averyblank/2019/04/28/female-leaders-take-non-traditional-career-paths-study-says-how-you-can-too/#25281bcd7862.

"I did everything from investment banking": Emily Fields Joffrion, "How Vimeo's 34-Year-Old CEO Mastered the Nonlinear Career Path," *Forbes,* June 7, 2018, https://www.forbes.com/sites/emilyjoffrion/2018/06/07/how-vimeos-34-year-old-ceo-mastered-the-non-linear-career-path/#1b8d5 79f1628.

10 *others "don't accelerate to the top":* Elena Lytkina Botelho, Kim Rosenkoetter Powell, and Nicole Wong, "The Fastest Path to the CEO Job, According to a 10-Year Study," *Harvard Business Review,* January 31, 2018, https://hbr.org/2018/01/the-fastest-path-to-the-ceo-job-according-to-a-10-year-study.

taking a smaller job: Botelho et al., "The Fastest Path."

a large LinkedIn study: Neil Irwin, "How to Become a C.E.O.? The Quickest Path Is a Winding One," *New York Times,* September 9, 2016, https://www.nytimes.com/2016/09/11/upshot/how-to-become-a-ceo-the-quickest-path-is-a-winding-one.html.

"The quickest path is a winding one": Irwin, "How to Become a C.E.O.?"

11   *"The dangers of life are infinite":* Christoph von Toggenburg, "7 Inspirational Leadership Lessons from an Adventurer," *Forbes,* July 29, 2016, https://www.forbes.com/sites/worldeconomicforum/2016/07/29/7-inspirational-leadership-lessons-from-an-adventurer/?sh=232d2896d990.

companies over a fifteen-year period: Chris Bradley, Martin Hirt, and Sven Smit, *Strategy Beyond the Hockey Stick: People, Probabilities, and the Big Moves to Beat the Odds* (Hoboken, NJ: John Wiley & Sons, 2018), 109, 143–44, 169.

CHAPTER 2: PUMP YOUR RISK-TAKING MUSCLES

15   *"patented cyclonic action system":* "The Original Cyclonic Action Cleaning System," *Filterqueen,* accessed October 15, 2020, https://www.filterqueen.com/stories.

16   *There were Gary and Sarah:* I've changed the names of individuals in this paragraph.

17   *"Do one thing":* Mitch Ditkoff, "50 Awesome Quotes on Risk Taking," *HuffPost,* updated September 29, 2017.

"the act or fact of doing something": Merriam-Webster Online, s.v. "risk-taking," accessed November 5, 2020, https://www.merriam-webster.com/dictionary/risk-taking?src=search-dict-hed.

20   *to learn and grow:* For a discussion of the relationship between betting and learning, please see chapter 3 of Annie Duke, *Thinking in Bets: Making Smarter Decisions When You Don't Have All the Facts* (New York: Portfolio, 2018).

"A man would do nothing": David Mills, "The Wise and Witty New Saint, John Henry Newman," *Stream,* October 13, 2019, https://stream.org/new-saint-john-henry-newman-say.

23   *"I felt like I had hit rock bottom":* I tell this story based on an interview my research team conducted with "Gina." I have changed this person's name and other identifying details to protect their privacy.

25   *"I can't swim":* Reshma Saujani (author of *Brave, Not Perfect* and founder

of Girls Who Code), interview with the author's research team, August 2020.

CHAPTER 3: THE POWER OF PIPELINING IN PARALLEL

32 *having too many choices:* See S. S. Iyengar and M. R. Lepper, "When Choice Is Demotivating: Can One Desire Too Much of a Good Thing?" *Journal of Personality and Social Psychology* 79, no. 6 (2000): 995–1006, https://doi.org/10.1037/0022-3514.79.6.995 and Schwartz, *Paradox.*

If we don't discipline ourselves: As an example of a text affirming the general importance of focusing, see "Harnessing Willpower to Meet Your Goals," *American Psychological Association,* updated December 9, 2019, https://www.apa.org/helpcenter/willpower-fact-sheet. The text concerns itself primarily with willpower and not focus, but it includes the following statement: "Psychologists have found that it is more effective to focus on a single, clear goal rather than taking on a list of goals at once."

33 *"We didn't really know":* Ashvin Kumar (founder of Tophatter), interview with the author's research team, June 2020.

CHAPTER 4: WHY PROXIMITY BEATS PLANNING

40 *millions each week:* Jeff Kaye, "British Satellite TV Networks Plan to Merge," *Los Angeles Times,* November 3, 1990.

44 *"I think what they can miss":* Shea Kelly (chief people officer at the data analytics company Sumo Logic), interview with the author's research team, July 14, 2020.

45 *"What motivates our investment":* Oliver Burkeman, *The Antidote: Happiness for People Who Can't Stand Positive Thinking* (New York: Farrar, Straus, and Giroux, 2012), 86.

46 *young aspirants have traditionally learned their crafts:* See, for instance, Sue George, "Tanners, Tailors and Candlestick Makers: A History of Apprenticeships," *Guardian,* February 4, 2020, https://www.theguardian.com/global/2020/feb/04/tanners-tailors-and-candlestick-makers-a-history-of-apprenticeships. For a brief history of apprenticeships in Europe, please see David de la Croix, Matthias Doepke, and Joel Mokyr, "More Than Family Matters: Apprenticeship and the Rise of Europe," *VOX EU/CEPR,* March 2, 2017, https://voxeu.org/article/apprenticeship-and-rise-europe.

U.S. policymakers have looked to expand apprenticeships: See, for example, Greg Ferenstein, "How History Explains America's Struggle to Revive Apprenticeships," *Brookings,* May 23, 2018, https://www.brookings .edu/blog/brown-center-chalkboard/2018/05/23/how-history-explains-americas-struggle-to-revive-apprenticeships, and Jeffrey J. Selingo, "Why Are Apprenticeships a Good Idea That Have Never Really Taken Off in the U.S.?" *Washington Post,* December 22, 2017, https://www.washington post.com/news/grade-point/wp/2017/12/22/why-are-apprenticeships-a-good-idea-that-have-never-really-taken-off-in-the-u-s.

"social learning theory": "Social Learning Theory," *Psychology Today,* accessed October 15, 2020, https://www.psychologytoday.com/us/basics/social-learning-theory.

neuroscientists have discovered that social learning: Natalie Parletta, "Sometimes We Need to Learn from Others," *Cosmos,* August 20, 2020, https://cosmosmagazine.com/health/body-and-mind/sometimes-we-need-to-learn-from-others.

"inadvertently filter information": Christoph Grüter, Ellouise Leadbeater, and Francis L. W. Ratnieks, "Social Learning: The Importance of Copying Others," *Current Biology* 20, no. 16 (August 24, 2010): R683–85, https://www.sciencedirect.com/science/article/pii/S0960982210008006.

highly successful practitioners: Sydney Finkelstein, *Superbosses: How Exceptional Leaders Master the Flow of Talent* (New York: Portfolio, 2018), 171 and throughout.

47 *"networks of success":* Finkelstein, *Superbosses,* chapter 8. The Alice Waters example referenced here appears on pages 171–73.

48 *"I was inspired by these clients":* Alyssa Nakken (assistant coach for the San Francisco Giants), interview with the author's research team, August 2020.

CHAPTER 5: FOMO > FOF = ACTION

53 *And the day came:* Although this quote is widely attributed to Nin, some question exists whether she actually wrote it (e.g., "Who Wrote 'Risk'? Is the Mystery Solved?" *Official Anais Nin Blog,* March 5, 2013, http://anaisninblog.skybluepress.com/2013/03/who-wrote-risk-is-the-mystery-solved).

54 *"I am the greatest":* Norbert Juma, "155 Positive Thinking Quotes for a

New Perspective," *Everyday Power,* July 17, 2020, https://everydaypower
.com/positive-thinking-quotes.

"*The positive thinker*": Juma, "155 Positive Thinking Quotes."

55   "*impeded people in the long term*": Gabriele Oettingen, *Rethinking Positive
Thinking* (New York: Current, 2014), 16.

a veteran practitioner: David Lesser (executive coach), interview with the
author's research team, September 8, 2020.

56   *Type 1 decisions are "one-way doors"*: Jeffrey P. Bezos, "To our Shareholders," *Securities and Exchange Commission,* accessed October 15, 2020,
https://www.sec.gov/Archives/edgar/data/1018724/000119312516530910/
d168744dex991.htm.

58   "*Give me the young man*": Robert Louis Stevenson, "*Virginibus Peurisque*"
and Other Papers (New York: Current Literature Publishing Co., 1910),
95.

60   *Ade built Formstack:* Ade Olonoh (founder of Formspring and Formstack), interview with the author's research team, August 2020.

62   "*I kind of liked the idea*": Hilary Brueck and Skye Gould, "A 57-Year-
Old Google Engineer Performed the Highest Human Free-Fall, Jumping from 135,890 Feet Up in the Stratosphere: A Documentary on Net-
flix Reveals How He Did It," *Business Insider,* February 7, 2019, https://
www.businessinsider.com/google-engineer-alan-eustace-free-fall-from-
stratosphere-2019-2.

63   *from an engineering standpoint:* Alan Eustace (former senior vice president of Knowledge at Google), interview with the author's research team,
October 26, 2020.

"*Daredevils are people*": Brueck and Gould, "A 57-Year-Old Google Engineer."

65   "*It definitely felt pretty risky*": Ade Olonoh (founder of Formspring and
Formstack), interview with the author's research team, August 2020.

reaching almost 28 million users: Boonsri Dickinson, "Formspring Started
as a Side Project, but Now Has Nearly 28 Million Users and $14 Million
in Funding," *Business Insider,* January 9, 2012, http://static.businessin-
sider.com/formspring-started-as-a-side-project-but-now-has-nearly-28-
million-users-and-14-million-in-funding-2012-1.

66   *realistic optimist:* Jim Collins examines a mentality that merges realism
and optimism in his account of Admiral Jim Stockdale and the "Stock-

dale Paradox." See Jim Collins, *Good to Great: Why Some Companies Make the Leap and Others Don't* (New York: Harper Business, 2001), 83–87.

CHAPTER 6: PUT *WHO* BEFORE *WHAT* WHEN TAKING A RISK

78   *"Your old friends"*: David Burkus, *Friend of a Friend: Understanding the Hidden Networks That Can Transform Your Life and Your Career* (Boston: Houghton Mifflin Harcourt, 2018), 13.

80   *"Aside from their basic humanity"*: Finkelstein, *Superbosses*, 24.

82   *superbosses tend to display*: Finkelstein, *Superbosses*, 29–33.

84   *"Every single person"*: Stacy Brown-Philpot (CEO of TaskRabbit), interview with the author's research team September 17, 2020.
      "Superbosses are the great coaches": Finkelstein, *Superbosses*, 14–15.

CHAPTER 7: IT'S NOT ALL ABOUT YOU

88   *"The need for control is biologically motivated"*: Lauren A. Leotti, Sheena S. Iyengar, and Kevin N. Ochsner, "Born to Choose: The Origins and Value of the Need for Control," *Trends in Cognitive Sciences* 14, no. 10 (October 2010): 457–63, https://www.ncbi.nlm.nih.gov/pmc/articles/PMC2944661.

89   *"the future is often a bit like the past"*: Spyros Makridakis, Robin M. Hogarth, and Anil Gaba, "Why Forecasts Fail: What to Do Instead," *MIT Sloan Management Review*, January 1, 2010, https://sloanreview.mit.edu/article/why-forecasts-fail-what-to-do-instead/?use_credit=0e7e05fa1026b0c5459267608ae320b8.

90   *macro-environments*: For a basic introduction to macro-environments and their affects on companies, see "Macro Environment," *Investopedia*, January 30, 2020, https://www.investopedia.com/terms/m/macro-environment.asp.
      companies that identify: See, for instance, chapter 6 in Chris Bradley, Martin Hirt, and Sven Smit, *Strategy Beyond the Hockey Stick: People, Probabilities, and Big Moves to Beat the Odds* (Hoboken, NJ: Wiley, 2018).

91   *"The organization was deeply divided"*: Satya Nadella, *Hit Refresh: The Quest to Discover Microsoft's Soul and Imagine a Better Future for Everyone* (New York: HarperCollins, 2017), 55.

92   *"A leader must see"*: Nadella, *Hit Refresh*, 62.

93   *headwind situations allow us:* For a discussion of the career opportunities available in times of crises, please see Natasha D'Souza, "How to Crisis-Proof Your Career," *Harvard Business Review,* July 14, 2020, https://hbr .org/2020/07/how-to-crisis-proof-your-career.

94   *"Fraser made a name":* Claire Zillman, "How Jane Fraser Broke Banking's Highest Glass Ceiling," *Fortune,* October 19, 2020, https://fortune.com/ longform/citi-ceo-jane-fraser-first-woman-wall-street-bank-citigroup -glass-ceiling.

      Girls Who Code: Reshma Saujani, *Brave, Not Perfect: How Celebrating Imperfection Helps You Live Your Best, Most Joyful Life* (New York: Currency, 2019), 142; Reshma Saujani (founder of Girls Who Code), interview with the author's research team, August 2020.

95   *corporate executives can dramatically accelerate their path:* Elena Lytkina Botelho, Kim Rosenkoetter Powell, and Nicole Wong, "The Fastest Path to the CEO Job, According to a 10-Year Study," *Harvard Business Review,* January 31, 2018, https://hbr.org/2018/01/the-fastest-path-to-the-ceo-job -according-to-a-10-year-study.

97   *raising over $141 million:* This data comes from the Crunchbase.com website, search performed November 10, 2020.

98   *a respectable $450 million valuation:* This figure comes from email correspondence between the author and Anil Arora, chief executive officer of Envestnet/Yodlee, November 9, 2020.

      story told in Daniel P. Simon's The Money Hackers: Daniel P. Simon, *The Money Hackers: How a Group of Misfits Took on Wall Street and Changed Finance Forever* (New York: HarperCollins Leadership, 2020).

100   *"You have brains in your head":* Quoted in Leotti, Iyengar, and Ochsner, "Born to Choose."

CHAPTER 8: WELL, SOME OF IT IS (HOW TO BET ON OURSELVES)

101   *I'll call her Margaret:* I've altered certain details in this story to protect the subject's privacy.

104   *"The two most important days":* Vishnu Verma, "These 31 Quotes Will Inspire You to Follow Your Passion," *Calling Dreams,* February 10, 2016, https://callingdreams.com/follow-your-passion-quotes.

105   *our educational credentials and experience:* James Whittaker, *Career Superpowers: Succeeding on Purpose* (Kindle, 2014).

106 *"I do not believe"*: Kim Scott, *Radical Candor: Be a Kick-Ass Boss Without Losing Your Humanity* (New York: St. Martin's Press, 2019), 64.

"rather stable broad life goals": Laura Parks-Leduc, Gilad Feldman, and Anat Bardi, "Personality Traits and Personal Values," *Personality and Social Psychology Review* 19, no. 1 (2015): 3–29, https://www.deepdyve.com/lp/sage/personality-traits-and-personal-values-kF1fPSdIdR?key=sage.

107 *"although 95% of people"*: Tasha Eurich, "Working with People Who Aren't Self-Aware," *Harvard Business Review*, October 19, 2018, https://hbr.org/2018/10/working-with-people-who-arent-self-aware.

Knowing ourselves can prove challenging: See Adam Grant, "People Don't Actually Know Themselves Very Well," *Atlantic*, March 1, 2018, https://www.theatlantic.com/health/archive/2018/03/you-dont-know-yourself-as-well-as-you-think-you-do/554612/; Robert W. Firestone, "You Don't Really Know Yourself," *Psychology Today*, November 26, 2016, https://www.psychologytoday.com/us/blog/the-human-experience/201611/you-dont-really-know-yourself; and Tasha Eurich, "What Self-Awareness Really Is (and How to Cultivate It)," *Harvard Business Review*, January 4, 2018, https://hbr.org/2018/01/what-self-awareness-really-is-and-how-to-cultivate-it.

Self-awareness can also become more difficult: Eurich, "What Self-Awareness Really Is."

108 *"We simply do not have access"*: Eurich.

112 *"really kind of inspired"*: Nick Grudin (vice president of Media Partnerships at Facebook), interview with author's research team, July 2020.

CHAPTER 9: BIGGER LEAPS

118 *"let our advance worrying"*: This quote is widely cited online and attributed to Winston Churchill, but I have been unable to locate its original source.

124 *a quick judgment with origins that remain somewhat mysterious to us*: Carlin Flora, "Gut Almighty," *Psychology Today*, May 1, 2007, https://www.psychologytoday.com/us/articles/200705/gut-almighty. For more on gut thinking, see chapters 3 and 4 of John Coates, *The Hour Between Dog and Wolf: How Risk Taking Transforms Us, Body and Mind* (New York: Penguin, 2012).

"rules of thumb": Claudia Dreifus, "Through Analysis, Gut Reaction Gains

Credibility," *New York Times,* August 28, 2007, https://www.nytimes.com/2007/08/28/science/28conv.html.

"*I can't explain always*": Dreifus, "Gut Reaction Gains Credibility."

125 unconscious "*pattern match*": Al Pittampalli, "When Should You Trust Your Gut? Here's What the Science Says," *Psychology Today,* November 16, 2017, https://www.psychologytoday.com/us/blog/are-you-persuadable/201711/when-should-you-trust-your-gut-heres-what-the-science-says.

CHAPTER 10: THE MYTH OF RISK AND REWARD

142 *mastery of the game improves:* Daniel Weinand, "The Perils of Linear Life," *Mission* (blog), August 21, 2017, https://medium.com/the-mission/the-perils-of-linear-life-e2a95ea6aaa1.

"*Decades of research in cognitive psychology*": Bart de Langhe, Stefano Puntoni, and Richard Larrick, "Linear Thinking in a Nonlinear World," *Harvard Business Review,* May–June 2017, https://hbr.org/2017/05/linear-thinking-in-a-nonlinear-world.

143 *emphasize linear thinking:* Richard E. Nisbett et al., "Culture and Systems of Thought: Holistic Versus Analytic Cognition," *Psychological Review* 108, no. 2 (2001): 291–310, https://doi.org/10.1037/0033-295X.108.2.291.

"*analytic thinkers*": Nick Hobson, "Our Anxiety Is Rooted in the American Tradition of Over-Analyzing," *Vice,* March 29, 2018, https://www.vice.com/en_us/article/ne9vv8/our-anxiety-is-rooted-in-the-american-tradition-of-over-analyzing.

145 *on a business career:* Corey Thomas (chairman and CEO of Rapid7), interview with the author's research team, August 25, 2020.

146 "*Sometimes life twists everything*": Corey Thomas interview.

CHAPTER 11: TO SUCCEED, FORGET SUCCESS

152 "*a significant or major effect*": *Merriam-Webster Online,* s.v. "impact," accessed November 5, 2020, https://www.merriam-webster.com/dictionary/impact.

153 *lengthy process of developing:* Mathai Mammen (global head of R&D for the Janssen Pharmaceutical Companies of Johnson & Johnson), interview with the author's research team, November 1, 2020.

157 *performing his basic duties:* Simon Chen (former executive assistant at Joyus), interview with the author's research team, October 26, 2020.

158　*"motivated* iteration": George E. P. Box, "Science and Statistics," *Journal of the American Statistical Association* 71, no. 356 (December 1976): 791.

159　*small business owners:* Leonard A. Schlesinger, Charles F. Kiefer, and Paul B. Brown, "Act, Learn, Build: Lessons Small Business Owners Should Take from Serial Entrepreneurs," *Washington Post,* May 14, 2012, https://www.washingtonpost.com/business/on-small-business/act-learn-build-lessons-small-business-owners-should-take-from-serial-entrepreneurs/2012/05/14/gIQATLefPU_story.html.

　　"get stuck in potential consequences": Julia Ries, "Here's What Happens to Your Body When You Overthink," *Huffington Post,* updated February 6, 2020, https://www.huffpost.com/entry/overthinking-effects_l_5dd2bd67e4b0d2e79f90fe1b.

162　*speak the truth in ways that others can hear it:* Orit Ziv (chief human resources officer at Sony Playstation), interview with the author's research team, October 26, 2020.

166　*"I could have certainly failed":* Daniel Alegre, president and chief operating officer at Activision and former Google executive, email correspondence with the author, November 15, 2020.

167　*10,000 hours:* Malcolm Gladwell, *Outliers: The Story of Success* (New York: Back Bay Books, 2009).

　　In a large study: Guy Berger, "How to Become an Executive," *LinkedIn,* September 9, 2016, https://www.linkedin.com/pulse/how-become-executive-guy-berger-ph-d-/?published=t)In.

CHAPTER 12: IMPACT FAILS

175　*now famous memo:* Eugene Kim, "This Internal Memo from 10 Years Ago Shows Yahoo Still Hasn't Solved Its Biggest Problem," *Business Insider,* February 7, 2016, https://www.businessinsider.com/peanut-butter-manifesto-still-holds-true-for-yahoo-2016-2.

　　much headway on any of them: For more on the problem of spreading ourselves too thin at the individual level, see chapter 2 of Morten T. Hansen, *Great at Work: How Top Performers Do Less, Work Better, and Achieve More* (New York: Simon & Schuster, 2018).

178　*"trillion dollar coach":* See Eric Schmidt, Jonathan Rosenberg, and Alan Eagle, *Trillion Dollar Coach: The Leadership Playbook of Silicon Valley's Bill Campbell* (Hodder & Stoughton, 2019).

182 *experiences with discrimination:* Ade Olonoh, "I Can't Breathe," Ade Olonoh.com, June 2020, https://adeolonoh.com/i-cant-breathe.

wrote a powerful blog post: Susan Fowler, "Reflecting on One Very, Very Strange Year at Uber," SusanJFowler.com, February 19, 2017, https://www.susanjfowler.com/blog/2017/2/19/reflecting-on-one-very-strange-year-at-uber.

similar allegations: Johana Bhuiyan, "A Former Uber Engineer Is Suing the Company for Discrimination and Sexual Harassment," Recode, May 21, 2018, https://www.vox.com/2018/5/21/17377588/uber-engineer-sexual-harassment-lawsuit-discrimination-ingrid-avendano.

183 *One British study of 1,400 employees:* Georgina Fuller, "Half of Employees Have Witnessed Racism at Work, Says Survey," *People Management,* March 2, 2018, https://www.peoplemanagement.co.uk/news/articles/half-employees-witnessed-racism-work.

184 *fired and successfully sued:* Carlos Granda, "UCLA Hospital Worker Awarded $1.5 Million in Racial Harassment Lawsuit," *ABC 7 News,* August 9, 2019, https://abc7.com/society/ucla-hospital-worker-awarded-$15-million-in-harassment-suit/5453517.

CHAPTER 13: THE SINES OF GROWTH

199 *"People who don't take risk":* Robert P. Miles, *Warren Buffett Wealth: Principles and Practical Methods Used by the World's Greatest Investor* (Hoboken, NJ: Wiley, 2004), 157.

200 *gig economy marketplace TaskRabbit:* Stacy Brown-Philpot (CEO of TaskRabbit), interview with the author's research team, September 17, 2020.

201 *"I'd had to take some personal risks along the way":* Stacy Brown-Philpot.

204 *about 12.5 percent:* Millie Beetham, "The 2020 Automotive Dealer Benchmarks Report," *Four Eyes,* January 17, 2020, https://foureyes.io/learn/the-2020-automotive-dealer-benchmarks-report.

spinal fusion surgery: Stephen P. Montgomery, "TLIF Back Surgery Success Rates and Risks," *Spine Health,* May 7, 2003, https://www.spine-health.com/treatment/spinal-fusion/tlif-back-surgery-success-rates-and-risks.

205 *posted win rates:* See, for instance, the data given on teamrankings.com, https://www.teamrankings.com/nba/player-stat/ts-percentage.

"recursive process": Darren J. Gold (executive coach and managing part-

ner at the Trium Group), interview with the author's research team, September 2, 2020.

207 *"It's not because things are difficult"*: David Stevenson, *Secrets of Wealthy People: 50 Techniques to Get Rich* (New York: McGraw-Hill, 2014), 1.

208 *"rebuilding the beast"*: Festus Ezeli, email message to the author, November 4, 2020.

CHAPTER 14: POSSIBILITY AND POWERFLOW

210 *"as a victim who reacts"*: Gary Zukav, *Soul to Soul: Communications from the Heart* (New York: Free Press, 2007), 196.

215 *A staggering 84 percent*: Sukhinder Singh Cassidy, "Tech Women Choose Possibility," *Vox,* May 13, 2015, https://www.vox.com/2015/5/13/11562596/tech-women-choose-possibility.

217 *When John was four*: John Krause (entrepreneur and founder of Big House Beans), interview with author's research team, May 14, 2020.

220 *"birthing potential"*: "Second Chances," *Big House Beans,* accessed October 31, 2020, https://bighousebeans.com/pages/ourstory.

INDEX